A BOOK OF FAMOUS

COMPLETE UNITS FOR TEACHERS OF CHILDREN AGES 4-8

BLACK AMERICANS

CAROL TAYLOR BOND

Editing and Portrait Line Drawings

Joyce Beecher King

Includes Day-by-Day Activities, Bulletin Boards, Songs, Fingerplays, Games, Poems, Flannel Board Activities, Recipes, Worksheets, Patterns, and More!

Published by PARTNER PRESS INC.
Box 124
Livonia, MI 48152

ISBN 0-933212-38-0

Distributed by:

Gryphon House
3706 Otis Street
Mt. Rainier, Maryland 20822
1-800-638-0928

This book is dedicated to

Joyce Beecher King

whose tireless collaboration
has added so much in "substance and shine"
to my books and has brought
such joy and laughter to the experience.

Acknowledgements

I wish to thank the following people for their encouragement and support: Charlotte Murchison; my husband, Brantley, and my children, Amy, Scott, and Destin; my family and friends; and my former students for whom my first ideas were created.

Thanks to the following people for supplying information and assistance: Greg Gravel, Bonnie Hines, Dr. Tom Hathorn, Bill Taylor, Gladys Donahue, and Leola Honore and other members of the helpful staff of the Rapides Parish Public Library, Alexandria, Louisiana.

I gratefully acknowledge the authors, publishers, and friends listed below, for granting permission to reprint materials in this book. Every effort has been made to trace the ownership and to acknowledge the use of materials not written by the author. If any error inadvertently occurred, please notify the publisher for corrections in future editions.

Liz Cromwell and Dixie Hibner for the peanut butter recipe from Explore and Create, published by Partner Press Inc., Box 124, Livonia, Michigan 48152.

Table of Contents

Introduction

About the Book

A Book of Famous Black Americans is designed to introduce young students to famous blacks in American history. To include in one volume all the black Americans who have made important historical and cultural contributions would be impossible. Instead, I have tried to choose a cross section of historically significant people, past and present, who have in different ways benefited humanity and who can serve as role models for young children.

As I researched the lives of these special people, I discovered a reoccurring theme. Each person established a goal, usually at an extremely early age, which became the driving force of their lives. This goal may have been born as merely a strong desire or interest. But it was nurtured with unusual determination, grew strong in spite of the obstacles, and branched out to touch the lives of others.

The units of A Book of Famous Black Americans were written with the interests and abilities of a child in mind. The childhood of each famous person is included in the biographical information and extended to the unit activities so that the young student realizes that famous people were once "just like me." The activities not only relate to subject's important achievements but also to their various talents and interests.

The unit approach, which correlates learning activities around a central theme, is used to maintain high interest in all subject areas. For example, counting is much more interesting when popcorn is used (Jackie Robinson unit) or when it is used in a peanut game (George Washington Carver unit). Another benefit of the unit approach is that many skills can be integrated into one activity, for effective use of time and an enriched program.

How to Use the Book

Purpose

A Book of Famous Black Americans provides the teacher with complete learning units. Included are activities for each subject, step-by-step directions, ready-made worksheets, patterns and pictures of finished projects, words and actions of fingerplays and action songs, tunes for songs, recipes, and letters to parents. The teacher, therefore, is free to plan, gather and process materials, and concentrate on the actual teaching and evaluation processes. Due to copyright restrictions, the words to some songs could not be included. The titles of the books or records containing these songs are listed.

Scheduling the Units

Scheduling of the units is optional. They can be presented consecutively at any time of the year or during Black History Month in February. They can also be taught once a week, once a month, or on each subject's birthday. The famous black Americans in this book are arranged alphabetically; however, the Table of Contents includes each person's birthday (when known) and for those who are deceased, the date of their deaths.

Format and Methods Suggestions

Room Environment - General — This section provides a bulletin board and room decorations to be used when teaching the units in a consecutive manner. It also provides information on the learning centers which are used in each unit.

Room Environment — The room environment section in each unit includes bulletin boards, room decoration ideas, centers, and displays. Many of these are made with the children's assistance, or they are constructed using the children's art projects.

Biographical Information — The biographical information provides the teacher with background information on the subject of the unit. From this, the teacher extracts points of interest to be shared with the children during the discussion.

Discussion — Discussions are used to establish and introduce the daily topic. Using the biographical information, a foundation is established for the daily activities. Discussions should be more than just lectures. A variety of methods can be used to present the simple discussions in each unit. Have the children role-play or close their eyes and "visualize" the information. Place items relating to the information in a sack and take them out at the appropriate time. Dress up as a character described in the discussion, and let the children interview you. Before or after the discussion, hold a brainstorming session on the daily topic. Read a book or show a film which covers the subject matter. Use questions to check for understanding. Preceding or during the discussion, hold up pictures or "real" objects. Call on the children to tell what they know about the picture or object. Use the pictures and objects to strengthen understanding as you relate the information. Use your imagination and vary discussion methods. The children will respond with their interest and excitement.

<u>Pictures</u> – Pictures of the subject should be displayed during the unit. In addition to those included in Patterns, Pictures, Etc., pictures can be found in the books listed for this purpose. All of these books were found at the public library.

<u>Language Arts - Social Studies - Science Block</u> – In the Language Arts - Social Studies - Science block, a variety of activities are offered which further develop the unit concept. You may substitute appropriate books, films, videos, etc., which are available in your area. Reproducible sheets and patterns are found in the Patterns, Pictures, Etc. section following each unit.

Note: Opinions differ concerning the advisibility of using worksheets, particularly with younger children. Worksheets are provided for those who wish to utilize them. For those who do not, additional activities are found under each subject heading.

<u>Art</u> – On each day, two or three art activities are offered. This allows you to choose the art activity based on skill levels, time allotment, and the availability of materials. Even when patterns are used in the unit art activities, encourage creativity by offering choices of colors, materials, and design methods. It is also a good idea to set up an art station for small groups at activity time. Include easels and paints, clay, crayons, scrap paper, scissors, glue, and so forth. This practice allows the children to create artwork with few restrictions. Patterns and pictures of art projects are found in the Patterns, Pictures, Etc. section following each unit.

<u>Math</u> – The Math section offers nonsequential activities which teach basic skills such as counting, one-to-one correspondence, number values, positions, patterns, and sets. Ready-made sheets are found in the Patterns, Pictures, Etc. section following each unit.

<u>Music - Movement - Games</u> – Music - Movement - Games contains songs just for singing, action songs, movement activities, and games. Many of the songs are sung to the tune of other popular songs as indicated.

<u>Story Time</u> – Story Time is a time set aside each day, preferably before nap time or after lunch, for the children to relax and enjoy a story. You may substitute any appropriate books or stories for those listed in the book. The books used for Story Time, which either pertain to the topic or relate to the black theme, were all found at the public library.

<u>Cooking in the Classroom</u> – Cooking is an excellent activity which develops many skills and teaches many concepts. For cooking activities, assemble ingredients and tools. Write the recipe on an experience chart

illustrating each ingredient. At the bottom of the page, draw and label the tools used to prepare the recipe. Spread the ingredients and tools on a covered table. Read the recipe to the class, passing around samples of the ingredients. Encourage the children to describe the appearance, feel, taste, and smell of each ingredient. Present each tool and discuss the appearance, use, and operation of each. Allow the children to do as much of the measuring, mixing, and pouring as possible. Be certain the children understand all safety rules and are not allowed near the actual cooking area. A food fund can be set up for expenses.

Patterns, Pictures, Etc. — This section follows each unit and contains pictures of bulletin boards and displays, patterns, project pictures, ready-made worksheets, and letters to parents.

Valuable Junk

Below is a list of valuable junk you will be using with each unit. The corresponding activity title is in parentheses. You may wish to send this list to parents before presenting the units.

Room Environment - General

medium-sized corrugated cardboard box (Famous Black Americans Learning
    Center)

Marian Anderson

scraps of material   (Sewing Demonstration)
old magazines   (How We Travel)
scraps of yarn, curling ribbon   (Singing Faces)
flower seed and bulb catalogs   (Marian's Flower Garden)

Louis Armstrong

oatmeal boxes, 5-6" in diameter   (Parade Hats)
cardboard toilet paper rolls   (Trumpets)
crockery jug or bottle with narrow opening   (Jug Band)
coffee cans   (Jug Band)
old inner tubes   (Jug Band)
large nails   (Jug Band)
bottle caps   (Jug Band)
cigar boxes   (Jug Band)

Mary McLeod Bethune

pieces of sandpaper   (Big Pencils)
old crayons   (Apples for the Teacher)

Guion Bluford

refrigerator box   (Classroom Rocket)
one medium-sized corrugated cardboard box   (Classroom Rocket)
one small corrugated cardboard box   (Classroom Rocket)
one cardboard ice cream cylinder   (Classroom Rocket)
milk jug caps, plastic medicine vials   (Classroom Rocket)

Ralph Bunche

scraps of burlap   (Brainwork Center)
cardboard toilet paper rolls   (Barber Shop)
two men's suits and shoes   (The Suitcase)

George Washington Carver

clothes hangers   (Clothes Hanger Masks)
nylon stockings or pantyhose   (Clothes Hanger Masks)

Shirley Chisholm

seashells   (Brainwork Center)
dried beans, aquarium gravel   (Sand Activities)
plastic cups, bowls, spoons   (Sand Activities)
old sifters and strainers   (Sand Activities)
old newspapers   (Sand Art)
shell macaroni   (On the Beach)

Althea Gibson

old sports magazines and catalogs   (Time for Tennis bulletin board)
egg cartons   (Brainwork Center)
buttons   (Brainwork Center, Button Rings, Button Activities)
corrugated cardboard boxes with divided compartments   (Mail Clerk -
    Alphabet Activity)
old tennis racket   (Tilda Tennis Racket)
yarn scraps   (Tilda Tennis Racket)

Martin Luther King, Jr.

burlap sacks (Burlap Sack Race)

Thurgood Marshall

dried beans, peas, macaroni, popcorn   (Seal of the Supreme Court)
cardboard toilet paper rolls   (Gavel)

Jesse Owens

old catalogs, magazines   (Brainwork Center)
aluminum foil   (Class Olympics - Medals)
scraps of yarn   (Class Olympics - Medals)
hay, leaves, or old blankets   (Class Olympics - Broad Jump)
broomsticks   (Class Olympics - Javelin)
plastic milk jugs and similar containers   (Class Olympics - Weight Lifting)
styrofoam egg cartons   (Egglympic Torches)

Jackie Robinson

refrigerator box   (Room Decorations - Popcorn Booth)
occupation hats   (Discussion)
old newspapers   (Padded Baseballs)

Wilma Rudolph

old magazines   (Basic Four Food Group Activities)
bottle caps   (Mini Olympics - Discus Throw)
egg carton   (Mini Olympics - Broad Jump)
buttons   (Mini Olympics - Broad Jump)
baby food jars   (Mini Olympics - Swimming Contest)

Sojourner Truth

aluminum pie pans   (The Life of Sojourner Truth - Mural)

Harriet Tubman

pint-sized plastic tub   (Weather Vane)
aluminum pie pans   (Harriet's Escape - Crayon Resist)
waxed paper   (North Stars)
scraps of string or thread   (North Stars)
star-shaped cereal   (Stars Counting Sheet)
small paper bags   (Trail Food)

Booker T. Washington

plastic plates, cups, utensils   (Tuskegee Learning Skills - Setting the
     Tables)
scrap lumber, nails   (Tuskegee Learning Skills - Building)
aluminum pie pans   (Booker T. Washington - Wet Chalk Picture)
scraps of string   (Paper Plate Snake)

Phillis Wheatley

pieces of corrugated cardboard   (Pierced Tin Lanterns)

ROOM ENVIRONMENT - GENERAL

BULLETIN BOARDS

Famous Black Americans

Cover the bulletin board with white paper and trim with a red, white, and blue border. Mount pictures of famous black Americans on the bulletin board. These may be purchased or you may use the line drawings found near the beginning of each Patterns, Pictures, Etc. section. (See example on page 3.)

Room Decorations

From colored construction paper or poster paper, make a symbol for the person featured in each unit. For Harriet Tubman, make a train engine; for Guion Bluford, a space shuttle; for Althea Gibson, a tennis racket and so forth. Tie pieces of string or fishing line to paper clip hangers; then attach to the symbols. Hang from the ceiling and/or from light fixtures and add red, white, and blue crepe paper streamers. Place small American flags around the room. Cut footprints from construction paper and tape on the floor in a path from the door to the discussion and/or center areas. At the beginning of the path, tape a construction paper square which reads "Follow the Famous Footprints."

DISPLAYS - LEARNING CENTERS

Famous Black Americans

Cut three sides from a medium-sized corrugated cardboard box and cover with bulletin board paper or burlap. Cut out letters for the title and staple at the top. See the Room Environment section of each unit for specific ideas for using the center. (See example on page 3.)

Note: Place the following books on the table in front of the center to be used as a permanent part of the display: Famous Black Americans by Langston Hughes, Great Negroes Past and Present by Russell L. Adams, Great Black Americans by Ben Richardson and William A. Fahey.

Brainwork Center

Fold a 16" x 10" piece of poster paper in half so that the two sides each measure 8" x 10". Write the title of the center at the top. Stand the center on a table. For a matching activity, draw or trace small pictures of famous black Americans and mount on small tagboard cards. On corresponding cards, glue matching items or symbols. Examples: Louis Armstrong - trumpet, George Washington Carver - peanut, Jackie Robinson - baseball. Laminate the cards. Place in the center. Other activities for this center are found in the Room Environment section of each unit. (See example on page 3.)

Famous Black Americans

George Washington Carver

Thurgood Marshall

Jesse Owens

Mary McLeod Bethune

Wilma Rudolph

Louis Armstrong

Ralph Bunche

Shirley Chisholm

Booker T. Washington

Guion Bluford

Sojourner Truth

Phillis Wheatley

Harriet Tubman

Marian Anderson

Martin Luther King, Jr.

Althea Gibson

Jackie Robinson

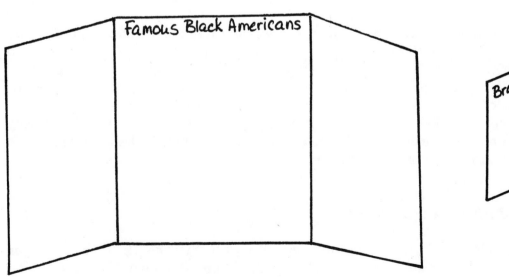

Famous Black Americans

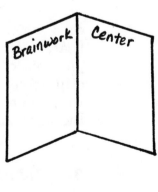

Brainwork Center

MARIAN ANDERSON

(1903 -   )

ROOM ENVIRONMENT - BULLETIN BOARD

"Sing, Sing a Song"

Cover the bulletin board as desired and staple the title at the top. Mount the "Singing Faces" (see Art) on the bulletin board. Make large musical notes from white construction paper and outline in black. Write each child's favorite song on one of the notes using a black marker. Staple the notes in the remaining space on the bulletin board. (See example on page 13.)

ROOM ENVIRONMENT - LEARNING CENTERS

Famous Black Americans - (See Room Environment - General - Learning Centers)

Staple a picture of Marian Anderson (see page 12) on the learning center. In front of the center, place books about Marian Anderson and books about orchestras and opera such as What Makes an Orchestra by Jan Balet, and The Fabulous World of Opera by Dorothy and Joseph Samachson.

Brainwork Center - (See Room Environment - General - Learning Centers)

Marian Anderson traveled all over the world giving concerts. To develop understanding about the various means of transportation, make a stand-up card which reads "Ways People Travel." Place the card and a toy car, boat, train, and plane on the table. On 4" squares of tagboard draw pictures of these vehicles; and on matching cards draw scenes such as a city street, a lake, a tunnel with railroad tracks, mountains, a country road, an ocean, a railroad bridge, a sky, and a forest. The children match the most suitable vehicle with each scene.

BIOGRAPHICAL INFORMATION

Marian Anderson is an American contralto who was the first black singer to become famous on the concert stage. She was also the first black soloist to sing with the Metropolitan Opera of New York City.

Marian Anderson was born on February 27, 1903, in Philadelphia, Pennsylvania. Her father, John Anderson, was employed at the Reading Terminal Market and did other odd jobs. Her mother Annie was formerly a teacher, but quit to stay home with Marian and her younger sisters, Alyce and Ethel. To earn extra money, she took in laundry or did domestic work, that is, housework for other people.

As a small child, Marian Anderson loved to sing. She saved money to buy a used violin, and when her father bought an old piano, she learned to play simple melodies by following a card which was marked with the notes.

When Anderson was twelve years old, her father died and the family moved in with his parents. Marian Anderson's unusual singing voice attracted the attention of the Union Baptist Church choirmaster, and she was invited to join the senior choir. Soon she was representing the church at recitals in neighboring churches. A black singing teacher, Mary Saunders Patterson, gave her free lessons, and the church members raised money for a fund they called "Marian Anderson's Future."

After graduating from high school, Anderson was introduced to the world-famous voice teacher, Giuseppe Boghetti. Mr. Boghetti already had too many students, but after hearing Marian Anderson sing, he quickly made room for her. Their relationship lasted for many years until his death.

In 1923 Marian Anderson became the first black woman to win the Philadelphia Harmonic Society's voice contest. In 1925 she won the Lewisohn Stadium Concert Award and had the privilege of singing with the New York Philharmonic Orchestra. During the next few years, Anderson received a scholarship from the National Association of Negro Musicians and a Rosenwald Fellowship which enabled her to further her studies in Europe.

Marian Anderson made her debut in Berlin in 1930, then toured the Scandinavian countries. She was an enormous success and critics began calling her the greatest singer in the world. After repeated requests, she returned in 1933 and gave 142 concerts in Norway, Denmark, Finland, and Sweden. She was decorated by the King of Sweden and the King of Denmark. She then made her Paris debut and gave successful concerts in all the European capitals. When Anderson returned home to America, she toured all over the country and became one of the country's favorite singers. She sang with the great symphony orchestras and appeared on radio and television many times. Her schedule increased each year until she was averaging over one hundred concerts a year in cities all over the world. Her repertoire consisted of over two hundred songs in many languages.

Despite her popularity, Marian Anderson experienced many unpleasant incidents resulting from racial prejudices. She was denied hotel accommodations and service in restaurants. In 1939 she was invited to sing at the White House, but in the same city was denied the use of Constitution Hall by its owners, the Daughters of the American Revolution. The people of America were shocked, and Mrs. Franklin D. Roosevelt protested by resigning her membership in the D.A.R. Mrs. Roosevelt and a committee of prominent citizens arranged to have the concert at the Lincoln Memorial. A platform was built before the statue of Abraham Lincoln, and Anderson sang before 75,000 people, one of the largest crowds ever gathered to hear a singer. Millions more listened to her on the radio.

During this same year, Marian Anderson was awarded the Spingarn Medal, an award given each year for the highest achievement by a black American, by the National Association for the Advancement of Colored People. (For explanation of NAACP, see Thurgood Marshall Unit, Biographical Information.) In 1941 she received the Bok Award, and with the $10,000 prize, she started the Marian Anderson Award. This award helps young people, without regard to race, color, or creed, to pursue an artistic career.

Anderson continued to be close to her family and friends in Philadelphia. Whenever possible, she returned to Philadelphia where she could relax and "talk gossip" with her old friends. Although she earned a great deal of money, she chose to live simply. She traveled without a secretary or maid; did her own packing, unpacking, and ironing; and carried along a sewing machine to mend her gowns.

In 1943 Marian Anderson married an architect, Orpheus H. Fisher. They built a beautiful home on a large farm near Danbury, Connecticut. There, between tours, Anderson relaxed by raising her own chickens, fruits and vegetables, and gardens of flowers.

Anderson fulfilled a lifelong dream when, in 1955, she made her debut at the Metropolitan Opera House in New York. She was the first black woman to become a member of the company.

As an ambassador of goodwill for the United States, Marian Anderson made a twelve-nation concert tour of the Far East in 1957. The tour was a success and improved relations between the United States and the Far East. In 1958 Anderson was appointed alternate delegate in the United States Mission to the United Nations. In this capacity she continued working towards improved international understanding.

In 1977 she was awarded the United Nations Peace Prize for her valuable contributions towards this goal. She had previously retired from the concert stage in 1965.

LANGUAGE ARTS - SOCIAL STUDIES - SCIENCE

Discussion

Play one of Marian Anderson's songs. (Recordings are available at public libraries.) Afterwards, summarize the Biographical Information and point out Pennsylvania and Washington, D.C., on a map and France, Germany, Norway, Denmark, Finland, and Sweden on a globe. Direct the children's attention to the various room displays.

Singing Demonstration

Invite a singer to perform for the class.

Learning About the Orchestra

Marian Anderson sang with many great symphony orchestras. To familiarize the children with this subject, display a poster of a symphony orchestra. Summarize the information and show the pictures in Let's Learn About the Orchestra by Carla Green. Discuss the instruments and the four groups in an orchestra: String Instruments, Woodwind Instruments, Brass Wind Instruments, and Percussion Instruments. Play the record and show the pictures of Peter and the Wolf by Serge Prokofieff, Walt Disney Productions (LP with pictures). Play the opera Hansel & Gretel by Engelbert Humperdinck and one of Marian Anderson's recordings in which she is accompanied by a symphony orchestra. Identify the various instruments by holding up pictures from the book (above) while the music plays.

Field Trip

Take the class to hear a symphony orchestra perform. Some orchestras offer special performances for school children.

Sewing Demonstration

Marian Anderson enjoyed needlework. To teach basic sewing, ask a parent to demonstrate sewing by hand or on a machine. Teach the children a simple running stitch and let them practice on scraps of material. For an easy sewing project, cut squares of material with pinking shears. Draw stitching lines. The children put two squares together, sew around three sides, fill half full with dried beans, and sew the fourth side together to make beanbags.

Musical Instrument Match

Duplicate and distribute the sheet on page 14. The children draw lines to match the two String Instruments, the two Woodwind Instruments, the two Brass Instruments, and the two Percussion Instruments, then color each. With younger children, a picture of each group should be displayed and each instrument should be identified again before completing the worksheet together, step-by-step.

Poem - "I'd Like to Be"

I'd like to be like Marian Anderson

And sing in a voice so clear,

Traveling around the world and back

So everyone could hear.

How We Travel

On a world map, show the class the various places where Marian Anderson performed and how she might have traveled to each place. Discuss ways we travel—by car, bus, train, ship, or airplane. Distribute old magazines, drawing paper, scissors, and glue to the students. Write "How We Travel" on the chalkboard and direct the students to copy this title in the middle of the sheets of paper. Then they should cut out pictures of the vehicles mentioned above and glue them on the paper to form a collage.

ART

Singing Faces

Preparation - Give each child a paper plate. Set out scraps of construction paper, curling ribbon, and yarn; scissors; glue; and markers.

Procedure - Create a singing face on the paper plate with markers, or by cutting features from the construction paper scraps and gluing them on the paper plate. Make the mouth open. Use the construction paper, yarn, or curling ribbon to make the hair. Glue in place. Dry. (See example on page 13.)

Note: To use on the "Singing Faces" on "Sing, Sing a Song" bulletin board, see Room Environment - Bulletin Board.

Musical Note Pin

<u>Preparation</u> - Purchase long black pipe cleaners and small safety pins. If you do not have a hot glue gun, purchase strong craft glue. Demonstrate forming a pipe cleaner musical note.

<u>Procedure</u> - Roll one end of the pipe cleaner into a circle and twist the end around the straight section of the pipe cleaner. Bend the top of the pipe cleaner so that it resembles a slightly drooping flag on a flagpole. Let the teacher make a puddle of glue on the back of the stem of the note and place the back of an open safety pin (vertically) in the glue. Dry thoroughly. Wear the pin on your shirt. (See example on page 13.)

MATH

Marian's Flower Garden

Gardening is one of Marian Anderson's favorite pastimes. To extend this theme, duplicate and distribute the sheet on page 15. Set out numerous pages torn from flower seed and bulb catalogs. Read the words on each section of the sheet. Direct the children to cut out and glue flowers of the correct number and color on each section.

Musical Instrument Counting Booklet

Duplicate the sheets on pages 16–18 so that each child has a complete booklet. Cut the pages in half, cut around the borders, and staple together. The students color the cover, then trace over the numbers and color the instruments on each page. When the booklet is completed, review the names of the instruments on each page.

MUSIC - MOVEMENT - GAMES

Song - "Sing" from <u>Sesame Street Tenth Anniversary Album</u> (LP)

Teaching Songs - "Row, Row, Row Your Boat," "Twinkle Twinkle Little Star," "Mary Had a Little Lamb"

To teach the children to understand and identify the rhythmic beat in music, use the songs above or other simple songs of your choice. First, recite each song as you would a poem, emphasizing the rhythmic beat with your voice and by clapping your hands. Then have the children repeat the procedure.   Once this skill is mastered, lead the children in singing the songs and clapping to the rhythmic beat.

High and Low Sounds

Explain that some sounds are high and some sounds are low.   Name some examples of high and low sounds (a factory whistle, a foghorn, an airplane's roar, the ring of a telephone).   Use a xylophone or piano to show a high note and a low note.   Direct the children to listen to the notes you play, then stand for high notes and squat down for low notes. Play 2 or 3 low notes and 2 or 3 high notes; then begin playing a series of high and low notes.   Pause between each series of sounds and check the children's responses.

STORY TIME

1.   Sing a Song - Mary Ann Johnston
2.   Harry and the Lady Next Door - Gene Zion

COOKING IN THE CLASSROOM

Marian's Favorite Golden Pound Cake

Note: Often when Marian Anderson's father returned from work, he brought the family a golden pound cake which they shared for dessert.   In later years, this was one of her special childhood memories.

1 cup margarine
2 cups granulated sugar
2 cups all-purpose flour, sifted
5 eggs
1 tablespoon vanilla

Preheat oven to 325°.   Cream margarine and sugar.   Add flour gradually, alternating with the eggs.   Mix in vanilla.   Pour into greased and floured 10-inch tube pan or 9" x 5" loaf pan.   Bake for 60-75 minutes.

Dear Parents,

On _____, we will learn about the famous black singer, Marian Anderson—her life and career. Please read below to find out ways you can help.

Things To Send: _____

_____

_____

Volunteers Needed To: _____

_____

_____

Follow-Up: At the end of the unit, ask your child the following questions:

_____

_____

_____

Thank you for your cooperation.

Sincerely,

MARIAN ANDERSON

Bulletin Board, Examples

Sing, Sing a Song

Singing Faces

Musical Note Pin

Musical Instrument Match

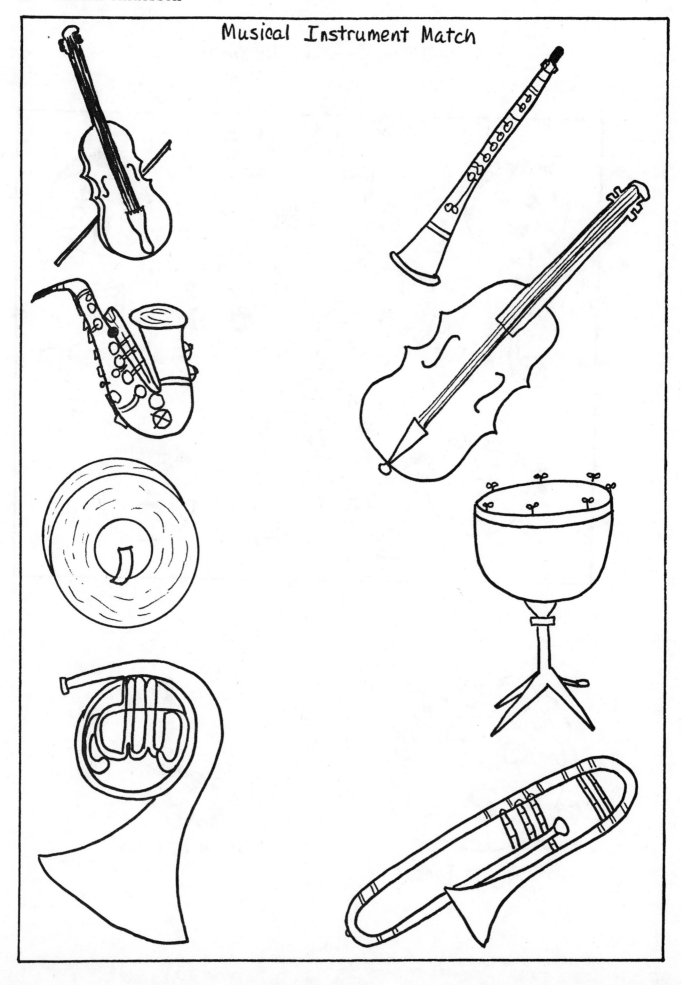

Musical Instrument Match

Marian's Flower Garden

1 red flower	2 blue flowers
3 orange flowers	4 yellow flowers

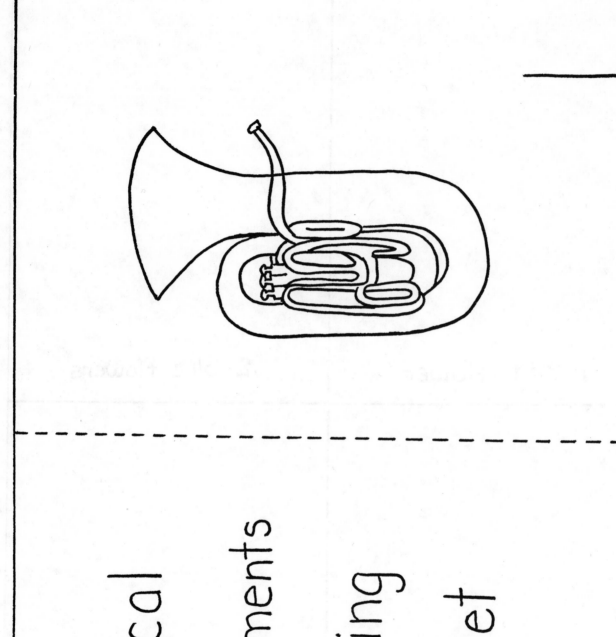

1

Musical Instruments Counting Booklet

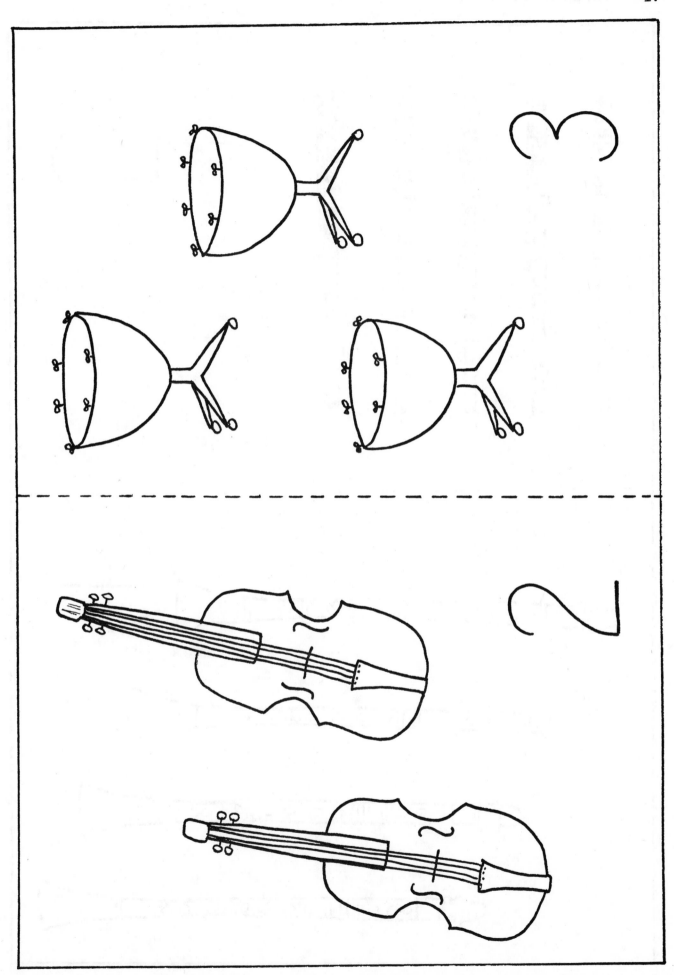

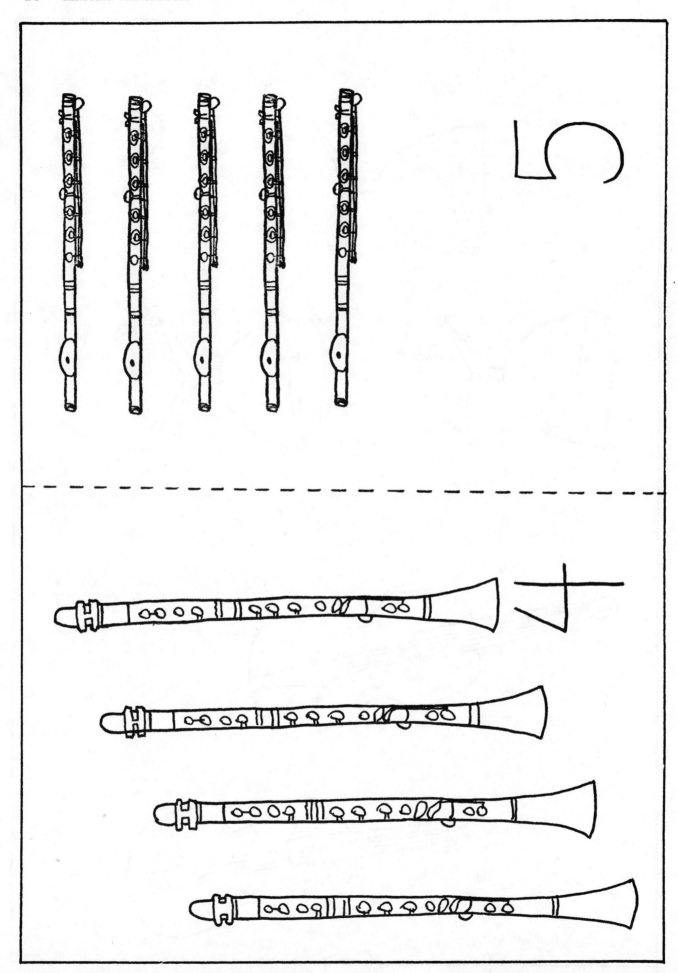

LOUIS ARMSTRONG

(1900 - 1971)

ROOM ENVIRONMENT - BULLETIN BOARD

"The Music Goes Round and Round . . ."

Cover the bulletin board with white paper and trim with a red border. Cut the letters for the title and musical notes from black construction paper. Mount the title at the top. Draw, color, and cut out instruments found in a jazz band—a trumpet, a cornet, a saxophone, a trombone, a guitar, a piano, and drums. Use a black marker to draw a spiral on the bulletin board as shown. Staple the musical instruments and notes on the spiral. Staple name cards under each instrument. (See example on page 30.)

ROOM ENVIRONMENT - LEARNING CENTERS

Famous Black Americans - (See Room Environment - General - Learning Centers)

Staple a picture of Louis Armstrong (see page 29) on the learning center along with scenes of New Orleans and Mardi Gras. If possible, borrow musical instruments to display in front of the center. Add books on Louis Armstrong's life such as Trumpeter's Tale: The Story of Young Louis Armstrong by Jeanette Eaton, Louis Armstrong by Genie Iverson, and Louis: The Louis Armstrong Story by Max Jones and John Chilton, and also books such as New Orleans: A Picture Book to Remember Her By designed by David Gibbon and Mardi Gras by Robert Tallant. Display Mardi Gras beads and doubloons.

Brainwork Center - (See Room Environment - General - Learning Centers)

Set up a listening station so that the children can hear the music of Louis Armstrong. His recordings are available at public libraries.

BIOGRAPHICAL INFORMATION

Louis Armstrong was a famous black American trumpet player. He was best known for his jazz solos and his gruff singing voice.

Louis Armstrong was born on July 4, 1900, in New Orleans, Louisiana. He lived with his mother Mayann and his sister Beatrice on Perdido Street in a poor section of town. His grandmother lived close by. Armstrong's father had divorced his mother and remarried when Armstrong was very young, so he could barely remember him. Armstrong's mother worked as a maid, so the children were left with Grandmother Josephine during the day. Grandmother Josephine had once been a slave and would tell them stories of her girlhood in New Orleans.

Louis Armstrong was called "Dipper" by his friends because of the size of his mouth. He and his friends played in the cluttered lots and dirty streets of the neighborhood. There were no decent houses or playgrounds, but since Armstrong had never known anything else, he was happy. He spent his time selling newspapers after school and listening to the music from the dance halls and bars on Perdido Street.

When he was twelve or thirteen years old, Louis Armstrong started his own band of singers. For weeks they practiced singing the new jazz songs they had heard around the neighborhood. Once they had learned the songs, the boys sang every night for the people on the streets. The crowds would applaud and throw money. On December 31, 1912, the people of Armstrong's neighborhood celebrated New Year's Eve as usual—by setting off fire crackers, blowing tin horns, and parading in wild costumes. The children liked this holiday even better than Mardi Gras. To add to the fun, Armstrong had found his father's old thirty-eight revolver and decided to fire it in the air. When a young boy fired a cap pistol at him, Armstrong raised his father's gun and fired it in the air to scare him. Armstrong was arrested and sent to the Colored Waif's Home where he stayed for a year and a half.

At first Armstrong was very unhappy at the home. He felt alone and afraid. But this was actually the turning point of his life. Soon he made friends, and it was here he was first called Satchel Mouth or "Satchmo" by one of the other boys. He kept this nickname for the rest of his life.

One of the teachers, Mr. Peter Davis, also conducted the band. He invited Armstrong to join and, along with the director of the home, Joseph Jones, taught him to play the cornet. The band was often invited to march in parades and play at club meetings and parties. Armstrong practiced hard and was proud of the band. When he was fourteen, he was sent back to live with his family. He quit school and found a job selling coal from a mule cart. At night he played his cornet at Matranga's Saloon. Whenever he had a chance, he listened to Joe Oliver play his trumpet. Oliver was the leader of Kid Ory's Band, New Orleans' most famous jazz group.

One night Joe Oliver stopped in Matranga's to hear Louis Armstrong play. The two men became good friends. In 1918 when Joe Oliver went to Chicago, Armstrong took his place in Kid Ory's Band.

The next job Armstrong had was playing in a riverboat band. The riverboat traveled from New Orleans to St. Paul, Minnesota, stopping at cities and towns along the way. When he returned, Armstrong worked in the New Orleans cabarets. Then Joe Oliver asked him to join his band in Chicago.

Armstrong was afraid to leave home and go north to Chicago, but he knew this was his big chance to become famous. So he went to Chicago and joined the band. For a while he was homesick but the audiences loved him. For the next few years he played with various bands in different cities in the North. Encouraged by a band leader, Armstrong changed from the cornet to the trumpet. He liked the deeper, richer tones of the trumpet.

The crowds loved "Satchmo." He was one of the first jazz musicians to sing "scat style"; that is, instead of words, he would sometimes sing nonsense syllables. This, along with his hoarse voice, wide smile, and "hot" trumpet solos brought the people to their feet.

As Louis Amstrong's fame grew, he was invited to play with different bands at popular cabarets with various groups. He made a series of records which are considered among the greatest in jazz.

During the 1930s and 40s, Armstrong led his own band. They toured the United States, then traveled to foreign countries to give concerts. Everywhere they went Armstrong and his band were greeted by thousands of fans. Armstrong was called the "King of Jazz" and the "greatest trumpeter in the world." Armstrong spent the rest of his life traveling and making music. He appeared in several motion pictures and made a number of hit records. He died on July 6, 1971, two days after his seventy-first birthday.

LANGUAGE ARTS - SOCIAL STUDIES - SCIENCE

Discussion

Discuss the room displays. Summarize the biographical information and show pictures from references (see Famous Black Americans, Room Environment - Learning Centers, page 19). Locate New Orleans, Louisiana, and Chicago, Illinois, on a map. Explain Mardi Gras and show pictures from Mardi Gras by Robert Tallant. Show and discuss the instruments in Picture Book of Musical Instruments by Marion Lacey. Borrow Louis Armstrong recordings from a library. Let the children listen to several selections (or parts of each). Identify the trumpet portions of the selections. Ask the children to describe what they heard. If available, show a film or video about Louis Armstrong.

King of Jazz - Choral Rap

Learn and recite the choral rap to the class, using the tone and rhythm associated with rap. Teach the children the last two lines of each verse, or divide the class into two groups and teach the last two lines of the first verse to one group and the last two lines of the second verse to the other group. Recite the rap once again and signal the proper groups to recite their lines.

Note: Older children can be taught the entire rap, then divided into groups to recite the various lines.

Note: You may wish to define razzmatazz which is a slang term for flashiness or liveliness.

Now Louis Armstrong was a very famous man,

He played his shiny trumpet in a swingin' jazz band,

But as a young boy he was just a little wild,

And his mother said, "Louis, you'd better calm down, child!"

Ca-ca-ca-calm down child; ca-ca-ca-calm down child,

And his mother said, "Louis, you'd better calm down, child!"

Then he got himself a horn and he learned to play,

He practiced on this trumpet each and every day,

And he became known as the King of Jazz,

'Cause people loved his music and his razzmatazz.

Ra-ra-ra-razzmatazz, ra-ra-ra-razzmatazz,

'Cause people loved his music and his razzmatazz.

Demonstration

Invite a jazz band or members of a high school band to visit the class. Ask if each band member can show and explain his or her musical instrument and play a few notes before the band plays all together.

Listen

Play parts of a lullaby, a march, a country song, a classical instrumental, a pop song, and a jazz record. After each selection, ask the children:

How did the music make you feel?
Why do you think it made you feel that way?
Was it loud, quiet, fast, or slow?
What instruments could you hear?

Riverboat Color Sheet

Duplicate and distribute the sheet on page 31. If necessary, write color words on the board and color code them with marks of colored chalk beside each word. The students color each section of the riverboat as labeled.

ART

Trumpets

Preparation - Purchase gold-colored foil and cone-shaped paper cups. Collect one cardboard toilet paper roll per child. Give each child a sheet of foil, a paper cup, and a toilet paper roll. Set out scissors and tape.

Procedure - Cut the end off the paper cup and insert the small end of the cup into one end of the toilet paper roll. Tape in place. Cover the trumpet with the foil, molding it tightly to the body of the trumpet. (Be sure to cover the inside of the cup.) Tuck the ends of the foil inside the center of the cup and inside the "mouth" end of the roll. (See example on page 32.)

Note: Rolls of gold foil are available at craft stores.

Parade Hats

Preparation - Collect oatmeal or similar containers, 5–6" in diameter. You will need one per child. Discard the tops and punch a hole on either side about an inch from the open end. On large sheets of construction paper, draw lines as shown on page 32. For chin straps, cut 20" pieces of $\frac{1}{4}$" elastic. Set out pencils, scissors, glue, and star stickers. Distribute oatmeal containers, construction paper, and elastic chin straps.

Procedure - Cut on the solid line of the construction paper. On the dotted line, fold back the rounded part, which will be the bill of the parade hat. Turn over the construction paper so that you cannot see the folded bill and spread with glue. Wrap it around the container to cover. Use a pencil to punch through the construction paper and into the two holes. Attach elastic. Decorate the hat with the star stickers. (See example on page 32.)

Variation: Cut small slits near the ends of each piece of elastic and secure to the hat with paper fasteners.

Note: Older children can use regular construction paper, cut out the bills, and attach with glue.

Firecrackers

Preparation - Give each child a half-sheet of red construction paper (6" x 9") and a paper straw. Set out scraps of construction paper, scissors, glue, markers, and staplers.

Procedure - For the firecracker, fold the red construction paper in half to measure 3" x 9". Decorate with the construction paper scraps. For the fuse, mash the straw so that it is flat and color the end orange or yellow. Slip the straw between the folds of the firecracker so that it protrudes at the top. Unfold the construction paper and glue or staple the straw in place. Fold the construction paper once again and staple together the edges. (See example on page 32.)

MATH

Counting Sheet

Duplicate and distribute the sheet on page 33. Direct the students to count the items in each section, circle the correct number below, and color the sheet.

Dot-to-Dot Trumpet

Duplicate and distribute the sheet on page 34. The children complete the picture by connecting the numbered dots and coloring the trumpet.

MUSIC - MOVEMENT - GAMES

Song - "When the Saints Come Marching In"

Source: Best Loved Songs of the American People Denes Agay

Jug Band

Form a jug band using any of the instruments below. Choose those that are appropriate for your age group. Once the children have learned to play their instruments, let the band play along with their favorite records. You can also play a marching song and let the children put on their Parade Hats (see Art) and parade around the room.

Jug
- A crockery jug or any bottle with a narrow opening. Hold the opening under the bottom lip and blow into it with puckered lips. Several jugs or bottles holding different amounts of water will produce different tones.

Drums
- Cover the open ends of different-sized coffee cans with circles cut from inner tubes. The circles should be a few inches bigger than the openings. Secure with string. Strike the drums with wooden spoons or the hands. Use other cans to make different sounds. Collect a variety of sizes, turn the cans over, and hit the metal surface with a stick or cooking utensil.

Spoons
- Hold two spoons together with the backs of the bowls almost touching each other. The handle of one spoon is held loosely between the first and second fingers; the handle of the other is held loosely between the second and third fingers. Slap the spoons in the palm of the other hand to produce the sound.

  Note: This activity is for older children. Younger children can hold a spoon loosely and upside down in one hand and strike the bowl lightly with another spoon.

Washboard
- Put sewing thimbles on the thumb and fingers of your "writing hand." Put your other arm around the washboard and grasp the far edge with your hand. Prop the washboard on your knee and play by running the thimbles up and down the slats in time to the music.

Kazoo
- Purchase a toy kazoo and hum into it to produce a unique sound.

Nails
- Collect a variety of large nails. Tie a piece of string to each nail head. Tie the strings to the bottom of a clothes hanger so that the nails hang in a row. Hang the clothes hanger on the back of a chair, on the edge of an overhanging shelf, or from a string suspended from the ceiling. Play the nails by striking them with a large nail or spoon.

Tambourine   - Take apart the two rings of a metal embroidery hoop. Collect bottle caps and punch a hole in the middle of each with a hammer and nail. Thread a short piece of string through two or three bottle caps and tie to the inner ring of the embroidery hoop. Continue until there are five or six "groups" of caps spaced around the hoop. Fit the outer and inner rings of the embroidery hoop together. Hold the tambourine in one hand and shake it, hit it with the other hand, or hit it against one leg in time to the music.

Bells   - Purchase jingle bells and large colored pipe cleaners. Thread several bells on each pipe cleaner and twist the ends together to form a circle. Shake the bells to the rhythm of the music.

Rubber Band Guitar   - Obtain a cigar box and punch corresponding holes, about an inch apart, through the ends of the box. (The number of holes and rubber bands depend on the size of the box.) Collect rubber bands of various widths and thicknesses. Loop one end of a rubber band around a metal paper fastener, put the fastener through a hole and spread apart; then stretch the rubber band across the box and attach to the opposite hole in the same manner. Repeat for each rubber band. Hold the guitar in front of you and pluck or strum the "strings."

Cymbals   - Saw a coconut in half, remove the contents, and sand the edges smooth. Hold a coconut shell (half) in each hand and hit the edges together as you would regular cymbals. The tops of two cooking pots can also be used as cymbals.

STORY TIME

1. Benjie on His Own - Joan M. Lexau
2. "Little Eight John" from The People Could Fly told by Virginia Hamilton
3. Goggles - Ezra Jack Keats

COOKING IN THE CLASSROOM

Louisiana Pralines

1 cup granulated sugar
1 cup brown sugar
1 cup cream
1 cup water
1 teaspoon vanilla
2 1/2 cups pecans

Combine the first four ingredients in a 3-quart saucepan. Stir to dissolve sugar and boil over medium heat until it reaches the soft ball stage (238° on a candy thermometer). Remove from heat. Beat until mixture is creamy. Stir in vanilla and pecans. Drop by tablespoonfuls onto a wax paper sheet. Cool. Patties may be individually wrapped in wax paper. Yield: fifteen 3" patties (or make smaller patties, one per child)

Dear Parents,

On _____, we will learn about Louis Armstrong, the great black jazz trumpeter. Please read below to find out ways you can help.

Things To Send: _____

_____

_____

Volunteers Needed To: _____

_____

_____

Follow-Up: At the end of the unit, ask your child the following questions:

_____

_____

_____

Thank you for your cooperation.

Sincerely,

LOUIS ARMSTRONG

Bulletin Board

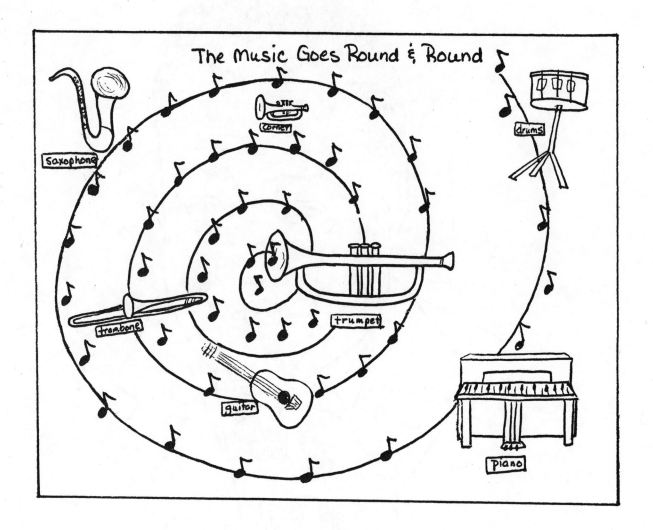

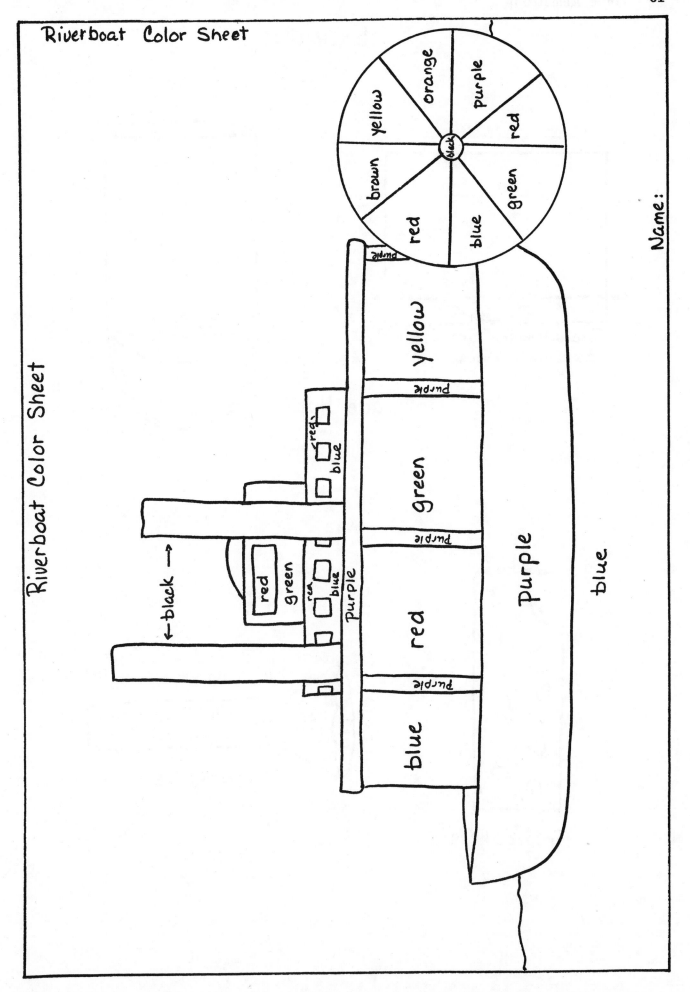

Riverboat Color Sheet

Name:

31

Examples

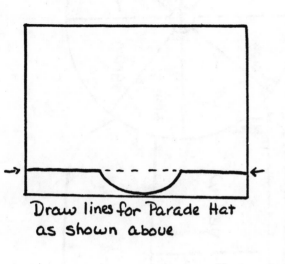

Draw lines for Parade Hat
as shown above

Parade Hats

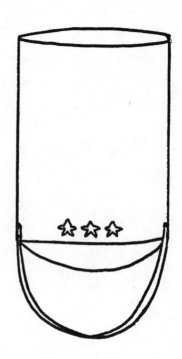

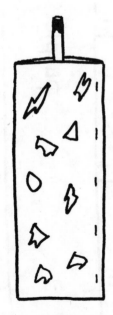

Firecrackers

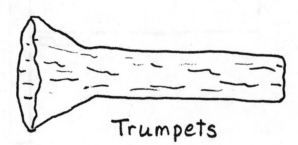

Trumpets

Counting Sheet   Name:

1   2   3

1   2   3

4   5   6

4   5   6

1   2   3

4   5   6

Dot-to-Dot Trumpet

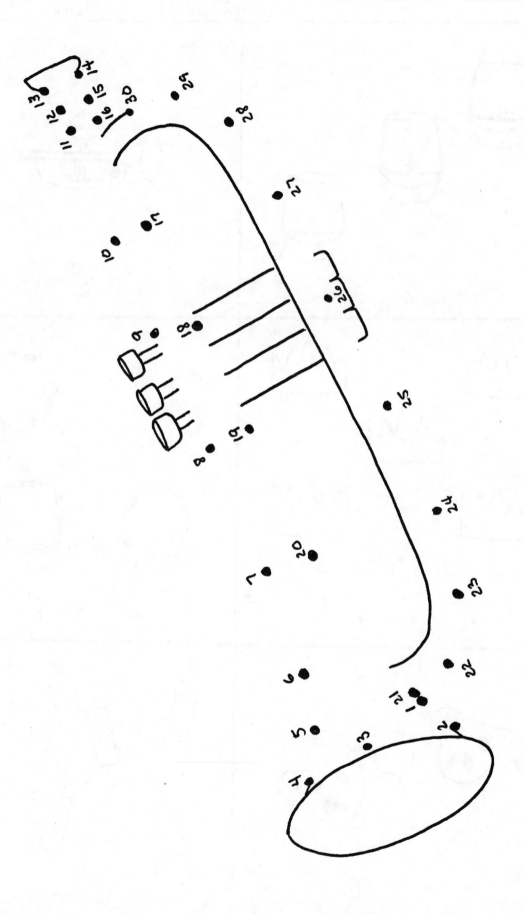

MARY McLEOD BETHUNE

(1875 - 1955)

ROOM ENVIRONMENT - BULLETIN BOARD

"What We Learn in School"

Cover the bulletin board with green paper and trim with a yellow border. Cut the letters for the title from blue construction paper and staple at the top. Make a red schoolhouse and mount in the center of the bulletin board. In the remaining space, position and staple the "Big Pencils" (see Art). (See example on page 46.)

Room Decorations - Door Display

"Welcome to Our Schoolhouse"

Measure the frame of the classroom door. From kraft paper, cut two strips 9" wide and the height of the door frame. Cut the schoolhouse roof as shown on page 48. Add 22" to the width measurement of the door frame and make the base of the roof that wide. Paint the side strips and roof red and the details, such as lines for shingles and bricks, black. Draw and cut out a bell for the tower. Paint it yellow and glue in place. Place a welcome mat in front of the door.

ROOM ENVIRONMENT - LEARNING CENTERS

Famous Black Americans - (See Room Environment - General - Learning Centers)

Staple a picture of Mary McLeod Bethune, page 45, on the learning center. Draw and color a picture of a log cabin and a picture of Bethune-Cookman College and mount on either side of Mrs. Bethune's picture. In front of the center, place books such as Mary McLeod Bethune by Rackham Holt, I Want to Be a Farmer by Carla Greene, Wake Up, Farm! by Alvin Tresselt, The First Book of Cotton by Matilda Rogers, Cotton: From Farm to Market by Winifred Hammond, Rice by Sylvia A. Johnson, Let's Find Out About School by Martha and Charles Shapp, Family by Seymour Rossel, and Discovering Others by Peter H. Martorella, Cleo Cherryholmes, and Gary Manson. Display a cotton plant, a rice plant, cotton balls, cotton material, and processed rice.

Brainwork Center - (See Room Environment - General - Learning Centers)

Place numbered picture cards depicting different kinds of families, drawing paper, and crayons in the center along with a tape recorder and prepared tape.   On the tape, explain what a family is and how families are composed of different members.   Discuss Mary McLeod Bethune's family. Convey the idea that Mary had acquired important values from her parents.   The desire to better herself and others by working hard and thinking quickly were two of these qualities.   In such a large family she also learned the values of sharing and cooperation.   Direct the child's attention to each numbered picture.   Ask him or her to (silently) count and name the family members shown in each picture and note their appearances.   At the end of the tape, direct the child to draw and color his or her family on a piece of the drawing paper.   Display the pictures around the center.

BIOGRAPHICAL INFORMATION

Mary McLeod Bethune was a black educator, lecturer, and executive who devoted her life to improving opportunities for blacks and relations between blacks and whites.

Mary McLeod was born in Mayesville, South Carolina, on July 10, 1875. Until 1863 when slaves were first freed, Mary's parents, Samuel and Patsy, and their fourteen children, had been slaves. Mary was the fifteenth child and the first to be born free.

After the Emancipation Proclamation, Patsy McLeod continued to work for her former master. She saved her money and bought five acres of land near Mayesville. Samuel McLeod and his sons built their home, called The Homestead, on this land.

The Homestead was a log cabin with a large middle room and two bedrooms on either side. The porch in front stood under a huge live oak tree.   In back was a kitchen and a wash shed for washing clothes and bathing. Fireplaces were used for warmth and cooking.

Mrs. McLeod believed in cleanliness and thriftiness, and her children were taught the same. She insisted they be neat and clean and keep everything in and around the cabin spotless. Food was grown and stored for the winter, and money was saved to buy thirty more acres of farm land.

The McLeods were hard working and deeply religious. The family worked together on their farm picking cotton and cutting rice. At age nine Mary could pick 250 pounds of cotton a day. Family prayer meetings were held each morning and evening. On Sundays the family traveled five miles to and from Mayesville to attend services at the Methodist Episcopal Church.

Before Mary McLeod was born, her mother had prayed for a child to "show them the way out." When Mary was born, her parents could tell that she was different and her grandmother claimed that Mary was born to be a leader. Mary herself felt this difference. She longed to go to school but at that time there were no schools for black children.

Then one day Miss Emma Wilson was sent by the Trinity Presbyterian Church to start a school for blacks in Mayesville. Mary was delighted to walk the five miles each way to go to school. In the evenings she shared what she had learned with her family, none of whom could read or write.

After six years Mary learned all that she could at the Mayesville school. In Denver, Miss Mary Chrissman, a Quaker school teacher, wished to pay for the education of a worthy child. Miss Wilson chose Mary, and she was sent to Scotia Seminary in Concord, North Carolina.

There she was taught English, math, science, Latin and, most importantly, that the color of a person's skin has nothing to do with his or her mind.

After graduating from Scotia, Mary studied for two years at the Moody Bible Institute in Chicago, then began teaching at Haines Institute in Augusta, Georgia. She married another teacher, Albert Bethune, and retired from teaching for a year when their son Albert was born. She then taught for a year in Palatka, Florida.

Mary McLeod Bethune had dreamed of being a missionary in Africa. But after teaching for nine years, she decided to dedicate herself to the education of blacks in the United States. Her dream was to have her own school, and she set about making this dream come true.

In 1904 Mrs. Bethune found a building in Daytona Beach, Florida, which rented for $11 a month. She gave the owner her savings of $1.50 as a down payment and started her school, The Daytona Literary and Industrial School for Training Negro Girls.

To keep the school going, Mrs. Bethune asked anyone and everyone for donations of money, used furniture, and secondhand clothes. She and her students searched the city dumps and trash sites for broken furniture, kitchenware, and anything that could be repaired and used. In less than two years the school, which had started with five pupils, had grown to two hundred and fifty. The rented building was too small, so Mrs. Bethune put five dollars down to buy one of the town dumps called Hell's Hole. She and her students cleared the land, and with contributions from generous people and donated labor, a new school was built. Mary McLeod Bethune's school continued to grow and was successful because she was never afraid to ask for help. She was constantly calling on people for donations, writing articles, handing out leaflets, and speaking to churches, clubs, and any interested groups.

In 1923 the school joined together with Cookman Institute and became Bethune-Cookman College, an institution for educating both men and women. Mary McLeod Bethune served as its president until 1942.

Mrs. Bethune had become widely known for her work. From 1935 to 1944 she served as President Franklin D. Roosevelt's Special Adviser on Minority Affairs. As Director of Negro Affairs of the National Youth Administration from 1936 to 1944, she became the first black woman to head a federal agency. In addition, she helped found and was president of The National Council of Negro Women and was vice president of the Commission on Interracial Cooperation of the National Urban League.

Mary McLeod Bethune received many awards and honorary degrees. Among these were an M.A. degree from Wilberforce University in Ohio, an LL.D. from Lincoln University, the NAACP's (for an explanation of the NAACP, see the Thurgood Marshall Unit, Biographical Information) Spingarn Medal given annually for highest achievement by a black American, and the Francis A. Drexel Award for distinguished service to her race. In 1931 Ida M. Tarbell, the foremost woman journalist of the country, named Mary McLeod Bethune one of the fifty outstanding living American women.

Mrs. Bethune continued her work to open the doors of education to all and to help create a world where one's color was not important. On May 18, 1955, at age eighty, she died at her home in Daytona. This home, which she called "The Retreat," is now The Mary McLeod Bethune Foundation. Besides providing various services, it houses all of Mrs. Bethune's school records and the many keepsakes of her full and productive life.

LANGUAGE ARTS - SOCIAL STUDIES - SCIENCE

Discussion

Before the discussion, place a piece of chalk, a red pencil, a ruler, and a textbook in a paper bag. Set the bag in the center of the discussion area. Ask the children to name various occupations. Take the items out of the bag, put them in front of the children, and say, "The person we are going to learn about today had a special occupation. These are some of the tools of her occupation. Can you tell me what she was?" After receiving the correct response, emphasize that Mary McLeod Bethune was a teacher and a person who worked to improve education in America. Summarize the Biographical Information and show pictures from various references. (See Famous Black Americans, Room Environment - Learning Centers, page 35.) Locate South Carolina and Florida on a map. Read The First Book of Cotton by Matilda Rogers or any simiiar book on cotton. Show and explain the various room displays.

Choral Poem - "In the Shining Sun"

Familiarize the class with the poem. Read the poem, allowing the children to recite their lines.

Teacher: In a neat log cabin 'neath an old oak tree
A baby girl was born and she was born free,
And her mother said, "You're a special one,"

All: And they rocked and they rocked in the morning sun.

Teacher: The girl grew tall and worked on the farm,
Quick of mind and strong of arm,
Worked until the day was done,

All: And she picked and she chopped in the burning sun.

Teacher: To school she went 'til she was grown,
Then she opened a little school of her own,
A school that was open to everyone,

All: And the school still stands in the shining sun.

What's Missing Sheet

Duplicate and distribute the sheet on page 47. The children look at both pictures on each row, find what's missing in the second picture, and draw the missing part. The sheet can then be colored.

Tongue Twisters

During the time when Mary Bethune went to school, tongue twisters were used to teach good speech. For fun, let the children recite any of the following tongue twisters several times each.

1. She sells seashells by the seashore.
2. Peter Piper picked a peck of pickled peppers and put them on a pressed pewter platter.
3. Three gray geese gaze at the green grass growing.
4. The swan swam the sea but shunned the sun.
5. Quizzical Quinn, kiss me quick.
6. Neddy Nooper nipped his naughty neighbor's noggin.
7. Sam Slick sawed six slender slippery sticks.
8. How much wood would a woodchuck chuck if a woodchuck could chuck wood?

Teachers for a Day

Invite parents to the class to be the students for one morning. Divide the children into groups of "team teachers" and assign each a different subject to teach. Let the groups meet and discuss what they will teach and how they will teach it. Be available for advice and assistance and to provide each group with the necessary materials. Encourage simple but fun lessons. Let the "team teachers" practice their lessons on the rest of the class. Write the schedule for the morning on the board. When the parents arrive, the team teachers take over the class. The parents sit in the children's seats, and the children (not teaching) sit in another area.

Alphabet Scavenger Hunt

Mary McLeod Bethune and her students frequently scavenged junk piles and garbage heaps to find things they could repair and use in their school. To have an Alphabet Scavenger Hunt, make sure you have an item in the room for each alphabet letter. Divide the class into two teams and designate a table for each. "Deal" alphabet cards to both teams, giving **A** to the first team, **B** to the second, and so forth, until all the cards are distributed. (You may wish to briefly review the name and sound(s) of each letter as you distribute the cards.) At the signal, the teams find something in the room that starts with each letter. Each team member may work individually, or several team members may work together to find an item. When an item is found, it is placed with the alphabet card on that team's table. The first team to find all their items wins the game.

Variation: If this is too difficult for your class, distribute a lesser number of alphabet cards to each team. To further simplify the activity, set out items beginning with each letter so that they are visible to the children and/or attach name cards to each item so that the children can see the beginning letters.

ART

Big Pencils

Preparation - Make several cardboard patterns of the Big Pencil parts on page 49 for the children to share. Cut yellow construction paper in thirds to measure 4" x 9" per piece. Cut red or pink construction paper and pieces of sandpaper into 4" squares. Set out scissors, glue, and black crayons. Have a black marker available.

Procedure - Trace around the pencil shaft pattern on the yellow construction paper, around the eraser pattern on the red or pink construction paper, and around the pencil point on the sandpaper. Cut out and glue together to form a pencil. Color the point of the pencil with the black crayon.

Note: Ask each child what he or she has learned in school. Write the answer on the pencil. Older children can write their own responses. (See "What We Learn in School" bulletin board - Room Environment section.) (See example on page 46.)

Apples for the Teacher

Preparation - Collect old crayons, red and green, and remove the paper from each. (Parents are a good source for these.) Make tagboard versions of the apple pattern on page 48. On waxed paper, trace two apple shapes for each child. Cut lengths of fishing line or heavy thread for hanging the finished apples and tie one end of each to a paper clip. Set out scissors, hole punchers, and the old crayons in bowls. Distribute a sheet of heavy paper to each child and the apple shapes to work on. Provide the hanging lines at the end of the activity.

For the crayon-shaving process, let the children use one of the following: one blade of a pair of blunt scissors, potato peelers, plastic pencil sharpeners, or cheese graters. Set up an ironing board and iron in an area away from the children. Set the iron on low and cover the ironing board with sheets of newspaper. An adult should do the ironing in this activity.

Procedure - Put one waxed paper apple shape on your sheet of paper. Cover the apple portion with red crayon shavings and the leaf and stem portions with green crayon shavings. Place the other waxed paper shape on top. Carry the shape on the sheet of paper to the ironing area. The teacher will cover the apple shapes with a sheet of newspaper and press them to melt the crayons and seal the waxed paper layers together. Punch a hole at the top and attach a hanging line. Hang the apple in a window.

Variation: For a simpler art activity, let the children trace around the tagboard apple pattern on white construction paper, cut it out, and sponge-paint it with red (apple) and green (leaf and stem) tempera paints. Hang as explained above.

MATH

The School Bell

Duplicate and distribute the sheet on page 50. The students fill in the missing numerals on the bell.

Classroom Counting Activity

Place the numeral flashcards 1–10 (or 1–20) on the chalkboard ledge. Call on different children, one at a time, to count various classroom items which you have placed on a table such as pieces of chalk, erasers, crayons in a basket, desks, blocks, pencils in a box, plants, books on a shelf, and so forth. After each child counts the items, as directed, he or she walks to the chalkboard ledge and holds up the flashcard that shows the total number of items counted.

MUSIC - MOVEMENT - GAMES

Song - "Mary McLeod Bethune"

Tune: "John Jacob Jingleheimer Schmidt"

A famous black American
Was Mary McLeod Bethune,
She worked for her concern
That everyone should learn,
Hurray for Mary McLeod Bethune.
(Hip hip hurray, hurray, hurray.)

Song - "School Days" by Will D. Cobb and Gus Edwards

Source: The New York Times Nostalgic Years in Songs (Book) edited by Irving Brown

Action Song - "The Teacher Who Couldn't Talk" - from Creative Movement and Rhythmic Exploration (LP) by Hap Palmer

Game - Jumping Rope

Let the children jump rope to traditional jump rope rhymes found in Wee Sing and Play by Pamela Conn Beall and Susan Hagen Nipp.

STORY TIME

1. Morris Goes to School - B. Wiseman
2. Fox at School - Edward Marshall
3. "Talk" from The Cow-Tail Switch and Other West African Stories - Harold Courlander and George Herzog
4. "Bruh Alligator Meets Trouble" from The People Could Fly told by Virginia Hamilton

COOKING IN THE CLASSROOM

Red Beans and Rice

1 lb. dried kidney beans
1 ham bone or leftover chunks of ham
6 cups water
1 small onion, chopped
1 stalk celery, chopped
3 tablespoons grated carrot
1 teaspoon sugar
1/8 teaspoon cayenne
Salt, pepper, and garlic powder to taste
3 cups cooked rice

Wash beans; cover with cold water. Soak overnight; drain. Put all ingredients, except the rice, in a large cooking pot or kettle. Bring to a boil; reduce heat. Cook slowly for several hours until the beans are tender. Stir frequently to prevent sticking and add more water if the mixture gets too thick. Add red pepper sauce if you desire a spicier taste. Serve over rice. Yield: 6 generous servings

Dear Parents,

On _____, we will learn about Mary McLeod Bethune, a famous black educator, lecturer, and executive. We will begin with her childhood and cover her many contributions to education. Please read below to find out ways you can help.

Things To Send: _____
_____
_____

Volunteers Needed To: _____
_____
_____

Follow-Up: At the end of the unit, ask your child the following questions:
_____
_____
_____

Thank you for your cooperation.

Sincerely,

MARY McLEOD BETHUNE

Bulletin Board

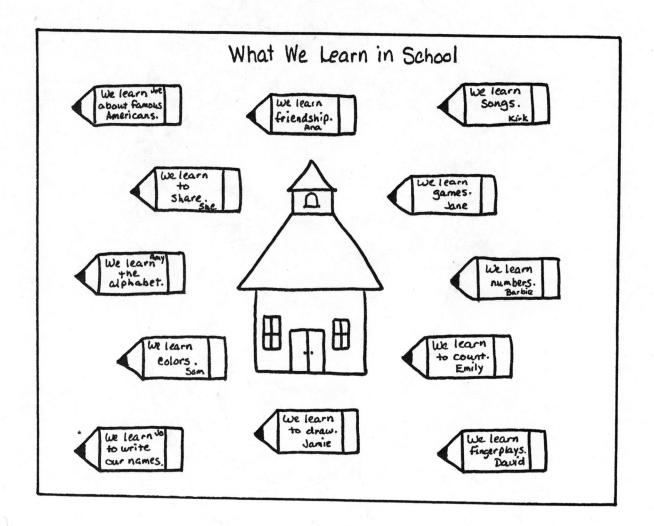

What We Learn in School

We learn about famous Americans.

We learn friendship.
Ana

We learn Songs.
Kirk

We learn to Share.
She

We learn games.
Jane

We learn the alphabet.
Amy

We learn numbers.
Barbie

We learn colors.
Sam

We learn to count.
Emily

We learn to write our names.

We learn to draw.
Janie

We learn fingerplays.
David

What's Missing Sheet

Name:

Examples

Door Display
" Welcome to Our Schoolhouse "

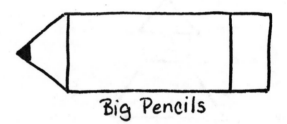

Big Pencils

Apples for the Teacher

Big Pencils

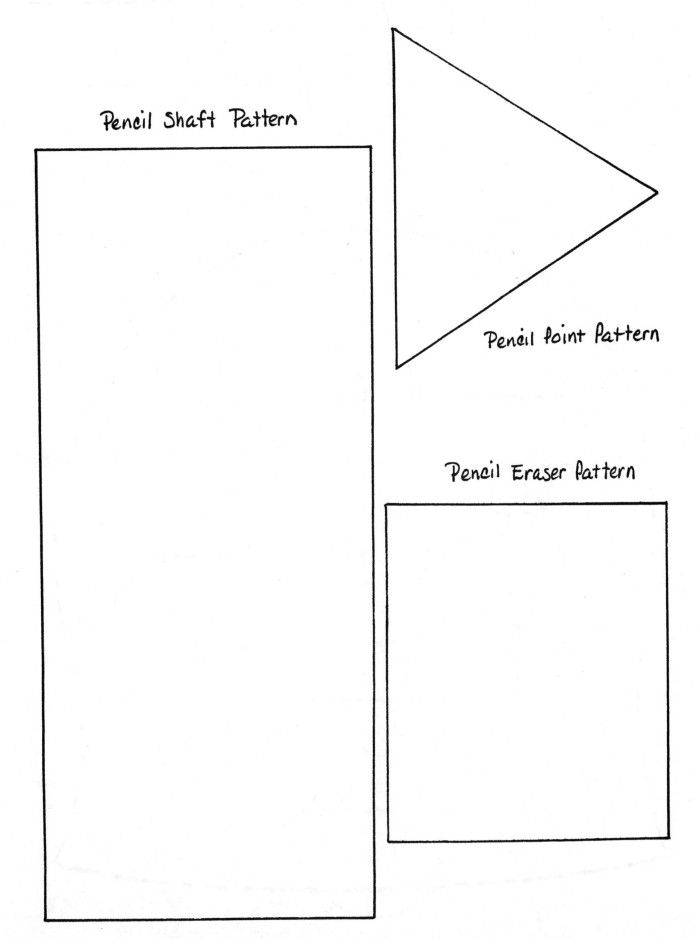

Pencil Shaft Pattern

Pencil Point Pattern

Pencil Eraser Pattern

The School Bell

Name: _____

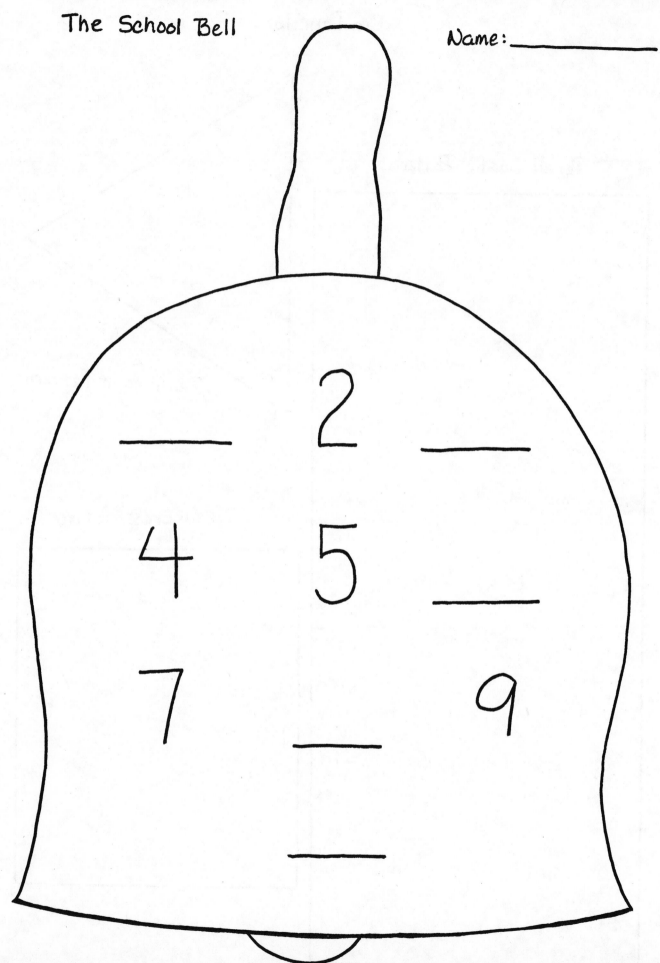

GUION S. BLUFORD, JR.

(1942 -   )

ROOM ENVIRONMENT - BULLETIN BOARD

"Blast Off!"

Cover the bulletin board with black or royal blue paper and trim with a yellow border. Cut the letters for the title from yellow construction paper and staple at the top. Mount a picture of Guion Bluford (see page 62) in the center of the bulletin board with a piece of construction paper underneath which reads "Guion Bluford, First Black American in Space." On the remaining area of the bulletin board, staple pictures of shuttles, satellites, rockets, and men in space (see sources below). If desired add a moon, planets, and small glitter (or sticker) stars. (See example on page 63.)

Note: For pictures of men in space, write National Aeronautics and Space Administration, Audio Visual Branch, Public Information Division, Code LFD-10, 400 Maryland Avenue, S.W., Washington, D.C. 20546. Pictures of shuttles, satellites, and rockets are found in Rockets and Satellites by Franklyn M. Branley.

Room Decorations

On poster paper draw, color, and cut out the planets, our moon, and numerous stars. Hang with fishing line from the ceiling. Make comets by punching a hole in the bottoms of yellow paper cups. Insert yellow crepe paper streamers in the holes, pull through, and knot or tape to secure. Hang from the ceiling with fishing line so that the comets are horizontal. If available, hang strings of tiny white Christmas lights from the ceiling to resemble stars. (You will need extension cords.) Draw and cut out a large space shuttle from white bulletin board paper. (See example on page 64.) Write "Welcome to Our Space Shuttle" on the body of the shuttle. Mount "We're Astronauts" (see Art) on and around the shuttle.

Classroom Rocket

Obtain a refrigerator box, one medium and one small corrugated cardboard box, and one cardboard ice cream cylinder (available at ice cream stores). Cut away the bottom of the refrigerator box and cut a door in one side. Cut "fins" from tagboard and tape to each side of the box. Spray-paint the box and fins white, or let the children paint with white tempera paint. Stack the medium box and the small box on top of the refrigerator box and tape in place.   Cover this top section with blue bulletin board paper to make it appear rounded.   Cut strips of the blue bulletin board paper long enough to extend from the top edges of the refrigerator box to the center top of the small box.   Tape in place.   Paint the ice cream cylinder red and tape in place on top of the small box.   Stand a small American flag in the cylinder.   Let the children paint dials, levers, and controls on the inside walls of the rocket.   Plastic milk jug caps and medicine vials may be glued on to serve the same purpose.   (See example on page 64.)

Note: A hot glue gun works better than tape but can only be used by adult participants.

ROOM ENVIRONMENT - LEARNING CENTERS

Famous Black Americans - (See Room Environment - General - Learning
    Centers)

Staple Guion Bluford's name and related pictures on the center. In front of the center, place a filmstrip on space and a viewer (and/or a children's Viewmaster with pictures on space); books such as Our Future in Space by Tim Furniss and The Space Race by Pearce Wright; and a model of our solar system.

Brainwork Center - (See Room Environment - General - Learning Centers)

Purchase a book of activities on space which contains mazes, dot-to-dot pictures, color-by-number sheets, and so forth. These can be found at teacher supply stores or in the coloring book sections of discount or drug stores. Reproduce and set in the center or laminate for continued use and supply wipe-off crayons and cloths for cleaning.

BIOGRAPHICAL INFORMATION

Guion Steward Bluford, Jr., became the first black American astronaut to travel in space. On August 30, 1983, the space shuttle Challenger blasted off for its third flight with Daniel C. Brandenstein, Dale A. Gardner, William E. Thornton, Richard H. Truly, and Guion S. Bluford, Jr., aboard.

Guion Bluford, Jr., was born on November 22, 1942, in Philadelphia, Pennsylvania. Guion, pronounced "Guy-on," was the oldest of three sons. His father, Guion S. Bluford, Sr., was a mechanical engineer and his mother, Lolita Harriet Bluford, was a special education teacher.

Guion, Jr., called Guy, was different from his two younger brothers, Eugene and Kenneth. His favorite toys were mechanical. He enjoyed taking them apart, studying their construction, then putting them back together. Best of all, he loved to watch and study things that fly. Until Guy went to college, he never felt different because he was black. His family lived in Philadelphia which was an integrated community. He and his brothers went to integrated schools. Guy's parents taught them that if they worked hard enough they could achieve whatever they desired, and it was their obligation to do so. Color was not a factor.

Guy Bluford's dream was to design and build airplanes. After reading about the space program, Guy became determined to work on the design, construction, and operation of spacecraft as an aerospace engineer.

After graduating from Overbrook High School in 1960, Bluford entered the aerospace engineering program at Pennsylvania State University. There, he was one of about four hundred blacks in a student body of several thousand. For the first time in his life Bluford felt different because of his color, but he had little time to think about it. He had to work hard at the courses he was taking such as calculus and aerospace engineering. He had enrolled in the Air Force ROTC program after his first ride in an Air Force T-33 plane and decided to go into the Air Force as a pilot. He thought that if he became a pilot he would be a better engineer.

After graduating from Pennsylvania State, Guy Bluford trained for combat crew duty and was sent to Vietnam where he flew 144 combat missions and was awarded the Vietnam Campaign Medal, the Vietnam Service Medal, the Vietnam Cross of Gallantry with Palm, ten Air Force medals, and three outstanding unit awards.

When Bluford returned from Vietnam, he was sent to Sheppard Air Force Base in Texas where he taught cross-country and acrobatic flying. In 1971 Bluford attended Squadron Officers School and became an executive support officer to the deputy commander of operations at Sheppard Air Force Base. In 1972 he entered the graduate program at the Air Force Institute of Technology and two years later graduated with a master's degree in aerospace engineering. He continued his studies and in 1978 received his Ph.D. degree in aerospace engineering. He then applied for the astronaut program.

In January 1978 Guy Bluford was chosen by NASA, the National Aeronautics and Space Administration, to be an astronaut. He was one of the 35 chosen out of the 10,000 people who had applied. Another of the 35 was Sally Ride who later became the first American woman in space.

At the Lyndon B. Johnson Space Center in Houston, Bluford began his year-long training program. Some of the courses it included were space-navigation, geology, celestial mechanics, oceanography, and crew station design.   There were also programs in physical fitness, flights on T-38 jet trainers, and field trips to other NASA space centers.   After the year of training, Bluford was eligible to fly in a space shuttle.

Space shuttles are reusable spaceships which can do various jobs in space. They can be used to launch communications satellites that send telephone messages and television programs all over the world or weather satellites that take pictures of storms and clouds.   They can launch other craft further into space and can build space stations where astronauts and space engineers can live and conduct experiments in laboratories.

Columbia was the first space shuttle.   It was launched in 1981 and completed its fourth flight in 1982.   Challenger was the second space shuttle.   Its first flight was in May 1983.   Its second flight was in June 1983, and one of its three mission specialists was Dr. Sally K. Ride, the first American woman in space.   Guy Bluford was chosen for Challenger's third flight.

Bluford was more excited about actually flying the shuttle than being the first black American astronaut in space.   Naturally quiet and unassuming, he did not consider himself a hero.   Others, however, were pleased that he would be the first.   With his keen intelligence, dedication, and strong values, Guy Bluford was the perfect role model.

Bluford was equally qualified to be a pilot or a mission specialist.   For the Challenger flight, he was one of two mission specialists.   The mission specialists have different responsibilities such as conducting scientific experiments and launching satellites.

The lift-off of the Challenger was at 2:32 a.m. on August 30, 1983.   In order to launch a communications and weather satellite for the government of India, it was launched at night, the first shuttle to do so.   As the flight got under way, the crew members used their training and quickly adjusted to the lack of gravity.   Without gravity they could just as easily walk on the ceiling as on the floor.   They began carrying out the various experiments and tests that were to be done.   They ate their meals which were various dehydrated foods stored in plastic containers.   The food was mixed with water and heated, then served on plates; however, the food was chosen for its ability to stick to the plate.   Otherwise it would float away.

On the shuttle flight's second day, the Indian satellite Insat-1B which was Bluford's main responsibility was successfully launched.   The satellite spun in space for about forty-five minutes.   Then it made a smooth climb to an altitude of about 22,000 miles above the earth and went into orbit.

On September 5, 1983, at 3:40 a.m., the Challenger landed on the runway in California's Mojave Desert to complete its successful flight.   Crowds cheered as the five astronauts climbed out of the shuttle. The astronauts were again cheered in Houston where they returned for medical examinations and debriefings. After that, there were press conferences and interviews. Bluford accepted many invitations for public appearances, but he most enjoyed those at which he addressed young blacks. To them he passed on what his parents had taught him, to set your goals high and then work hard to achieve them.

Among the many honors and awards Guy Bluford has received are the NAACP Image Award, the NASA space flight medal, the Ebony Black Achievement Award, the Distinguished National Scientist Award, and several honorary university degrees.

LANGUAGE ARTS - SOCIAL STUDIES - SCIENCE

Discussion

Show a film or video on our space program. Discuss the film or video; then introduce the unit and point out the various room displays and centers. Summarize the Biographical Information and show pictures from Space Challenger: The Story of Guion Bluford by Jim Haskins and Kathleen Benson. Locate Pennsylvania and Texas on a map.

Blast Off! - Review Game

To check for understanding, play "Blast Off!" Draw a large rocket on the board as shown on page 64. Divide the class into two teams and alternate asking questions (see samples below). If the answer is correct, write it by that team's "number 10" on the rocket; the next correct answer will be number 9, and so forth. The first team to answer ten questions correctly is the winner and gets to "blast off."

Note: If sample questions are too difficult, compose a list of questions which suits the needs of your class.

Sample Questions
1. What is space?
2. Why do we want to go into space?
3. How is a person carried into space?
4. How do you eat in space?
5. Why do things float in space?
6. What is a satellite?
7. Why are satellites useful?
8. What is a space station?

9.   Guion Bluford flew on the space shuttled named _____ .

10. Was he a pilot or a mission specialist on the flight?

11. Bluford's shuttle was the first to lift off at _____ ?

12. Was the flight a success?

Challenger Poem and Pictures

Duplicate and distribute the sheets on pages 65 and 66. Give each child three half-sheets of black construction paper. The children color the pictures, then cut out the pictures and verses on the dotted lines. Three cloud shapes are cut from the black construction paper. Each picture is glued on one cloud shape. Details (stars, moon, runway lights) are added using white or yellow crayons. Corresponding verses are glued on the back of each cloud shape. (See example on page 68.) Teach the verses. The children hold up the correct picture as they recite the verses of the poem.

See the Challenger space shuttle,
The countdown seems so slow,
5-4-3-2-1, LIFT OFF!
Watch the shuttle go!

See the night sky blazing,
Hear the shuttle's roar,
Up in the sky, then into space
And we can see no more.

The runway lights are shining
And sonic booms we hear,
The Challenger makes its landing,
The crowd gives it a cheer!

Junior Astronauts - Alphabet Sheet

Before duplicating the sheet (see page 67), write in random order an upper-case alphabet letter on the front of each astronaut's spacesuit at the top of the sheet. Likewise, write the corresponding lower-case alphabet letters on the astronauts at the bottom of the page. Duplicate and distribute. The students draw lines to match the spacesuits and helmets, then color.

Variation: Use numbers and number dots instead of alphabet letters.

Books - Read Rockets and Satellites by Franklyn M. Branley and/or Let's Find Out About the Moon by Martha & Charles Shapp.

ART

We're Astronauts

Preparation - Distribute manila paper, crayons, and scissors. Display pictures of astronauts. Demonstrate drawing a person.

Procedure - Draw yourself as an astronaut. Include a spacesuit and space helmet. Color and cut out. Write your name on the spacesuit. (See example on page 68.)

Note: "We're Astronauts" may be used on the shuttle display. See Room Decorations, page 51.

Flying Rockets

Preparation - Purchase cone-shaped paper cups, one per child. On each cup, make a dot 2" under the rim. Turn the cup around and in the same manner make a dot on the opposite side. Give each child a cup and a 24" piece of string. Set out scissors and markers.

Procedure - To make a rocket, decorate the cup with the point as the top. Cut two thin wedges from the cup, starting at the rim and ending at each dot. Place the ends of the string in each hand and hold the string so that it is slack. Have a friend place the rocket on the string, inserting the string in the cut-out wedges. As soon as the friend lets go of the rocket, pull sharply on the ends of the string. The rocket will fly into the air. (See example on page 68.)

Variation: Make space capsules by using regular paper cups.

Boomerangs

Preparation - Duplicate the patterns on page 69 and cut apart. Give each child a pattern, a piece of cardboard, and scissors. Set out crayons or markers, staplers, and staple removers.

Procedure - For Guion Bluford's senior thesis, he investigated the flight of the boomerang. To make your own boomerang, staple the pattern to the cardboard. Cut out, following the lines of the pattern. Remove the staples and discard the pattern. Decorate the boomerang.

To "launch" the boomerang, hold the inside of the "elbow" between your pointer finger and thumb with your pointer finger on top. The two ends of the boomerang will be pointing at you. Raise it to eye level, then loosen your grip so that you are barely holding it between your finger and thumb.   Hold up the pointer finger of your other hand and use it to sharply strike one end of the boomerang. With practice, the boomerang will fly back to you.

MATH

Flannel Board Rockets - Positions and Counting Activity

Use the pattern on page 68 to make ten felt or pellon rockets. Cut a circle for the moon, and a square to use as the launch pad. Cut two pieces of yarn and place parallel at the bottom of the flannel board to represent the runway. Put the moon, the launch pad, and one rocket on the flannel board.

Ask different children to put the rocket on the launch pad, above the runway, under the moon, beside the launch pad, below the runway, on the moon, and so forth. Remove everything and place the rockets in a pile. Call on children to put three shuttles on the flannel board, five shuttles on the flannel board, etc. If desired, hold up flashcards or write the numbers on the chalkboard. To teach the concepts of addition and subtraction, have the children add or remove shuttles as directed.

Note: To teach colors, make each rocket a different color and include color identification in the directions above.

Short and Tall Shuttles

Place modeling clay on a table. Use masking tape to make a line on the floor or carpet or on a long table. Direct the students to break off a piece of clay, "work it" until it is soft, then form the shape of a shuttle. (Show pictures if necessary.) After the shuttles are completed, place them (in vertical positions) side by side on the "launch pad" (the masking tape line.) Have the students decide which shuttle is shortest, which is tallest, and which shuttles are of the same height. If desired, rearrange the shuttles in order of height.

MUSIC - MOVEMENT - GAMES

Song and Game - "Let's Go 'Round the Sun"

Tune: "Here We Go Looby-Loo"

Verse 1:

Let's go 'round the sun
Let's go 'round the moon

Let's go 'round them both

Back to the earth before noon.

Verse 2:

(child's name) go 'round the sun

_____ go 'round the moon

_____ go 'round them both

Back to the earth before noon.

The children stand in a circle with two children, "the sun" and "the moon," standing a few feet apart in the center. All the children sing the first verse while clapping to the beat. For the second verse, choose a child to skip in a circle around the sun and around the moon, in a big circle around them both, and then back to his or her place. The rest of the children clap and sing as usual, using the chosen child's name in the song.

Game - Parachute Play

The children stand around the parachute, holding it with two hands. Give the following directions:

1. Lift arms as high as possible, watch as the chute swells and then sinks to the floor. Lower arms and repeat.

2. Lift arms as high as possible, watch the chute swell, then quickly crouch and bring edges to the floor.

3. (Tap every other child and have these children choose a partner who is standing "across the chute" from him or her.) Lift arms as high as possible. Partners run under the chute and change places.

4. Lift arms as high as possible. When the chute has swelled, pivot and change hand positions so that you are under the chute, facing outward. Pull the chute down over your heads.

5. (Throw a ball into the center of the chute.) Move your arms up and down to make the ball bounce around on the chute.

STORY TIME

1. Marty McGee's Space Lab, No Girls Allowed - Martha Alexander
2. Garp and the Space Pirates - David Ross

COOKING IN THE CLASSROOM

Shuttle Mix

Purchase packages of dried fruit (apples, peaches, bananas, pineapple, etc.). Let the children pour the fruit into large bowls and stir to mix. Divide into equal portions and serve in ziplock bags. Cups of orange juice are an added treat.

Note: If you wish to show the class how apples are dried, peel and core several apples, slice horizontally into rings approximately one-fourth inch thick, pass a length of heavy string through the holes in the rings, and hang (clothesline-fashion) in the warmest area of your room.

Allow up to two weeks to dry. When dried, the rings will resemble leather and have a "chewy" texture like those which are commercially prepared.

Dear Parents,

On _____, we will learn about Guion S. Bluford, Jr., the first black American astronaut to travel in space. Please read below to find out ways you can help.

Things To Send: _____
_____
_____

Volunteers Needed To: _____
_____
_____

Follow-Up: At the end of the unit, ask your child the following questions:
_____
_____
_____

Thank you for your cooperation.

Sincerely,

GUION BLUFORD

Bulletin Board

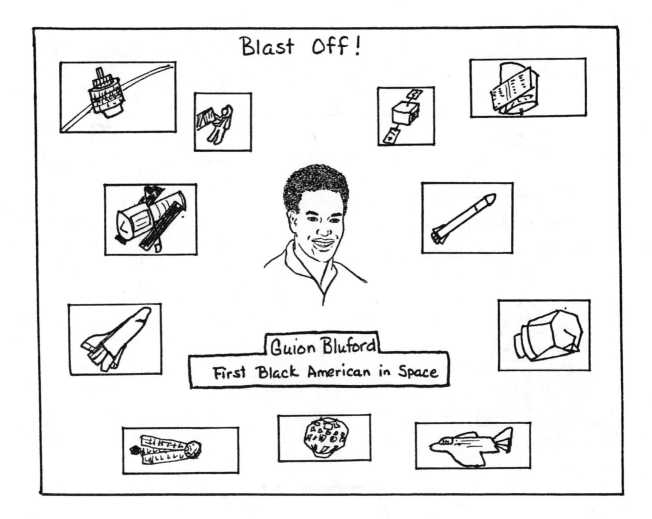

Blast Off!

Guion Bluford
First Black American in Space

Examples

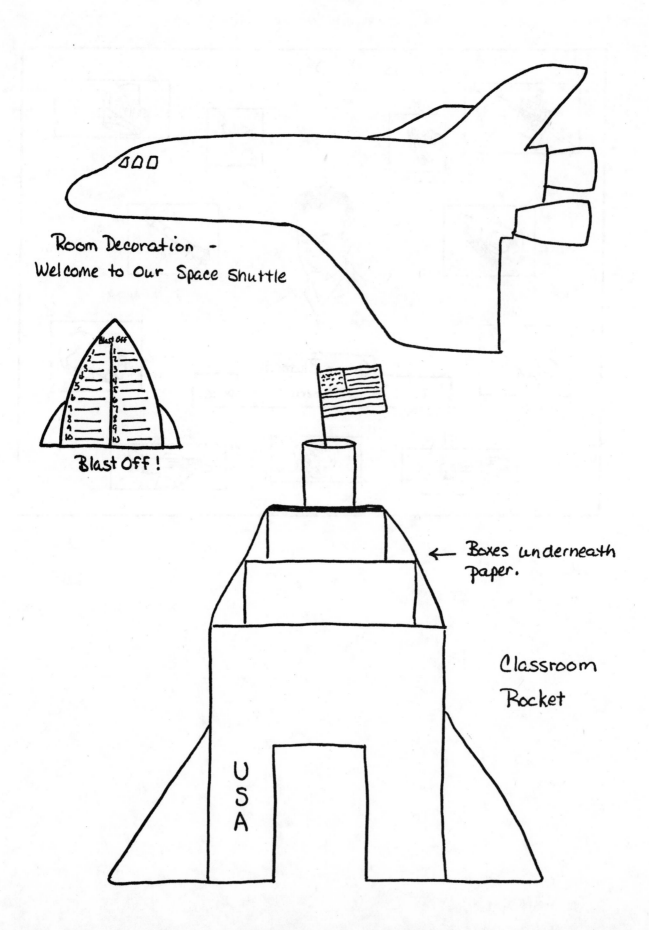

Room Decoration -
Welcome to Our Space Shuttle

Blast Off !

← Boxes underneath paper.

Classroom
Rocket

CHALLENGER POEM

1.

See the Challenger space shuttle,
The countdown seems so slow,
5-4-3-2-1, LIFT OFF!
Watch the shuttle go!

2.

See the night sky blazing,
Hear the shuttle's roar,
Up in the sky, then into space
And we can see no more.

3.

The runway lights are shining
And sonic booms we hear,
The Challenger makes its landing,
The crowd gives it a cheer!

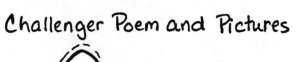

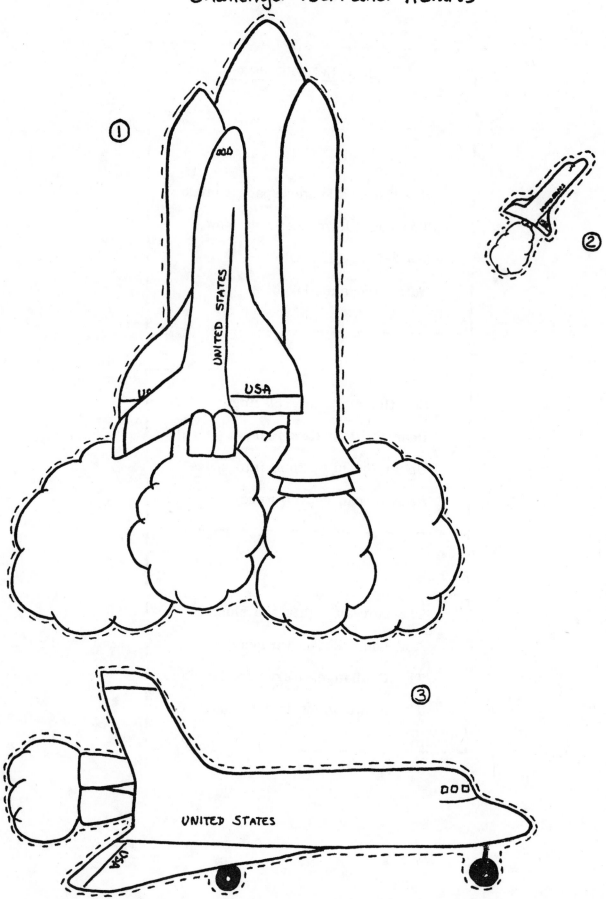

Junior Astronauts

Name:

Examples, Pattern

Challenger Poem & Pictures

We're Astronauts

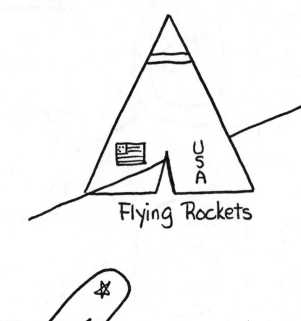

Flying Rockets

Boomerangs

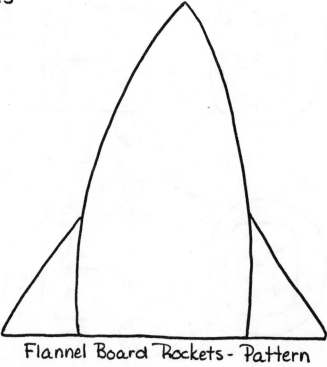

Flannel Board Rockets - Pattern

Boomerangs

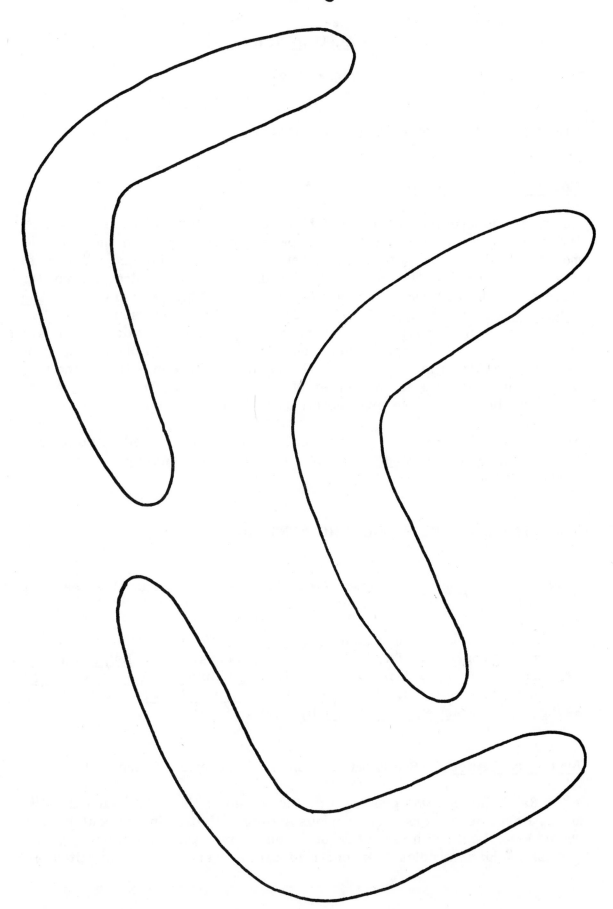

RALPH BUNCHE

(1904 - 1971)

ROOM ENVIRONMENT - BULLETIN BOARD

Countries for World Peace - The United Nations

Cover the bulletin board with light blue paper and trim with a red border. Use a different color of construction paper for each word in the title and mount the first four words at the top. Let each child use markers to draw and color the flag of a different nation on white drawing paper. Have one volunteer make the flag of the United Nations. (Refer to The International Flag Book in Color by Christian Fogd Pedersen, "Flags" in the World Book Encyclopedia or references of the individual nations.) Draw and cut out clasped hands from manila paper. Staple the flags of different countries in a circle with the hands in between. Mount the flag of the United Nations in the center of the circles and, below it, the last words of the title. (See example on page 83.)

Note: To check for the nation's membership in the United Nations, see the current World Almanac published annually by Newspaper Enterprise Association Inc.

ROOM ENVIRONMENT - LEARNING CENTERS

Famous Black Americans - (See Room Environment - General - Learning Centers)

Staple a picture of Ralph Bunche (see page 82) and the United Nations on the learning center. In front of this, display books such as Ralph Bunche: Champion of Peace by Jean Gay Cornell, Ralph Bunche: A Most Reluctant Hero by James Haskins, The Story of the United Nations by Katharine Savage, and Israel and the Arabs by Geoffrey Regan.

Brainwork Center - (See Room Environment - General - Learning Centers)

When Ralph Bunche was growing up, the women of the family earned extra money doing needlework. Put various sewing activities in the center. Let the children begin with sewing cards; then provide scraps of burlap, yarn, and large plastic needles. Demonstrate making a simple running stitch on the burlap. Once this is mastered, the children can follow a simple shape or letter drawn on burlap with a permanent marker. For the last project, introduce simple needlepoint. Purchase needlepoint canvas that has large squares. The children use yarn and a large plastic needle to fill in the squares. The needle is put underneath the canvas, inserted in the hole of a square, and then pulled through the square. Next the needle is inserted in

the square diagonally above the first square, then pulled through from the back. Stitches will look like those in the picture above. The stitches are continued until the canvas is filled. Colors may be varied.

Note: Explain and give all demonstrations to the class so the children can work independently at the center.

BIOGRAPHICAL INFORMATION

Ralph Bunche was an American statesman who became the first black to win the Nobel Peace Prize in 1950. Appointed to the United Nations Palestine Commission in 1947, he worked as a mediator and brought about an end to the Arab-Israeli war in 1949. He was awarded the Peace Prize for this accomplishment.

Ralph Johnson Bunche was born in Detroit, Michigan, on August 7, 1904. His father owned a barber shop in the black section of Detroit, and above the shop was an apartment where the family lived. Here Ralph was born and lived with his father, Fred Bunche; his mother, Olive Agnes; his grandmother, Lucy Johnson; and his two aunts, Nelle and Ethel Johnson.

Like most of their neighbors, the Bunche family was poor. The women of the family took in washing and needlework or worked as maids, and Ralph Bunche sold newspapers to bring in extra money. In desperate times, other families in the neighborhood helped out and the Bunches reciprocated.

One day a social worker visited the family to encourage them to keep Ralph in school. She had seen his school records which showed him to be extremely brilliant. It was then that Grandma Lucy Johnson became determined to see her grandson fully educated.

When Bunche was about ten years old, his sister Grace was born. Two months later his mother became ill with rheumatic fever. His father was also in ill health with a persistent, racking cough. For this reason, the family moved to sunny Albuquerque, New Mexico, where the air was dry. Bunche entered a new school and, with his love of history, enjoyed meeting his first native American and learning some of the Indian language.   He and his grandmother and aunts worked at whatever jobs they could find and took turns watching his sister Grace.

In the fall of 1916 Ralph Bunche's mother died, and three months later his father died of tuberculosis. Grandma Johnson decided it was best to move the family to Los Angeles, California. Two years later Bunche graduated from elementary school, receiving prizes in history and English. He then entered Jefferson High School where he was a member of the debating team and the football, basketball, baseball, and track teams. Grandma Johnson worked as a maid and a seamstress so that he could enjoy high school and participate in sports. Each summer Bunche worked to help out.

After high school, Bunche attended the University of California at Los Angeles on an athletic scholarship. He worked as a gymnasium janitor to pay for his books and, in 1927, graduated summa cum laude (with highest honors). He was class valedictorian (honor student who gives the farewell address at graduation), earned five medals in various subjects, and won a scholarship to Harvard University. He was also presented one thousand dollars for his other college expenses by the people of his community who were so proud of him.

Bunche's grandmother, whose work and determination had gotten him through school, died a few days before he left to go to Harvard. In later years Bunche attributed much of his success to her, for she had shown him the values of strength and thriftiness and the ability to laugh.

Bunche studied political science at Harvard and received his master's degree a year later. He then established a department of political science and taught at Howard University in Washington, D.C. He headed the department, taking several leaves, until 1950.

In 1930 Bunche married Ruth Harris. They later had three children, Joan, Jane, and Ralph, Jr. In 1931 a Rosenwald Fellowship enabled Bunche to go to Europe and Africa to gather material for his doctorate. In 1934 he received his Ph.D., the first American black to receive a doctorate in political science. He later traveled with Gunnar Myrdal and prepared thousands of pages of research data for Myrdal's book on the race problem entitled An American Dilemma.

When World War II broke out, Dr. Bunche worked for the Office of Strategic Services. There he researched and supplied valuable information on Africa which was used to plan African airbases. He was so successful that after the war he was selected Associate Chief of the Division of Dependent Territories, and therefore was the first black to be in charge of an office in the State Department. In this capacity, he was assigned to the United Nations Conference on International Organization where he wrote the trusteeship portions of the charter for formation of the United

Nations. The trusteeship portions concerns regions or colonies that are administered by other countries.

Established in 1945, the United Nations is an international organization of nations formed to maintain world peace and security. Its headquarters is located in Manhattan, N.Y. The charter, which is the basic laws and principles of the organization, was signed on June 26, 1945, by fifty nations and went into effect on October 24, 1945. On October 24 of each year, United Nations Day is recognized all over the world.

In 1946 Dr. Bunche was chosen to head the U.N. Trusteeship Division and in 1947 flew to Palestine to help the United Nations Special Committee negotiate peace between the Arabs and the Jews. Since 1936 serious conflicts had developed between the two groups who, for centuries, had both occupied the same land. The assignment was very dangerous, and once Dr. Bunche's car was fired on by snipers and his chauffeur was killed. Soon after that, the U.N. Mediator, Folke Bernadotte, was assassinated and Dr. Bunche took his place in the negotiations.

Bringing about peace between the Israelis and Arabs seemed impossible. Many times the two groups would get angry and refuse to talk to each other. Besides the points of disagreement, there were the differences in customs and the language barrier. Dr. Bunche worked day and night and used patience and determination to bring about the end of the war. In 1949 he won the Spingarn Medal, the NAACP's annual award for highest achievement by a black American, and in 1950 he became the first black to receive the world's most distinguished award, the Nobel Peace Prize.

Dr. Bunche continued his work at the U.N. and became an undersecretary to the Secretary General in 1955. Because of his severe diabetes, Dr. Bunche attempted to retire in 1967. The people who worked at the United Nations were crushed. Dr. Bunche treated everyone, regardless of their position, with the same respect and kindness. Every letter he received was answered personally, and at Christmas the members of his large staff received gifts he had chosen himself. Dr. Bunche was persuaded not to retire and remained there until his death on December 8, 1971.

LANGUAGE ARTS - SOCIAL STUDIES - SCIENCE

Discussion

Summarize the Biographical Information, referring to the room displays and showing pictures from various references (listed above). As they are mentioned, point out Detroit, Albuquerque, Los Angeles, New York and Palestine on a map or globe. On a calendar, circle October 24 which is United Nations Day.

Stand Up-Sit Down Review Drill

Read the students a series of statements about the Biographical Information (see samples below). If the statement is true, the students stand; if the statement is false, the students sit down.

Sample Statements:

1. Ralph Bunche was an American stadium.

    Ralph Bunche was an Armenian statesman.

    Ralph Bunche was an American statesman.

2. Ralph Bunche was born in Detroit, Michigan.

    Ralph Bunche was born in Albuquerque, New Mexico.

    Ralph Bunche was born in Cattle Gap, Egypt.

3. Ralph's parents were named Frankie and Johnnie Bunche.

    Ralph's parents were named Fred and Olive Branch.

    Ralph's parents were named Fred and Olive Bunche.

4. Ralph did well in school.

    Ralph barely passed in school.

    Ralph did not go to school.

5. Ralph's family moved to Albuquerque because of a potato famine.

    Ralph's family moved to Alabama to see the Hot Air Balloon Festival.

    Ralph's family moved to Alabama because the dry air would help his sick mother.

6. After Ralph's parents died, he moved to New York.

    After Ralph's parents died, he moved to Los Angeles.

    After Ralph's parents died, he moved to India.

7. The person who made sure Ralph got his education was Grandma Lucy Johnson.

    The person who made sure Ralph got his education was Grandpa Luther Jones.

    The person who made sure Ralph got his education was Granny Clampett.

8. Ralph graduated from UCLA summa cum laude.
   Ralph graduated from UCLA with his laundry.
   Ralph graduated from UCLA with his dog, Lawrence.

9. Ralph got his master's degree in social science.
   Ralph got his master's degree in political science.
   Ralph got his master's degree in science fiction.

10. Ralph Bunche was the first black to be in charge of a State Department office.
    Ralph Bunche was the first black to be in charge of a Highway Department office.
    Ralph Bunche was the first black to be in charge of a complaint department office.

11. Ralph Bunche helped write the United States Charter.
    Ralph Bunche helped write the U.S. Constitution.
    Ralph Bunche helped write the United Nations Charter.

12. The United Nations was formed for business reasons.
    The United Nations was formed for maintaining world peace.
    The United Nations was formed in order to have another holiday.

13. Dr. Bunche went to Palestine to negotiate peace between the Arabs and the Jews.
    Dr. Bunche went to Palestine to negotiate peace between the French and the Indians.
    Dr. Bunche went to Palestine to negotiate peace between the Eskimos and Italians.

14. For his efforts, Dr. Bunche received the Pulitzer Prize and a Purple Heart award.
    For his efforts, Dr. Bunche received the Spingarn Medal and the Nobel Peace Prize.
    For his efforts, Dr. Bunche received the Congressional Medal of Honor and the Distinguished Service Trophy.

15. For the rest of his life, Dr. Bunche taught political science.
    For the rest of his life, Dr. Bunche was Secretary of State.
    For the rest of his life, Dr. Bunche was an undersecretary of the United Nations.

Flags - Flannel Board Activity

Make a cardboard rectangle measuring 3" x 4". Use the pattern to make several felt flags of each of the following colors: red, blue, yellow, green, purple, orange, brown, black, and white. Put one of each color on the flannel board and call on volunteers to identify the colors. The volunteers should use complete sentences such as "That flag is red," or "Red is the color of that flag." Remove the flags from the flannel board, and place them in a pile. Call on children to find a certain color in the pile and place it on the flannel board. Once all flags are on the flannel board, call on other children to remove certain colors and place them in a pile.

Poem - Read "Hug O' War" from Where the Sidewalk Ends by Shel Silverstein.

I'm Going to Palestine - Alphabet Game

Seat the children in a circle. Hold up a flashcard of the letter **A**. The first child says, "I'm going to Palestine and I'm taking an alligator (or any appropriate **A** word)." Hold up the letter **B**. The next child says, "I'm going to Palestine and I'm taking a bicycle (or any appropriate **B** word)." The game continues in this manner until all letters have been used. If a child cannot think of a word, others may volunteer answers. For younger children, place an object for each letter in the center of the circle. The first child says the first part of the sentence as usual but finds the **A** object and uses it to end the sentence.

Nobel Peace Prize and Junior Peacemakers Activity

Information: Alfred Nobel was a Swedish chemist who invented dynamite and became one of the world's richest men. In his later years, Nobel became more and more distressed that his invention, which he had created for peaceful purposes, had caused so many injuries and deaths. So in his will he set up a fund of $9,000,000 with the interest to be divided yearly among the five winners of the Nobel prizes. Three of the prizes are given for the most important invention or discovery in physics, in chemistry, and in physiology or medicine. One prize is given for literature and one for the most effective work toward world peace.

Discussion

Define peace. On the chalkboard, draw the symbols for peace—a dove and an olive branch. Ask the students for words or phrases that mean the same as the word peace. Then ask for words or phrases that mean the opposite. List these in two columns on the chalkboard. Relate the Nobel

Peace Prize information above; then ask, "Why was Ralph Bunche awarded the Nobel Peace Prize in 1950?"

Junior Peacemaker's Dramatizations

Tell the students, "This week you will all try to be Junior Peacemakers and, like Ralph Bunche, find ways to solve problems peacefully." Divide the class into groups and let each group act out a situation such as the samples listed below. After each scene, brainstorm for peaceful ways to solve the problem. Use this same method to solve problems during the week.

Note: Numbers 1 and 2 are samples designed for younger children; numbers 3 through 5 are for older children.

1. Both John and Robert want to play with the wagon at playtime. John grabs it and starts to run, with Robert chasing him.

2. Mother gave Sara and Martha permission to cook whatever they want. Sara wants to bake a cake. Martha wants to make a pizza. They begin arguing.

3. Jason looks on Anna's paper during a test. Anna tells the teacher and Jason gets an F. Jason gets mad and tells all his classmates to avoid Anna. They do and Anna begins to cry.

4. Two teams are playing baseball. A player runs for home. The catcher tags him, but the runner claims he missed touching him with the ball. There is no umpire. Both teams get into the argument.

5. Buster is a bully who enjoys picking on younger children. William overhears him threatening a little boy, Joey. Buster tells Joey he has to give him his lunch money every day or else he will beat him up. William doesn't know what to do.

ART

Junior Peacemaker Badges

Preparation - Purchase yellow or gold tissue paper, large safety pins, and blue gift tie ribbon (3/4" wide). Make several cardboard patterns of the 3 1/2" circle (see page 84) for the children to share. Transfer the Junior Peacemaker pattern on page 84 to a ditto master and duplicate. Give each child a 4" square of tagboard, an 8" square of tissue paper, two 5" pieces of blue ribbon, a safety pin, and the duplicated badge. Provide staplers, glue, pencils, markers, hole punchers, and scissors.

<u>Procedure</u> - Trace the circle pattern on tagboard and cut out. Cover with the tissue paper square and staple in place. Use the two pieces of ribbon to make an inverted **V** and staple with the ends overlapping to the center of the circle. Color and cut out the duplicated badge. Glue in the center of the circle (dry well). Punch a hole at the **X,** insert a safety pin, and pin to your shirt. (See example on page 84.)

Barber Shop Painting

<u>Preparation</u> - Cut cardboard toilet paper rolls in half lengthwise. (Cut down the length of each side.) Mix tempera of different colors. Set out in aluminum pie pans along with paintbrushes and glue. Give each child a toilet paper roll half and a sheet of newsprint or butcher paper.

<u>Procedure</u> - Paint Mr. Bunche's barber shop. To make a barber pole, paint the cardboard roll white. Allow it to dry; then add red stripes. Put a line of glue on each edge and glue the barber pole in front of the barber shop. (See example on page 84.)

MATH

Albuquerque Cactus - Counting Activity

Explain that cactuses are plants which grow well in dry areas such as Albuquerque, New Mexico, where Ralph Bunche lived for several years. Show pictures of cactuses and point out the prickly spines.

Give each child some green modeling clay and a piece of cardboard. Set out crayons and bowls of uncooked spaghetti broken into 3–4 inch pieces. Direct the children to form a clay cactus on the piece of cardboard, then insert pieces of spaghetti to represent the spines. The children should count the "spines" as they push them into the clay, then write the total number at the bottom of the cardboard. Call on different children to count aloud the spines in their cactuses and read the totals.

Variation: Use paper plates instead of pieces of cardboard. Older children can use toothpicks rather than the uncooked spaghetti pieces.

Add-a-Star Flag Sheet

Duplicate the sheet on page 85. Give each child 21 star stickers. Direct the children to color the flags. They should then read the number in each section and stick that many stars on the flag as indicated by the **X**'s.

Variation: Use star-shaped cereal and glue instead of stickers.

MUSIC - MOVEMENT - GAMES

Song - "He's Got the Whole World In His Hands"

Sources: Folk Song Carnival (LP) by Hap Palmer
             Best Loved Songs of the American People (book) by Denes Agay

Song - "What a World We'd Have If Christmas Lasted All Year Long"

Sources: Holiday Songs and Rhythms (LP) by Hap Palmer

Game - The Suitcase

Divide the class into two teams. The teams stand in two lines facing each other, with the team members standing side by side. Give the end player in each line a small suitcase containing a man's suit (coat and pants) and shoes. Put a record on the record player and start the music. The players of each team pass the suitcase from player to player, down the line and back. Stop the music at any point. The players holding the suitcase must put them down, open them, and put on the clothing as quickly as possible. The first player dressed wins a point for his or her team. Continue to repeat the procedure until one team reaches a predesignated number of points and wins the game. If you prefer the game to be less competitive, eliminate scoring. Continue the activity as long as the children are interested.

Game - Going to Jerusalem

"Musical Chairs" evolved from this old favorite. The two games are played the same, but in this version the chairs are placed side by side in a line with the first one facing one wall, the second one facing the opposite wall, and so forth, down the line. There is one less chair than players. When the music starts, the players walk in a line around the chairs; and when it stops, they all attempt to sit in a chair. The player without a chair is eliminated. Remove another chair and let the eliminated child start and stop the music for the next round.

STORY TIME

1. The Trip - Ezra Jack Keats
2. Let's Be Enemies - by Janice May Udry
3. The Quarreling Book - Charlotte Zolotow

COOKING IN THE CLASSROOM

Peaceful Pancakes

Purchase pancake mix and prepare as directed. Drizzle the mix from a teaspoon onto the hot griddle or frying pan to form the shape of a peace pipe or dove. Cook until the top bubbles and the bottom is golden brown. Flip to the other side and cook until it, too, is golden brown. Place in a pan or an oven-proof dish, and set in a 200° oven to keep the pancakes warm until you are finished and ready to eat. Top with a pat of butter and the syrup of your choice.

Dear Parents,

On _____, we will learn about the famous black American statesman, Ralph Bunche. Please read below to find out ways you can help.

Things To Send: _____
_____
_____

Volunteers Needed To: _____
_____
_____

Follow-Up: At the end of the unit, ask your child the following questions:
_____
_____
_____

Thank you for your cooperation.

Sincerely,

RALPH BUNCHE

Bulletin Board

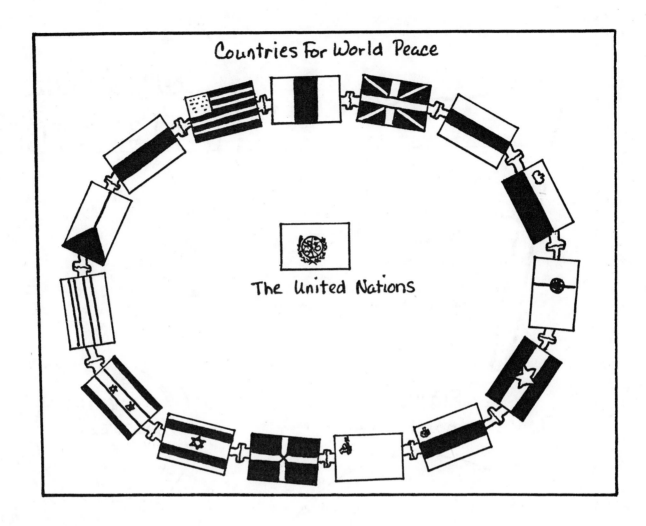

Countries For World Peace

The United Nations

Patterns, Examples

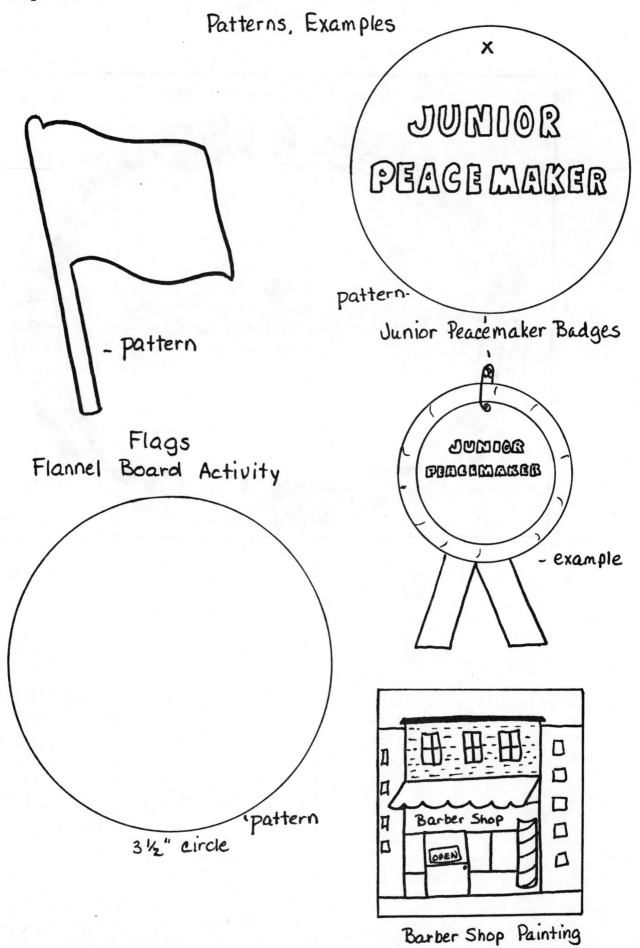

- pattern

Flags
Flannel Board Activity

3 ½" circle   'pattern

pattern.
Junior Peacemaker Badges

JUNIOR PEACEMAKER

- example

Barber Shop Painting

85

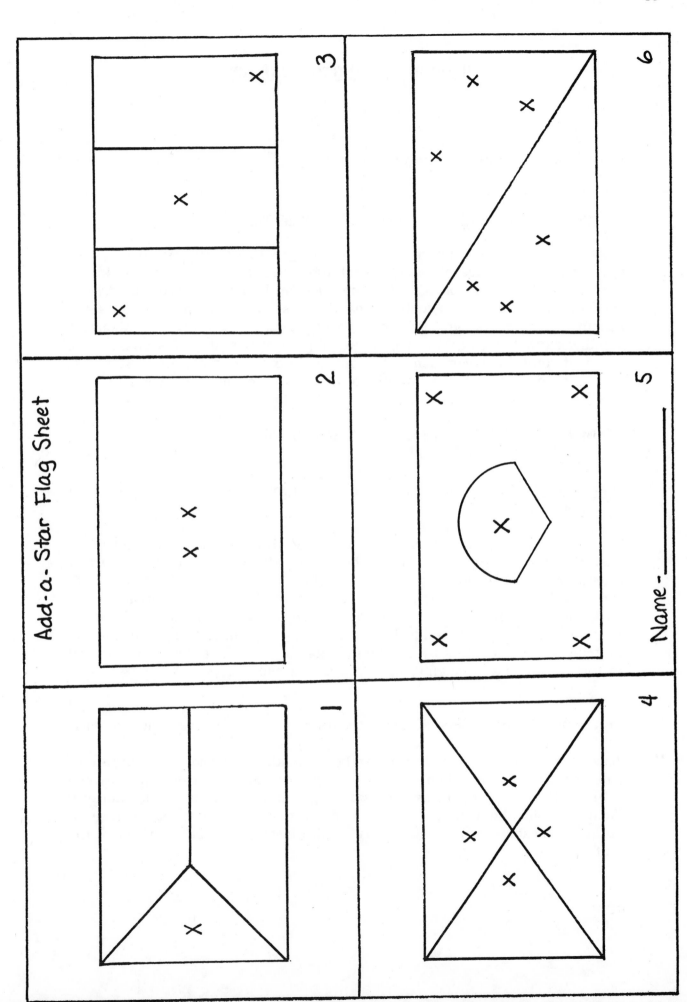

Add-a-Star Flag Sheet

Name -_____

GEORGE WASHINGTON CARVER

(1864 - 1943)

ROOM ENVIRONMENT - BULLETIN BOARD

George Washington Carver - Scientist, Educator, Author

Cover and trim the bulletin board as desired, and staple the title at the top. Mount a picture of George Washington Carver (see page 96) in the center of the bulletin board. Let the children look through old magazines and cut out pictures of lizards, frogs, insects, rocks, plants, peanuts and peanut products, sweet potatoes, books, artist supplies, greenhouses, laundry equipment, cooking tools, farm equipment, and farm scenes. Glue on construction paper which has been cut into various shapes. Staple on the remaining area of the bulletin board. (See example on page 97.)

ROOM ENVIRONMENT - LEARNING CENTER

Famous Black Americans - (See Room Environment - General - Learning Centers)

On the Famous Black Americans - Learning Center, staple George Washington Carver's name at the bottom of the center section. Draw, trace, or use an opaque projector to make simple scenes of Carver's life and mount on the learning center. In front of the center, display books on George Washington Carver, rocks, plants, peanuts, and other items mentioned in the Biographical Information. Encourage the children to contribute to the display by bringing frogs, lizards, insect collections, and so forth. Include a magnifying glass and a microscope.

Brainwork Center - (See Room Environment - General - Learning Centers)

Place a bowl of peanuts, an empty bowl, a kitchen timer, and a pair of tongs in the center. The children attempt to transfer peanuts from one bowl to the other with the tongs in one minute or less. Put numeral flashcards in the center. The children place the correct number of peanuts on each card. Simple activity sheets may also be included in the center.

BIOGRAPHICAL INFORMATION

George Washington Carver was a famous black American scientist, educator, and author. He made many important discoveries and dedicated his life to helping others.

George Washington Carver was born in 1864, the son of two slaves. His father was killed in an accident soon after George was born. His mother Mary was a slave owned by Mr. Moses Carver and his wife Susan. They were kind people who owned a farm in Diamond Grove, Missouri.

When George was a tiny baby, he and his mother were stolen by Night Riders. Night Riders were bands of outlaws who stole slaves and sold them in the South. Mr. Carver hired a man to find Mary and George but he only returned with George, who, because he was sick, had been left behind by the outlaws. Mary was never found.

George and his older brother Jim were not slaves since slavery was outlawed in 1863. Mr. and Mrs. Carver raised George and Jim as if they were their own sons. George Carver was a sickly baby and, as a child, was not as strong as Jim. Still, he did the outside chores for the Carvers, learned to cook, clean, iron, and mend clothes. When he was not busy with chores, he spent every minute studying nature. He collected pebbles, lizards, frogs, and any kind of insect he could find; but plants fascinated him the most. He had a secret garden in the woods where he experimented with flowers. He would plant the same kind of flower in different types of soil—clay, loam, and sand. He would also plant them in different locations—in the sun or in the shade. Then he would watch the flowers every day and see which grew to be the strongest. In this way, he taught himself about plants and soon became known as the "Plant Doctor." People for miles around brought him their sick plants to tend.

George Carver loved to learn, and everyone agreed that he had a fine mind. Mrs. Carver taught him to read and write from an old spelling book, but he dreamed of going to school. Because at that time there were fewer schools for black children, Carver had to set out on his own when he was only ten years old. He lived in many towns, going to school until he could no longer find work. Then he would move on to another town, another job, and another school. He had many different jobs such as ironing clothes, chopping wood, cleaning houses, cooking in a restaurant, driving oxen, harvesting wheat and oats, and working in a greenhouse.

Even though most of his time was spent working, going to school, and studying, Carver still found time to do things he enjoyed. He learned to crochet lace, draw and paint, write poetry, and play the accordion. And wherever he was, he always found time to observe the plants, insects, rocks, and soil of the area.

Sometimes Carver was taken in by kind people who helped him, and sometimes he was hungry and slept in barns or on the ground; but he never gave up. He graduated from high school and then opened a small laundry business. It was around this time that Carver added "Washington" as his middle name. This was because his mail had been going to another man in town named George Carver.

In 1890 George Washington Carver entered Simpson College in Indianola, Iowa, where he studied art and music. A year later he transferred to Ames College in Ames, Iowa, to study agriculture. He graduated in 1894 and received his master's degree in 1896.

After completing his education, George Washington Carver moved to Alabama to become head of the agriculture department at Tuskegee Institute, a college for blacks founded by the famous black educator, Booker T. Washington. It was there that Professor Carver won international fame for his work with peanuts. He made more than 300 products from peanuts including milk, butter, coffee, soap, face powder, breakfast foods, ink, and paper. He also made 118 products from sweet potatoes.

Besides his research, Professor Carver taught students about plants and soil, wrote bulletins and pamphlets on soil conservation, helped farmers learn better ways to farm, gave lectures on the many uses of peanuts, and worked to help blacks and whites get along better.

George Washington Carver received many awards and honors for his accomplishments. One of these awards was the Spingarn Medal which was given to him for his outstanding work in agriculture by the National Association for the Advancement of Colored People. Since Carver's death on January 5, 1943, Tuskegee University has established the George Washington Carver Research Foundation to continue research in agriculture. Also, the George Washington Carver National Monument was built on the Missouri farm where he was born.

LANGUAGE ARTS - SOCIAL STUDIES - SCIENCE

Discussion

Summarize the Biographical Information, examine the various room displays, and show pictures from George Washington Carver: An American Biography by Rackham Holt. Locate Missouri, Iowa, and Alabama on a map. Ask the students questions, such as the samples below, and discuss their responses. Afterwards, brainstorm for words to describe George Washington Carver and list on the board.

Sample Questions:

1. George Washington Carver dreamed of going to _____.
2. Have you ever really wanted something?
3. What was it?
4. To get what you wanted, would you set off on your own like George Carver did?
5. Why do you think going to school was so important to him?
6. How do you think he felt as he walked from one town to another? At his first day in a new school? When he couldn't find a place to sleep? When kind people helped him?

Poem - Read one of George Washington Carver's favorite poems entitled "Equipment" by Edgar A. Guest found in Collected Verse of Edgar A. Guest.

Plant Activities

Discuss George Washington Carver's experimental garden. Grow four bean plants, two in red cups and two in blue cups. Put one of the plants (red cup) in the sunlight and the other (red cup) in a closet. Observe and discuss what happens. Water one of the plants (blue cup) daily, and do not water the other (blue cup). Observe and discuss the results.

Observe three types of soil—sand, clay, and loam. Note the differences. Fill a cup with each type and plant a bean seed in each. Place in a window and water when the soil is dry. Observe and compare the growth of the three plants.

To grow a peanut plant, fill a large, deep pot with loose and slightly sandy soil. Purchase peanut seeds or raw (unroasted) peanuts. If you use the raw peanuts, either discard the shells and plant the peanuts (seeds) only, or crack the shells and plant the shell and seeds together. Plant the peanut seeds about 2" deep.

The peanut plant requires at least four months' growing time. The plant produces a stalk, leaves, and flowers. As the flowers wither, smaller stalks grow out of them and down into the soil where the peanut develops.

After the required amount of growing time, dig up the whole plant and allow to air-dry for 2–3 weeks. Then the shell pods may be removed. (See Cooking in the Classroom for peanut recipes.)

Make arrangements to tour a greenhouse.

<u>Skit</u> - "George Carver and the Horse Thieves"

The following play is taken from an incident described in the biography <u>George Carver: Boy Scientist</u> by Augusta Stevenson. George Carver was seldom punished, but he broke a very strict rule and played with Mr. Carver's hunting dogs. His punishment was to sleep in the loft of the barn for one night. What happened that night is described in the play below.

Choose one child to play George, one to play Mr. Carver, and the rest to be the horse thieves, the horses, and the hunting dogs. Use a table for the loft, a table on its side for the dog pen, and chairs for the horse stalls. If you wish to include masks, see Art.

George: I've never slept in the loft before, but Mr. Carver was right to punish me. I was wrong. (George yawns and goes to sleep.)

(Horse Thieves sneak in.) (George wakes up and watches from loft.)

Horse Thief I: Look at all the horses!

Horse Thief II: Yeah, and six more in the pasture!

Horse Thief I: No time for them. We'll take these.

Horse Thief III: Let's get 'em and get out of here!

(Horse Thieves begin to round up horses. Horses stamp and neigh.)

George: (Whispers) I've got to save the horses! But how? Oh, the hunting dogs!

(George climbs the hayloft, sneaks to the dog pen, and opens the gate.)

Dogs: (Rush out and run after Horse Thieves) Aarf, aarf, aarf!

(Thieves jump on their horses and gallop away with the dogs chasing. George leads the horses back into the stalls.)

Mr. Carver: George! I saw those thieves being chased away by our dogs! How smart you were, and brave too! You saved all of our horses. No hayloft for you tonight, and for this, I am giving you a horse of your very own! (George smiles. They walk away together.)

Demonstration

Ask someone who crochets, paints, or plays the accordion to give a demonstration to the class.

Fingerplay - "In Little George's Garden"

In little George's garden   (Extend one hand with palm up)

He rakes and then he hoes,   (Make a raking motion on palm with
                                3 fingers of other hand)

And now some tiny flower seeds   (Look in cupped hand)

He plants deep in the rows.   (Planting motion)

Each day the sun shines brightly   (Make circle with hands)

Or else the rain does fall   (Fingers flutter downward)

And little George's flowers   (Cup hands)

Grow and grow so tall.   (Slowly raise cupped hands)

ART

Clothes Hanger Masks

Preparation - Collect a wire clothes hanger and a nylon stocking (or pantyhose) per child. Distribute. Set out scraps of construction paper, crayons or markers, scissors, glue, and masking tape.

Procedure - Bend the clothes hanger into a diamond shape. Stretch the stocking over the hanger and tape to the hook end which will be the handle of the mask. Draw and cut out facial features from the construction paper and glue on the mask. Dry well. (See example on page 98.) If the masks are to be used for the skit, "George Carver and the Horse Thieves" (see Language Arts - Social Studies - Science), they should correspond to the children's assigned parts.

The Big Peanut

Preparation - Duplicate the pattern (see page 99) on white paper. Mix together brown and white fingerprint to make tan. Set out in aluminum pie pans along with pieces of brown construction paper, pencils, scissors, glue, and several spray bottles of water. Distribute the sheet.

Procedure - Cut out the peanut shell and spray lightly with water. Cover the surface with the tan fingerpaint. Allow this to dry while you draw and cut out two peanuts from the brown construction paper. Glue in place on the peanut shell. (See example on page 98.)

Nature Collages

Preparation - Go on a nature walk and let the children collect nature objects. For the collage activity, distribute construction paper and set out glue.

Procedure - Arrange the nature objects on the paper as desired; then glue in place. Use an ample amount of glue. Dry thoroughly. (See example on page 98.)

MATH

George Carver Washes Clothes

For each child, write a numeral (between 5 and 10) in the corner of a sheet of unlined white paper. Distribute. Direct the students to place the paper in front of them horizontally and draw a clothesline from edge to edge. After reading the numeral, they should draw that many items of clothing on the clothesline, number each item, and color to complete.

How Many Peanuts?

Put unsalted peanuts in a jar. Let the children guess how many are in the jar. Record guesses on the chalkboard. Open the jar and count the peanuts together. As a follow-up, divide the class into small groups. Each group sits on the floor in a circle with a bowl of peanuts and a stack of numeral cards in the middle. The children take turns drawing a numeral card and, counting aloud, putting that many peanuts on the card.

Peanut Game

Purchase dry roasted (unshelled) peanuts or roast your own. For every two players, put peanuts in a small paper bag. The players sit on the floor facing each other with the bag in between them. One player, the "Guesser," closes his or her eyes while the other player takes 1–5 peanuts out of the bag and hides them behind his or her back. The "Guesser" tries to guess how many peanuts the other player is holding. The peanuts are then revealed and counted. If the guess was correct, the "Guesser" gets the peanuts; if not, the other player keeps the peanuts. The game resumes, with the roles reversed, and continues until no peanuts remain. Partners then divide the peanuts and eat them.

MUSIC - MOVEMENT - GAMES

Song - "George Carver"

Tune: "Yankee Doodle"

George Carver was a little boy
Who had no dad or mother,
Lived in Kansas on a farm
Along with Jim, his brother.

    Chorus:
    George did have a special dream,
    Left his home to find it,
    Worked and earned so he could learn
    And never seemed to mind it.

George Carver went to school for years
And learned all that he could,
Used his mind to help mankind
Just like he knew he would.

    Chorus:
    George did have a special dream,
    Left his home to find it,
    Worked and earned so he could learn
    And became a famous scientist.

Game - Snatch the Sweet Potato

Divide the class into two equal teams. The teams form two horizontal lines and face each other with a space of 15-20 feet in between. In the center of the area, place a sweet potato on a stool. At the signal, the four end players run to the stool and attempt to snatch the sweet potato. The player who is successful must return to his or her team's line without being tagged by the two end players from the opposing team. If successful, the "Snatcher" scores two points for his or her team; if he or she is tagged, the opposing team scores one point. Return the sweet potato to the stool and resume the game with four new end players.

Variation: Let pairs of younger children "race" (walk quickly) while each holds a sweet potato in a serving spoon.

STORY TIME

1. <u>Why the Sun and the Moon Live in the Sky</u> - Elphinstone Dayrell
2. <u>The Plant Sitter </u> - Gene Zion
3. <u>The Carrot Seed</u> - Ruth Krauss
4. <u>The Poppy Seeds</u> - Clyde Robert Bulla
5. <u>The Little Red Flower</u> - Paul Tripp

COOKING IN THE CLASSROOM

Roasted Peanuts

Preheat oven to 350°. Place raw peanuts (unshelled) in a shallow pan. Roast for 20-30 minutes.

Peanut Butter

1 lb. roasted peanuts, shelled
Peanut oil
Salt
Crackers

Grind peanuts in a blender, adding peanut oil, a few drops at a time, until peanut butter is of the desired consistency. Salt to taste. Yield: 1 cup

Peanut Butter Snacks

Spread peanut butter on crackers or make peanut butter and banana sandwiches. Spread peanut butter on two slices of bread. Place banana slices on top of the peanut butter and assemble the sandwiches. Cut into fourths for "taster's portions."

Note: For more peanut recipes and detailed information on growing peanuts, send for Dr. Carver's "Bulletin 31 - How to Grow the Peanut and 105 Ways to Prepare it for Human Consumption" (current cost - <u>$1.61</u>-address below).

For other bulletins by Dr. Carver, books on Dr. Carver and other famous black Americans, Dr. Carver's lists of by-products from peanuts and sweet potatoes, and other related information, write for a mail order list from:

> Eastern National Park and Monument Association
> P.O. Drawer #10
> Tuskegee Institute, Alabama 36088-0010

Dear Parents,

On _____, we will learn about George Washington Carver, the famous black American scientist, educator, and author. Please read below to find out ways you can help.

Things To Send: _____

_____

_____

Volunteers Needed To: _____

_____

_____

Follow-Up: At the end of the unit, ask your child the following questions:

_____

_____

_____

Thank you for your cooperation.

Sincerely,

GEORGE WASHINGTON CARVER

Bulletin Board

George Washington Carver - Scientist, Educator, Author

Examples

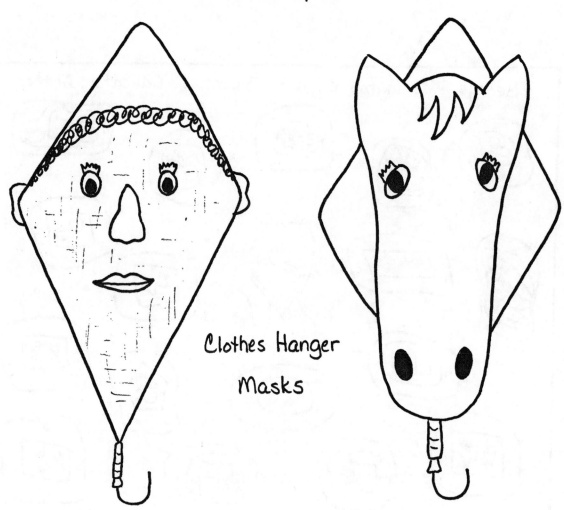

Clothes Hanger
Masks

The Big Peanut

Nature Collages

The Big Peanut

Pattern -

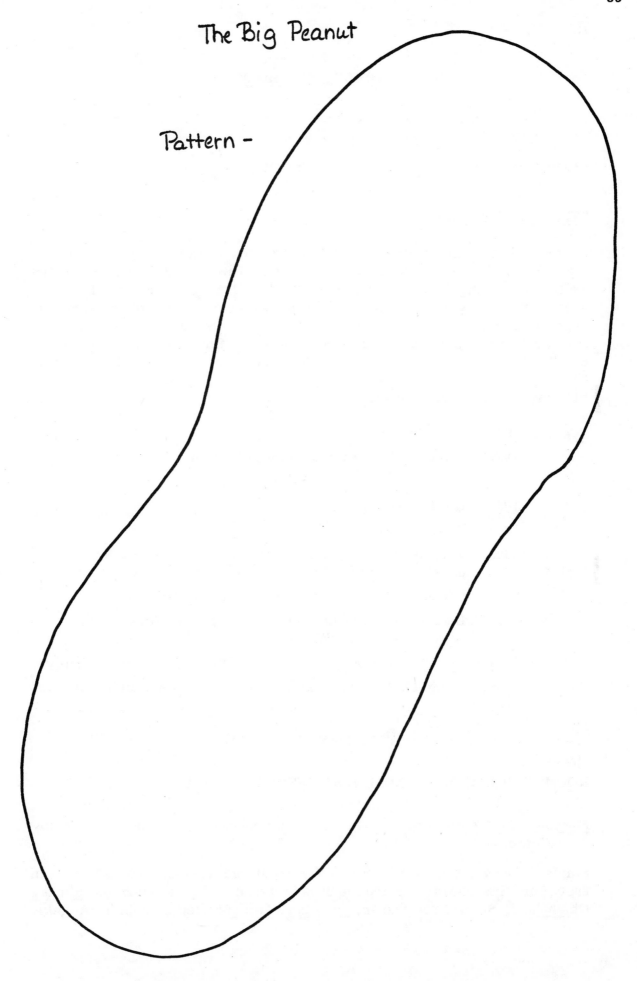

SHIRLEY CHISHOLM

(1924 -   )

ROOM ENVIRONMENT - BULLETIN BOARD

"The Chisholm Trail"

Cover and trim the bulletin board as desired, mounting the title at the top. Beginning in the lower right corner, draw a trail (as shown in the example), ending in the upper left corner. Draw, color, and label the events of Shirley Chisholm's life (listed below) on pieces of construction paper and mount at intervals along the trail. Also draw, color, and cut out the U.S. Capitol and a picture of Shirley Chisholm (see page 111). Staple the Capitol at the end of the trail and the picture of Shirley Chisholm in the upper right corner. Let the children assist according to their abilities. (See example on page 112.)

Events:
1924 - Born in Brooklyn, N.Y.

1927 - Lived in Barbados with grandmother

1935 - Returned to live with parents in Brooklyn

1942 - Graduated high school

1946 - Graduated college

1946 - Taught at child care center, earned master's degree, married Conrad Chisholm

1953 - Became director of a private nursery school

1959 - Became educational consultant for New York City's Bureau of Child Welfare

1964 - First black woman elected to New York State Assembly

1968 - Elected U.S. representative—first black woman in Congress

1971 - Ran for Democratic Party's presidential nomination

1983 - Retired after 15 years in the House of Representatives

ROOM ENVIRONMENT - LEARNING CENTERS

Famous Black Americans - (See Room Environment - General - Learning Centers)

Staple Shirley Chisholm's name and related pictures on the center. In front of the center, place various reference books such as Shirley Chisholm by Susan Brownmiller, Caribbean Lands edited by John P. Augelli,

Let's Visit the West Indies by John C. Caldwell, The Caribbean in Pictures prepared by Lancelot O. Evans, Sugar by O. B. Gregory, Underwater Life: The Oceans by Dean Morris, Who Lives at the Seashore? by Glenn O. Blough, Seahorse by Robert A. Morris, I Want to Be a Teacher by Carla Green, New York State and Niagara Falls: A Picture Book to Remember Her By designed by David Gibbon, Washington by Janice Anderson, and Congress by Harold Coy. Also display a stalk of sugar cane, some beach sand, several sea shells, campaign pins, bumper stickers, and pamphlets.

Brainwork Center - (See Room Environment - General - Learning Centers)

As a child Shirley Chisholm lived in Barbados with its beautiful beaches. To expand on this theme, make a small stand-up sign which reads "Let's Go to the Seashore." Place a tub full of seashells in the center along with paper, pencils, and colors. Write activity directions on pieces of paper, or record them on a tape recorder. Have the children observe and feel the shells and compare the different colors, shapes, sizes, and textures. The children can sort the shells using these attributes. Place them in order by size, count them, and use them for texture rubbings. If you have access to a large quantity of shells, each child can string the shells and make a necklace.

BIOGRAPHICAL INFORMATION

In 1969 Shirley Chisholm became the first black woman to be elected to the United States House of Representatives. After college she first taught nursery school, then became a day care center director. From 1959 to 1964 she was chief educational consultant for New York City's day care centers. In 1964 she was elected to the New York Assembly where she served until 1968.

Shirley St. Hill was born in Brooklyn, New York, on November 30, 1924. When she was three years old, she and her two sisters, Odessa and Muriel, were sent to Barbados to live with their grandmother. There was a depression in America and Shirley's parents, Charles Christopher and Ruby St. Hill, were having difficulty making enough money to support the family.

Shirley and her sisters lived on the Seales's farm in Barbados with Grandma Seales, Uncle Lincoln, Aunt Myrtle, and four cousins. Barbados is part of the West Indies, a group of islands located between Florida and the top of South America. Shirley loved Barbados with its beautiful fruit trees, coral beaches, and fields of sugar cane, corn, and cotton. She enjoyed Granny Seales's delicious meals and especially liked flying fish, which were caught by the local fishermen; ackee, a fruit that was cooked and eaten like a vegetable; green plantain, a fruit related to the banana; and yams, small, tasty sweet potatoes.

The people of Barbados believe strongly in a good education. Shirley and her sisters and cousins went to school in the village of Vauxhall. Discipline was strict and the children were expected to work hard on their lessons. Shirley loved school, and her teacher thought that one day Shirley would be a teacher also.

When Shirley St. Hill was eleven, she and her sisters went back to Brooklyn to live with their parents and their new baby sister Selma. It took some time for the three girls to get used to Brooklyn. After enjoying the tropical weather of Barbados, the girls were miserable during the first cold winter in Brooklyn. They missed the flowers, fruit trees, and wide open spaces.

Soon the girls grew accustomed to New York. They started school and made new friends. Mr. St. Hill worked hard in a burlap factory loading big burlap bags onto platforms. When Selma was old enough to go to school, Mrs. St. Hill found work as a maid. She was determined to earn extra money so the family could have a better apartment. It was Shirley's job to watch the other children after school while her mother worked. Mrs. St. Hill found a larger apartment and the family moved. Mrs. St. Hill tended the coal furnaces, put out the garbage cans, and mopped the stairs and the halls of the building in order to pay reduced rent for their apartment.

Shirley loved to dance, but most of all she loved to read. Her favorite books were about famous women in American history. She most admired Harriet Tubman, the slave who had risked her life to help over 300 slaves escape to the North; Susan B. Anthony, who had fought for the equal rights of women; and Mary McLeod Bethune, who had dedicated her life to provide education for blacks.

Shirley St. Hill was the first in her family to go to college. She went to Brooklyn College on a scholarship and majored in sociology. Because of her debating skills, one of her professors encouraged Shirley to enter politics. But after graduating with honors, Shirley decided to teach nursery school and work on her master's degree. She earned her M.A. degree in elementary education from Columbia University.

In 1949 Shirley St. Hill married Conrad Chisholm, a private detective and later investigator for the New York City Department of Social Services. From 1953 to 1959 she was director of Hamilton-Madison Child Care Center in Lower Manhattan, and from 1959 to 1964 she was educational consultant in the day care division of New York City's child welfare bureau.

Meanwhile, in 1953, Shirley Chisholm heard about a local black lawyer, Lewis Flagg, who had decided to run for judge. Mrs. Chisholm's neighborhood, Bedford-Stuyvesant, was nearly all black. But the white leaders of the Democratic Party were bringing in a white lawyer from outside the neighborhood to run against Lewis Flagg. Mrs. Chisholm volunteered to help, and from then on, was involved in politics.

In 1964 Shirley Chisholm was the first black woman to be elected to the New York State Assembly. Known for her honesty and independence, she was never afraid to fight for the needs of her district, and for this reason, she became known as "Fighting Shirley Chisholm."

In 1968 she was elected United States Representative from the Twelfth New York Congressional District. The campaign was long and difficult, but Shirley Chisholm was confident she would win because the people knew her and she had built a reputation for understanding their problems.

In January 1969 she took her seat as the first black woman in Congress. Soon after this, Mrs. Chisholm, who represented an urban district, was placed on the Agricultural Committee's subcommittee on forestry and rural villages. Mrs. Chisholm had been told that as a freshman representative, she should keep quiet and that committee assignments should be accepted. But knowing she could not help her district by serving on such a committee, Mrs. Chisholm shocked the House by asking to be changed to another assignment. She was then put on the Veteran's Affairs Committee and, after being reelected in 1970, was put on the House Education and Labor Committee which she had first requested.

Shirley Chisholm served as representative from 1969 to 1983. She spoke out against the seniority system in the House of Representatives which was eventually changed. She worked for improvements in the anti-poverty programs, equal rights for women, and changes in the Democratic Party procedures. She was always interested in the problems and opinions of America's young people. Mrs. Chisholm felt that through her work, she could make the world a better place.

LANGUAGE ARTS - SOCIAL STUDIES - SCIENCE

Discussion

Introduce the unit and examine the various displays. Summarize the Biographical Information, pointing out the various events of Shirley Chisholm's life on the bulletin board (see Room Environment - Bulletin Board). Locate Brooklyn, N.Y.; Barbados; and Washington, D.C., on a map. Show pictures from the references (see Famous Black Americans, Room Environment - Learning Centers, page 100).

Film or Book - Show a film on Barbados or show the pictures in the book _Caribbean Lands_ edited by John P. Augelli. Tell about the people, the climate, the land and how the island was formed, the natural resources, and the important farm products.

Sand Activities

Shirley Chisholm played on the beaches of Barbados where she lived with her grandmother. To familiarize the children with the properties of sand, use a sand table or sandbox, or make your own by purchasing sand from a building supply store and pouring it into an inexpensive child's plastic swimming pool. Use this for the activities below.

Remove a small amount of sand and place it on an old newspaper along with equal amounts of rice, dried beans and peas of various sizes, popcorn (unpopped), aquarium gravel, and small pebbles. Explain that sand is actually tiny grains of rock which were broken down by weathering. Let the children compare the look and feel of the sand with the other materials. Then experiment with sifting them through strainers and colanders of various sizes.

Supply the children with plastic cups, bowls, shovels, spoons, and a bucket of water for wetting the sand. Demonstrate molding sand and explain how to use this technique to build sand castles. Let the children create their own sand castles.

Furnish buckets, shovels, sifters, strainers, cups, bowls, spoons, toy cars and trucks, and plastic figures (army men, cowboys and horses, farm animals). Let the children play in the sand as desired.

Note: Some sand which is sold for use in children's sandboxes is actually too fine for this purpose. Ask for the coarser sand which is used in mixing cement.

Country Mouse and Town Mouse

Read _The Country Mouse and the Town Mouse_ by Aesop. Use two connecting sides of a corrugated cardboard box to make a display. Cover one side with blue and the other with green bulletin board paper. Label one side "Country" and one side "City." Discuss the two places where Shirley Chisholm lived during her childhood—Brooklyn, N.Y., and in Barbados. Direct the children to look through old magazines and find items and scenes of the country and of the city. Staple on the display.

Fingerplay - "City Mouse and Country Mouse"

This is a house in the city, and this is a country house, (Hold up one
    fist, then the other)

This is the mouse that lives in the city, and this is a country mouse,
    (Raise one thumb, then the other)

The city mouse rises to the sound of his alarm, (Hold one thumb
    horizontally, then vertically)

The rooster of the country mouse wakes up the farm. (Hold the other
    thumb horizontally, then vertically)

The city mouse travels to work far away, ("Walk" one thumb away from
    body)

The country mouse works on his land each day. ("Walk" one thumb
    toward body)

The city mouse goes to the store for cheese, (Act out opening a door)

From his cows the country mouse gets what he needs, (Act out milking
    a cow)

And both little mice when they lie down to rest (Hold both thumbs
    horizontally, then point toward chest)

Say, "I'm happy where I am, my life is best."

Book - Read and discuss I Want to Be a Teacher by Carla Greene and/or
Sugar by O. B. Gregory.

Class Elections

To give younger children a simple understanding of the election process,
bring to school two very different stuffed animals such as a tiger and a
rabbit. Tell the children, "Many teams in sports have mascots to bring
them good luck. (Give examples.) Today we will choose one of these
stuffed animals to be our Class Mascot. Who can tell me why the tiger
would be the better mascot? (Call on children to answer.) Who can tell
me why the rabbit would be the better mascot?" (Call on children to
answer.)

Now, using the President of the United States (or any other familiar
office), explain to the class how two people called candidates both want to
be President. Both of them travel around the country asking people to
choose them for President. Then on a certain day, the people vote for (or
choose) one of the candidates. The one who receives more votes gets to
be President.

Set out a shoebox with a slot cut out of the top. Situate the children so that no one is close to anyone else, and give each child a slip of paper and a pencil. Tell the children, "Now we will vote to see which stuffed animal will be our Class Mascot. If you like the tiger, draw a circle with stripes on your slip of paper; if you like the rabbit, draw two rabbit ears on your paper. (Use any simple symbols.) Then put your slip of paper into this box."

After everyone has voted, count the votes aloud, write the totals on the chalkboard and ask, "Which stuffed animal got more votes?" (Call on a child to answer.) Then say, "The _____ got more votes so it is our Class Mascot."

With older children, let them nominate two classmates to run for Class President or whatever office you choose. Divide the class into two parties, the Republicans and Democrats, and assign each party to one of the candidates. Let the children make campaign pins and posters, and speeches for their candidates. Hold a "debate" between the two candidates in which they answer your questions on why they are qualified, their platforms, etc. On election day, the children write the name of their choice on a slip of paper and place it in the ballot box (a shoebox with a cut out slot). Count the votes and announce the winner.

ART

Flying Fish Mobiles

Preparation - For each child, cut a 12" circle of green nylon net (or use the mesh from vegetable bags). Duplicate the sheet on page 113 and distribute one to each child. Set out crayons, scissors, hole punchers, and staplers. Distribute the net circles, cardboard patterns, and 4 paper clips per child.

Procedure - Cut a wedge from the nylon net and overlap the edges to form a cone shape. Staple in place and set aside. Cut out the flying fish and wings. On each fish, cut on the line to make a slit and insert the wing. Add details with the crayons. Punch a hole in each fish at the mouth, about $\frac{1}{2}$" from the edge. Bend the centers of the four paper clips upward so that they each resemble a tall, skinny letter **S**. Hook the big end of one paper clip through the net at the point of the "cone" to form a hanger. Hook one end of each remaining paper clip through the hole in each fish. Hook the other ends to the bottom edge of the nylon net. Hang. (See example on page 112.)

Note: If necessary, on each flying fish, put a dot of glue on the wing at the slit to secure.

Sand Art

Preparation - Set out sand in aluminum pie pans, construction paper of different colors, and bottles of glue. Cover the area with old newspapers.

Procedure - Use the glue to draw part of a design or scene on a sheet of construction paper. Sprinkle sand on the glue until it is completely covered. Shake the excess sand back into the pan. Continue this procedure until the design or scene is completed. (See example on page 112.)

MATH

On the Beach

Duplicate and distribute the sheet on page 114. Set out crayons, shell macaroni, and glue. Direct the students to color the bottom (beach) of each section yellow, the middle (ocean) of each section green, and the top (sky) of each section blue. Then the number in each section is read, and that many shells (macaroni) are glued on the beach. A "puddle" of glue should be used for each shell. Dry thoroughly.

Counting Votes

Use two shoeboxes with slots cut in the tops for the ballot boxes. Label the boxes "Candidate I" and "Candidate II." Use color chips or game tokens for the votes. Put the chips or tokens in a pile. Tell the children, "Today we are counting votes for two candidates." Hold up a numeral flashcard and direct a child to put that many "votes" into one box. Hold up another numeral flashcard and direct another child to put that many "votes" into the other box. Take the "votes" from each box and let the class count them aloud. Compare with the flashcards. Ask, "Who won—Candidate I or Candidate II? How do you know?" After receiving the correct response and emphasizing the concepts of more and less, repeat the procedure with different numerals and volunteers.

MUSIC - MOVEMENT - GAMES

Song - "Paw Paw Patch" ("Where, Oh, Where Is Pretty Little Susie?")

In Barbados, pawpaw is the local name for the melon-like papaya that grows on trees. Shirley and her friends would sometimes climb the trees and drop the pawpaws on people who were passing by. Sing the song and perform the actions in parenthesis.

Where, oh, where is pretty little Susie? (Shade eyes, look from
    side to side)
Where, oh, where is pretty little Susie? (Repeat same actions)
Where, oh, where is pretty little Susie? (Repeat same actions)
Way down yonder in the paw paw patch. (Pointing motion)

Chorus:
Picking up paw paws; put 'em in your pocket, (Bend down, pick up
    paw paws, put in pocket)
Picking up paw paws; put 'em in your pocket, (Repeat same actions)
Picking up paw paws; put 'em in your pocket, (Repeat same actions)
Way down yonder in the paw paw patch. (Pointing motion)

Come on, boys, let's go find her, (Wave "come on")
Come on, boys, let's go find her, (Repeat same actions)
Come on, boys, let's go find her, (Repeat same actions)
Way down yonder in the paw paw patch. (Pointing motion)

(Repeat Chorus)
Come on, boys, bring her back again, (Join hands with a partner, skip)
Come on, boys, bring her back again, (Repeat same actions)
Come on, boys, bring her back again, (Repeat same actions)
Way down yonder in the paw paw patch. (Drop hands, pointing motion)

(Repeat Chorus)

Marine Movement

Play appropriate music and direct the class to pantomime the following:

1. A wave in the ocean
2. A crab on the beach
3. A flying fish
4. A shark attacking
5. Seaweed on the ocean floor
6. A mermaid swimming
7. An octopus looking for food
8. A jelly-fish floating in the waves

STORY TIME

COOKING IN THE CLASSROOM

Napping Children

Cheese, individual slices
Pickles, sliced lengthwise
Ham, individual slices
Butter
Bread

Spread butter on the bread. Place the ham on the bread and lay three pickle slices side by side on the ham. Position the cheese on the pickles so all but the tops are covered. (These are the napping children covered with a blanket.) Toast under the oven broiler, or bake in a 400° oven until the cheese is melted and the edges of the bread are light brown.

Dear Parents,

On _____, we will learn about Shirley Chisholm, the first black woman elected to the United States House of Representatives. Please read below to find out ways you can help.

Things To Send: _____
_____
_____

Volunteers Needed To: _____
_____
_____

Follow-Up: At the end of the unit, ask your child the following questions:
_____
_____
_____

Thank you for your cooperation.

Sincerely,

SHIRLEY CHISHOLM

Bulletin Board, Examples

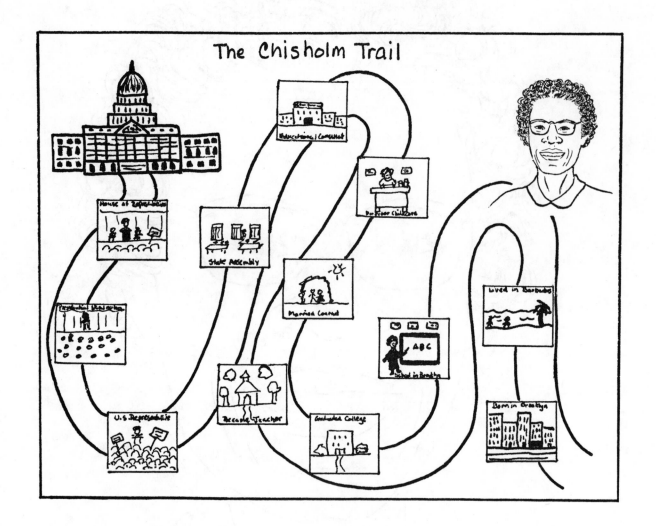

The Chisholm Trail

Flying Fish Mobiles

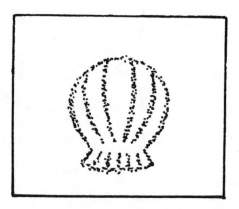

Sand Art

Flying Fish Mobiles

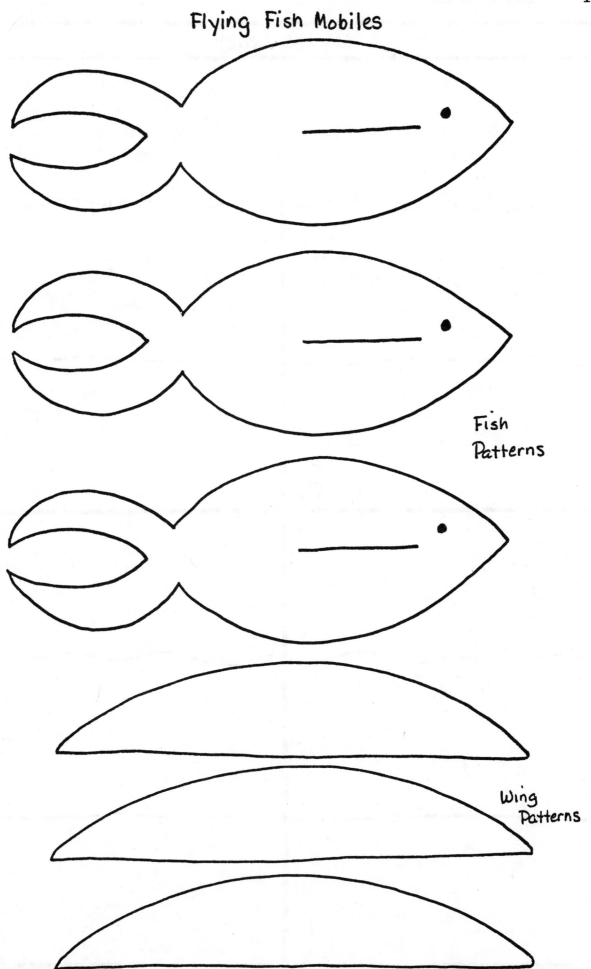

Fish
Patterns

Wing
Patterns

On the Beach

3

2

1

4

ALTHEA GIBSON

(1927 -   )

ROOM ENVIRONMENT - BULLETIN BOARD

Time for Tennis

Cover the bulletin board with yellow paper and trim with an aqua border. Make letters for the title out of white construction paper outlined in aqua and staple at the top. Make two clocks with tennis rackets for hands and mount on the bulletin board as shown. Let the children find action pictures of tennis matches and tennis equipment in sports magazines and catalogs and glue them on sheets of construction paper. Arrange and staple the sheets on the bulletin board. (See example on page 125.)

ROOM ENVIRONMENT - LEARNING CENTERS

Famous Black Americans - (See Room Environment - General - Learning Centers)

Staple a picture of Althea Gibson (see page 124) on the center underneath a strip of paper which reads "Althea Gibson, Tennis Champion." On the table in front of this, display a tennis racket, a tennis ball, tennis shoes, and tennis hats. Also include books such as I Always Wanted to be Somebody by Althea Gibson, 100 Greatest Women in Sports by Phyllis Hollander, Junior Tennis by Harry "Cap" Leighton, and Volleying and Lobs by Paul J. Deegan.

Brainwork Center - (See Room Environment - General - Learning Centers)

Althea Gibson worked for a while in a button factory. Tape-record the story "A Lost Button" from the book Frog and Toad Are Friends by Arnold Lobel. Use a bell to indicate when each page should be turned. Place the tape recorder, prepared tape, and book in the center. Cut the lids from several egg cartons and discard. Put the cup sections and a large bowl of buttons in the center. After listening to the story, the children sort the buttons by color, style, texture and/or size, placing each group in a cup of the egg cartons.

Note: Parents are a good source for these and other "valuable junk." Also, buttons in packages or cartons can be purchased at teacher supply stores and craft stores.

BIOGRAPHICAL INFORMATION

Althea Gibson became the first important black tennis player and the first black to win Wimbledon and to win the United States national singles title.

Althea Gibson was born on August 25, 1927, in the little town of Silver, South Carolina. She was the oldest of the five children of Daniel and Anna Gibson. Daniel Gibson and his brother were sharecroppers on a five-acre farm where they grew cotton and corn. Bad weather ruined the crops three years in a row, so the family moved to Harlem in New York City. Mr. Gibson got a job as a handyman but money was still tight.

When Gibson was seven or eight, she went to live with her Aunt Daisy Kelly in Philadelphia. She stayed with her, on and off, for about two years, then returned to the Gibson's apartment on West 143rd Street in New York.

Althea Gibson called herself a "traveling girl." She disliked staying in one place and was dissatisfied with school. She also didn't like people telling her what to do, so she was frequently punished. She skipped school all the time and spent her days at the movies or playing games with her friends.

Somehow Gibson managed to graduate from junior high school and attended trade school for a year. Then she got her working papers and held a variety of jobs. She was a waitress, a mail clerk, worked in a dressmaking shop, cleaned chickens in a butcher shop, and worked in a button factory. After she was unemployed for a while, the City Welfare Department gave her money to live on while she looked for a job. Instead, Gibson spent her days shooting pool, playing basketball, and playing paddle tennis.

One day when she was playing paddle tennis, a game played similar to tennis but with solid wooden rackets, a young musician named Buddy Walker stopped to watch her. He was working for the city as a play leader and, being a tennis fan, thought Althea Gibson had potential. He bought her a couple of secondhand tennis rackets and, after she practiced, took her to the Harlem River Tennis Courts to play. There, Juan Terrell, a black school teacher, saw her play and arranged for her to a be junior member of the Cosmopolitan Tennis Club. At the Cosmopolitan, she took lessons from the club's professional and began to learn about sportsmanship.

In 1942, when Althea Gibson was fifteen, she played in and won her first tournament, the all-black American Tennis Association's New York State Open Championship. There she met Dr. Hubert A. Eaton of Wilmington, North Carolina, and Dr. Robert W. Johnson of Lynchburg, Virginia, who became her sponsors.

Both men obviously felt Althea Gibson had the potential to be a great tennis player. They also hoped she could be the player to break the color barrier in the all-white national and international tournaments.

The two doctors convinced Gibson that she must develop her mind as well as her tennis game. For a year she lived with Dr. Eaton and his family and went to high school. She then spent the summer with Dr. Johnson and his family, played in various black tournaments, and won her first American Tennis Association national women's singles title—the first of ten in a row.

Gibson progressed well in high school and graduated in 1949. She went to Florida A & M on a scholarship where she gradually won the right to compete against white players in big tournaments. In 1950 she became the first black to appear on the courts of Forest Hills, Long Island, for the United States nationals and, in 1951, the first black to be invited to Wimbledon. She was eliminated from both tournaments but gained valuable experience.

In 1952 and 1953 her tennis was disappointing. She dropped in the national rankings from number seven to number thirteen and thought about quitting. She had graduated from college and had a job teaching physical education at Lincoln University in Jefferson City, Missouri.

In 1955 Gibson returned to New York. She met Sydney Llewellyn, a Harlem tennis teacher, who encouraged her to continue playing tennis and helped her improve her game. After a 1956 goodwill tour of Southeast Asia, Gibson won the French women's singles championship.

That same year Althea Gibson was eliminated at Wimbledon and at Forest Hills. She was frustrated but she refused to give up. Returning in July of 1957, she beat Darlene Hard in straight sets and became the first black to win Wimbledon. She was thirty years old at the time. She was presented the gold salver of victory by Queen Elizabeth II and was given a ticker-tape parade when she returned home to New York. On September 8, 1957, she won the United States women's singles title at Forest Hills.

In 1958 Gibson repeated her feat and won both the United States and Wimbledon women's championships. In both years she was awarded the Associated Press Woman Athlete of the Year Award—the first black so honored.

In 1959, at the age of thirty-two, Althea Gibson retired from tennis and turned to golf. Four years later she turned professional and once again broke the color barrier. In 1965 she married William A. Darben who had first proposed to her in 1953.

LANGUAGE ARTS - SOCIAL STUDIES - SCIENCE

Discussion

Prior to the discussion, tape record the sound of a tennis racket hitting a tennis ball, a foot kicking a football, a baseball bat hitting a baseball, and a basketball being dribbled.   Then tape portions of a televised tennis match, football game, baseball game, and so forth. Play the tape, allowing the children to identify the sounds.   Point out the various room displays and summarize the Biographical Information.   As they are mentioned, locate South Carolina, New York, Pennsylvania, Virginia, North Carolina, Southeast Asia, and England on a map or globe.

Things That Go Together

Seat the children in a circle. In random order in the center of the circle, display a tennis racket, a tennis ball, a golf club, a golf ball, a baseball bat, a baseball, a croquet mallet, a croquet ball, a hockey stick, and a hockey puck. Call on a child to pick up one item; then call on another to find the matching item. Continue until all items have been matched.

Word Story - Listening Activity

Read the story below and direct the children to listen for the word "tennis." When they hear the word, they should say "Whack!"—the sound of a tennis racket hitting a tennis ball.

Althea Gibson liked games.   Every day after work, she would play basketball or paddle **tennis**. Paddle **tennis** was her favorite. One day a man saw her playing paddle **tennis**. He said, "You have talent. You could be a famous **tennis** player!" He bought her two **tennis** rackets to use and arranged for her to take **tennis** lessons from a **tennis** professional. After that, she played in many **tennis** tournaments.   She won the women's championship in France but lost the **tennis** championship at Wimbledon in England. She then worked harder than ever to improve her **tennis** game. The next year she won the women's **tennis** championship at Wimbledon and at Forest Hills.   She was the most famous woman **tennis** player in the world.

Recall Restaurant

Remind the students that Althea Gibson worked for a time as a waitress. Set up a small table a couple of yards away from the housekeeping center (or use another table for the kitchen) and cover with a tablecloth or sheet.   Place a plastic plate and cup on a tray in the kitchen area. Choose one child to be the customer, one child to be the waitress, and one child to be the chef.   The waitress asks the customer for his or her order, and the customer lists three to four items.   The waitress walks to the kitchen and repeats the order to the chef.   The chef pretends to cook the meal, hands the waitress the tray, and says, "Here is the customer's _____," and lists the items of the order.   The waitress sets the plate and/or cup on the table and says to the customer, "Enjoy your _____," and repeats the order once again.   Continue the activity, allowing different children to play the parts of the customer, waitress, and chef.

Mail Clerk - Alphabet Activity

Decide how many alphabet letters you wish to include in the activity and obtain a corrugated cardboard box (or boxes) with that many divided compartments.   The compartments will be the post office boxes and each should be labeled with a different alphabet letter.   For the "mail," purchase inexpensive envelopes or use index cards as postcards.   Write a name beginning with each sound on the individual envelopes or cards; for example, Amy for **A**, Bill for **A**, and Carrie for **C**.   Mix up the cards and place them in a stack in front of the post office boxes.   Tell the children, "As a mail clerk, Althea Gibson had to sort many letters."   Call on a student to pick up the first envelope or card, read aloud the beginning letter, and put it in the correct post office box.   Continue until all letters have been filed.   Then call on one child at a time to pick up the mail by withdrawing the letter or card from a particular post office box.

ART

Paper Weave Tennis Rackets

<u>Preparation</u> - Duplicate the sheet (see page 126) on light colored construction paper.   Distribute along with construction paper of various colors.   Provide scissors and glue.

<u>Procedure</u> - Cut out the racket.   Bend the top back so that you can make small cuts on the **X**'s without making a fold.   Unbend, insert a blade of the scissors in each small cut, and cut on the lines in either direction, ending at the large dots.   Cut 6" x ½" construction paper strips of a contrasting color.   Beginning at the bottom, weave one of the strips <u>over</u> and <u>under</u>, over and under the strips of the racket.   Weave the second strip <u>under</u> and <u>over</u>, under and over the strips of the racket.   Continue weaving in this manner until the racket is "filled."   Glue the edges of the strips to the racket with dabs of glue and trim the excess.   Dry.   (See example on page 125.)

Button Rings

Preparation - Collect a variety of buttons with large holes (see note, Brainwork Center) and set out along with white pipe cleaners which have been cut in half.

Procedure - Choose a button that you like. Holding the top side up, insert an end of the pipe cleaner into one hole of the button and pull half of the pipe cleaner through to the back. Insert the other end of the pipe cleaner into the second hole and pull the rest of the pipe cleaner through to the back. Put the ring on your finger and twist the pipe cleaner sections one time so that you get the proper fit. Slide the ring off your finger and wrap one of the ends around and around the ring part of the pipe cleaner so that it lays flat. Do the same with the other end. If the ends are too long, let your teacher cut them with scissors. (See example on page 125.)

MATH

Bounce Count

Seat the children in a circle. Spread out numeral cards in the center of the circle and stand next to them holding a tennis ball. Ask the students to close their eyes and silently count the number of bounces. Bounce the ball so many times; then call on a child to find the numeral card which indicates the correct number of bounces. Continue in this manner; then allow various children to take your place.

Button Activities

Seat the children around a table. Have a bowl of buttons (see note, Brainwork Center) and 18" pieces of yarn available.

More or Less - Put several buttons on the table. Tell the children to close their eyes. Place two more buttons on the table and then ask, "Are there more or less buttons than before?" Repeat the procedure but remove one or two buttons; then ask the same question. Continue in this manner, increasing the number of buttons used.

Sets - Use the yarn pieces to make circles on the table. Ask different children to make sets by placing so many buttons within each circle. Have other children count aloud to check for accuracy. Point out two sets and ask, "Which set has more members? Which set has less?" Remove the buttons from the sets and let the other children make new sets.

<u>Patterns</u> - Place a red button, a blue button, and a red button in a row. Ask, "What color button comes next?" Let a child answer and place a blue button on the row. Then ask the question again. Continue the activity with different two-color, then three-color patterns.

MUSIC - MOVEMENT - GAMES

<u>**Song**</u> - "Did You Ever Play Tennis"

Tune: "Did You Ever See a Lassie"

The children form a circle and join hands. During the first two lines of each verse, the children take a half-step forward while raising their joined hands, then a half-step backwards while also swinging their joined hands in a backward motion. For the last two lines of the first verse, the children drop hands and make a right to left waving motion with their right hands. For the last two lines of the second verse, the children rotate their heads from side to side.

Did you ever play tennis, play tennis, play tennis?

If you ever played tennis, the ball goes like this,

Goes this way and that way, this way and that way,

If you ever played tennis, the ball goes like this.

Did you ever watch tennis, watch tennis, watch tennis?

If you ever watched tennis, your head goes like this,

Goes this way and that way, this way and that way,

If you ever watched tennis, your head goes like this.

<u>**Game**</u> - Tilda Tennis Racket

Make Tilda by gluing or taping eyes, a nose, and a mouth to an old tennis racket. For the hair, place long pieces of rug yarn side by side and tie together in the center with a shorter piece of yarn. Tie to the top and sides of the tennis racket with pieces of yarn. If you don't have an old tennis racket, stretch hose over a new racket and glue features to the hose. Poke holes in the hose to attach the hair.

The players stand in a circle with one player holding Tilda. Start the music. The players pass Tilda to the right until the music stops. The player holding Tilda when the music stops must give her a hug and say, "Oh Tilda, I wish I could look just like you!" Then the music is started again and the game continues.

STORY TIME

1. <u>Sometimes I Don't Like School</u> - Paula Z. Hogan
2. <u>The Snowy Day</u> - Ezra Jack Keats

COOKING IN THE CLASSROOM

Tennis Balls

Make "Rice Krispies Marshmallow Treats" by following the recipe on the Rice Krispies box. Instead of pressing the warm mixture into a buttered pan, shape into balls and roll in flaked coconut. If you wish to make yellow tennis balls, blend 1 teaspoon milk and a few drops of yellow food color. Add 1 1/3 cups flaked coconut and toss with a fork until evenly colored. Roll the balls in this mixture. Eat when cooled.

Dear Parents,

On _____, we will learn about the first important black tennis player, Althea Gibson. Please read below to find out ways you can help.

Things To Send: _____
_____
_____

Volunteers Needed To: _____
_____
_____

Follow-Up: At the end of the unit, ask your child the following questions:
_____
_____
_____

Thank you for your cooperation.

Sincerely,

ALTHEA GIBSON

Bulletin Board, Examples

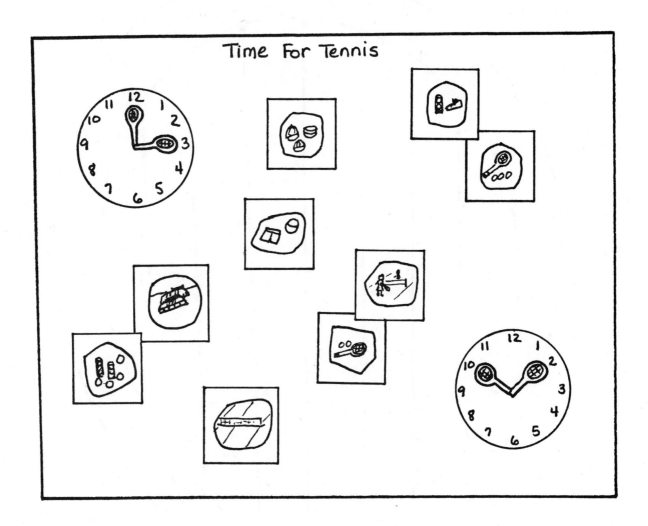

Time For Tennis

Paper Weave Tennis
Rackets

Button Rings

Pattern

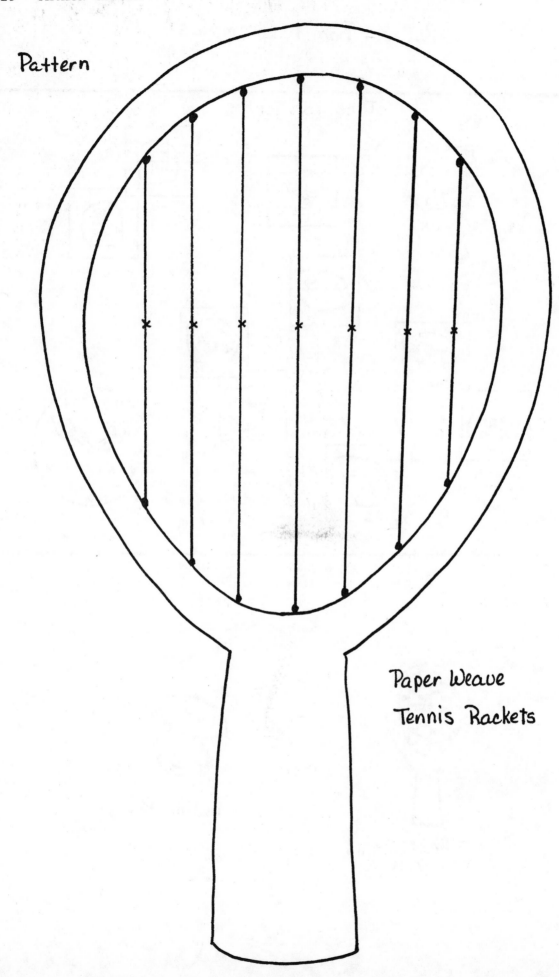

Paper Weave
Tennis Rackets

MARTIN LUTHER KING, JR.

(1929 - 1968)

ROOM ENVIRONMENT - BULLETIN BOARD

"I Have A Dream"

Cover the bulletin board as desired, mounting the title and a picture of Martin Luther King, Jr., (see page 136) at the top. On a piece of poster paper, write excerpts from Martin Luther King, Jr.'s "I Have a Dream" speech. Mount the speech in the center of the bulletin board. On strips of poster paper, write memorable quotes from Martin Luther King, Jr., (see below) and staple in various places on the bulletin board. Explain each quote; then assign various children to illustrate each one. Staple the pictures above the quotes.

Quotes from Martin Luther King, Jr. –

From Civil Rights March on Washington, D.C.:

"I have a dream that one day on the red hills of Georgia the sons of former slaves and the sons of former slave-owners will be able to sit down together at the table of brotherhood."

". . . I have a dream that one day this nation will rise up and live out the meaning of its Creed: 'We hold these truths to be self-evident; that all men are created equal.' I have a dream!"

Other quotes:

"We must meet the forces of hate with the power of love; we must meet physical force with soul force."

"Love your enemies, bless them that curse you, and pray for them that despitefully use you."

"I will never be in front of a violent march."

"Injustice anywhere is a threat to justice everywhere."

"If a man hasn't discovered something that he will die for, he isn't fit to live."

"Don't lose faith."

"Freedom has a price . . . a very high price."

"We still have a long, long way to go in this nation before we achieve
. . . brotherhood."

ROOM ENVIRONMENT - LEARNING CENTERS

Famous Black Americans - (See Room Environment - General - Learning
     Centers)

Staple various pictures of Martin Luther King, Jr., (see page 136) on the
center. In front of the center, display books such as Martin Luther King,
Jr. - A Picture Story by Margaret Boone-Jones, Martin Luther King:
Fighter for Freedom by Edward Preston, Martin Luther King, Jr.: A Man
to Remember by Patrick McKissack, Martin Luther King, Jr. by Jacqueline
L. Harris, Rosa Parks by Eloise Greenfield, and various references on
Africa and the civil rights movement.

Brainwork Center - (See Room Environment - General - Learning Centers)

Make a stand-up card which reads "Martin Luther King Was a . . .," then
shows a bookworm. Place story books in the center along with drawing
paper, crayons, and markers. The children read a book, then illustrate a
scene on the drawing paper. Post the pictures around the center.

BIOGRAPHICAL INFORMATION

In January we celebrate the birthday of Dr. Martin Luther King, Jr.
Dr. Martin Luther King, Jr., was a civil rights leader who dedicated his
life to helping blacks attain their basic rights as Americans.

Martin Luther King, Jr., was born on January 15, 1929, in Atlanta, Georgia.
His father, the Reverend Martin Luther King, Sr., was pastor of Ebenezer
Baptist Church. His mother, Alberta Williams King, was the daughter of
Reverend Alfred Williams. Reverend Williams and Reverend King were both
active in obtaining civil rights, the rights guaranteed to individuals by the
Constitution of the United States, for blacks. Both men were religious,
hard-working, self-made men who loved their families.

Martin Luther King, Jr., was called "M.L." as a child. He had an older
sister, Willie Christine, and a younger brother, Alfred Daniel, known as
"A.D." His whole family lived with his grandparents, Reverend and
Mrs. Williams, in a big house on Auburn Street. When M.L. was small, his
first friends were two white boys who lived in the neighborhood. When
they all started school, King went to a school for blacks, and his two

friends went to a school for whites. This is the way it had always been, so King was not concerned. But when he went to play with his friends after school, their parents said, "Don't come around here anymore. You are colored and they are white, so you can't play with them anymore."

This was King's first experience with segregation. His mother explained that some white people could not accept black people as equals. She told him not to let it make him sad and to always remember he was as good as anyone. M.L. always remembered what she said.

Like every child, Martin Luther King, Jr., loved to run and play. He loved sports, but he also loved books and studying. He graduated from high school and went to Morehouse College, a black college in Atlanta, Georgia, when he was only fifteen years old. He first thought he would study medicine but then decided to study sociology. Sociology is the science that explains how people live and work together. During his junior year, Martin decided he wanted to be a minister. He was ordained (admitted to the clergy) as a minister when he was only nineteen years old. Still he wanted to know more, so he went to Crozer Theological Seminary and graduated when he was twenty-two. He then earned his Doctor of Philosophy degree at Boston University.

In Boston Dr. King met and fell in love with Coretta Scott, a young music student. They were married in 1953 and moved to Montgomery, Alabama, where Dr. King became the pastor of Dexter Avenue Church. They eventually had four children—Yolanda, Martin Luther III, Dexter Scott, and Bernice Albertine.

On December 1, 1955, a black seamstress named Rosa Parks boarded a city bus and sat in the fifth row. She was tired and glad to be off her feet. The law in Montgomery required that when a bus filled up, black people had to give up their seats to white people. After the bus was full, two white people boarded. Mrs. Parks was told by the driver to give up her seat, but she refused. She was arrested and put in jail. A leader in the black community heard about it and called other black leaders including Martin Luther King, Jr. They organized a black boycott of the buses; that is, blacks refused to ride on the buses. Blacks were threatened and arrested. Martin Luther King, Jr., received phone threats, and one day a bomb was thrown on his porch. Luckily, no one was hurt. The case against segregation went to court and finally the Supreme Court ruled segregation on buses to be unconstitutional. This was a great victory for blacks, but it was largely ignored by many whites.

Martin Luther King, Jr., spent the rest of his life trying to make integration a reality. He was greatly influenced by Mahatma Gandhi, an Indian leader who had helped free India from British rule. Gandhi's philosophy was one of brotherly love. He felt that if people who did evil were met with love, they would give up their evil ways. Dr. King used this philosophy of nonviolence in his speeches for civil rights for blacks. He traveled all over the United States helping people who were working to change unfair laws.

The Civil Rights Movement grew.   When the President proposed a civil rights bill to Congress, a march on Washington, D.C., was organized to show support for the bill.   On August 28, 1963, more than 200,000 people gathered in Washington, D.C.   There were many speeches and songs, but the most memorable was Dr. Martin Luther King, Jr.'s, "I Have a Dream" speech.   The Civil Rights Act of 1964 was passed and signed by President Lyndon B. Johnson on July 2, 1964.

In 1964 Martin Luther King, Jr., was awarded the Nobel Peace Prize for his work to build peace among all Americans.

On April 4, 1968, Martin Luther King, Jr., was assassinated while he stood on the balcony of the Lorraine Motel, a black motel in Memphis, Tennessee.   The assassin, James Earl Ray, claimed that he was hired to kill Martin Luther King, Jr., but this has never been proven.   Ray was convicted of first degree murder.   On April 9, King was buried in Atlanta, Georgia.   On his tombstone are the words from an old spiritual that he used in his Washington speech, "Free At Last!"

Martin Luther King, Jr., will always be remembered.   His words, achievements, and ideas, which have changed America, live on.

LANGUAGE ARTS - SOCIAL STUDIES - SCIENCE

Discussion

Summarize the Biographical Information.   For a simple version of Martin Luther King, Jr.'s life, read Martin Luther King, Jr. – A Picture Story by Margaret Boone-Jones.   Show pictures from references (see Famous Black Americans, Room Environment - Learning Centers, above).   Point out Atlanta, Georgia, and Montgomery, Alabama, on a map.   Discuss Martin Luther King, Jr.'s life and what he believed in.

Film - Show a film or videotape on the life of Martin Luther King, Jr. Review the highlights of the film or videotape.

Hopscotch Drill

Make a list of review questions from the Biographical Information, one question per child.   Draw a hopscotch snail as pictured on page 137, marking off a space for each child.. Divide the class into two teams and have a different colored piece of chalk available for each team. A player from one team hops on one foot to the center of the "snail" where he stands and awaits a question. If he answers correctly, he hops to any square, writes his name in the center, and hops home. If he answers incorrectly, others on his team may volunteer the answer but the player doesn't get to sign his name in a square. Continue in this manner, alternating teams until all questions have been asked. Count the names in each color. Each name earns a point for one of the teams. The team with the most points wins the game.

Family Tree

Duplicate and distribute the Family Tree sheet (page 138). Explain to the class that Americans have always realized the value of their families. Martin Luther King, Jr., was deeply aware of his family's wonderful influence on his life. He, along with Alex Haley, the author of the book Roots, renewed an interest in our origins.

Direct the children to write their names on the tree trunks, then lightly color the tree. The trees are taken home to be filled in and returned as directed.

Poem - "Little Martin Luther King"

Little Martin Luther King,
Sat in church one day,
Listening to his daddy preach,
And listening to him pray.

"One day I'll talk like that," he said,
"And use those big words, too.
I'll make folks feel good inside."
Little Martin's words came true.

Ebenezer Baptist Church - Alphabet Dot-to-Dot

Duplicate and distribute the sheet (see page 139). Following the alphabet letters, draw a line from dot-to-dot to complete the church. Color.

Book - Read Jambo Means Hello: Swahili Alphabet Book by Muriel Feelings.

Sandwich Men

A sandwich man is a man who walks on sidewalks and streets displaying advertising on signs hung from his shoulders. One sign hangs in front and one in back. Let the children be "sandwich men" by making and wearing similar signs. Cut two pieces of poster paper for each child. Punch holes in the top and tie the signs together with nylon cord. There should be a few inches of cord between the signs to rest on the shoulders. Provide markers. The children write "Happy Birthday, Martin Luther King, Jr." on the front (or a similar message), then decorate. On the back, the children may choose to draw and color a picture of Martin Luther King, Jr., copy some of his quotes, or list facts about his life. The "sandwich men" can visit other classrooms and display their signs. (See example on page 137.)

Poem - Read "No Difference" from Where the Sidewalk Ends by Shel Silverstein.

ART

Martin Luther King, Jr., Silhouette

Preparation - Duplicate the Silhouette sheet (see page 140) and staple each to a piece of black construction paper. (The staples should be placed within the silhouette.) Give each child the two sheets, a sheet of white construction paper, scissors, and glue.

Procedure - Cut out the silhouette. Cut through both thicknesses. Remove the staples and discard the white copy. Glue the black copy in the center of the white construction paper.

Freedom Pins

Preparation - Purchase safety pins and red, white, and blue (tiny) glass beads which fit on the safety pins. Pass out the pins. Set out the beads in bowls. Tell the children, "Today we will make Freedom pins. Freedom pins show our gratitude for the many freedoms we enjoy in the United States today."

Procedure - Being very careful, open the safety pins. Slide the beads on the safety pin in any color arrangement you desire. Fill the pin up halfway, leaving room (about 1/8") for the safety pin to be pinned on your shirt and for the end to be closed. Pin on your shirt and wear in honor of Martin Luther King, Jr.'s birthday. (See example on page 137.)

Peace Doves

Preparation - Make cardboard patterns of the dove (see page 141). Set out the patterns, pencils, half-sheets of white construction paper, crayons, 24" pieces of string, paper clips, and hole punchers.

Procedure - Place the cardboard pattern on the half-sheet of construction paper and trace around it with a pencil. Be sure to mark the dot on the dove's wing. Cut out. On each side of the dove, draw an eye and color the beak with crayons. Punch a hole at the dot. Tie one end of the string through the hole and the other on the paper clip.

MATH

Birthday Cakes - Counting Sheet

Duplicate and distribute the sheet (see page 142). Direct the children to read the number in each block, draw that many candles on the cake, and color all of the cakes.

Fingerplay - "One Little Church"

Teach the fingerplay below. The children recite it, holding up one through ten fingers as designated in each line. You may also display corresponding numeral cards.

One little church with a bell in the steeple
Two open doors welcome all the people
Three giggling girls sitting in a front pew
With four little boys in suits brand new
Five tall ushers lead people to their places
Six bouquets of flowers on the altar in vases
Seven stained glass windows shimmer and shine
Eight robed choir members walking in a line
Nine bells ring and the people kneel to pray
At 10 o'clock sharp on a sunny Sabbath day.

MUSIC - MOVEMENT - GAMES

Song - "There's Nobody Just Like Me" from There's Nobody Just Like Me (LP) by Jamie, Hy, and Lynn Glaser

Song - "He's Got the Whole World in His Hands"

Source: <u>Folk Song Carnival</u> (LP) by Hap Palmer

Martin Luther King, Jr., Birthday Picnic

Plan a picnic in celebration of Martin Luther King, Jr.'s birthday. If the weather is unsuitable, obtain permission to use the gym or auditorium. Invite parents. Ask for volunteers to prepare Martin Luther King, Jr.'s favorite foods—fried chicken, sweet potatoes, black-eyed peas, corn bread, and peach cobbler. Ask additional parents to prepare cupcakes.

Suggested Picnic Activities –

Play a game of baseball (using plastic balls and bats), badminton, horseshoes, or kickball.

Supply ropes for rope-jumping and beanbags for tossing.

Play a game of Bingo.

Have a burlap sack race and a three-legged race.

Sing-along - Lead a sing-along of favorite folk and nursery songs.

(**Book**) - Tell the class, "In 1957 Martin Luther King, Jr., accepted an invitation to attend the Independence Day celebrations in Ghana, Africa. This country had just gained its independence from Great Britain. The following is a traditional story of the Ashanti people in Ghana." Then read <u>Anansi the Spider</u> by Gerald McDermott. Be sure to first read the prologue.

Song - "Happy Birthday"

Put one birthday candle in each cupcake. Light the candles and sing "Happy Birthday" to Martin Luther King, Jr. Each child blows out his or her candle and makes a wish. Since it is Martin Luther King, Jr.'s birthday, make an exception to the "keep the wish a secret" rule. Encourage the children to share their wishes.

Dear Parents,

On _____, we will learn about Martin Luther King, Jr. We will begin with his childhood and cover the many achievements of his life and his work in the civil rights movement. Please read below to find out ways you can help.

Things To Send: _____
_____
_____

Volunteers Needed To: _____
_____
_____

Follow-Up: At the end of the unit, ask your child the following questions:
_____
_____
_____

Thank you for your cooperation.

Sincerely,

MARTIN LUTHER KING, JR.

Bulletin Board, Examples

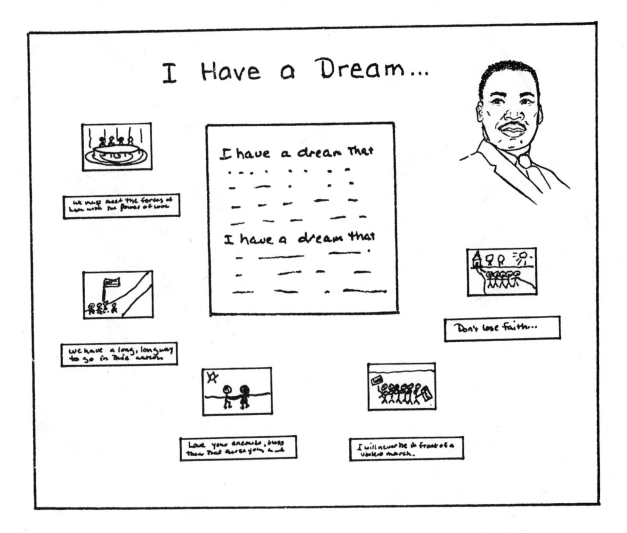

I Have a Dream...

I have a dream that
I have a dream that

Happy Birthday Martin Luther King, Jr.

Sandwich Men Signs

Hopscotch Snail

Freedom Pins

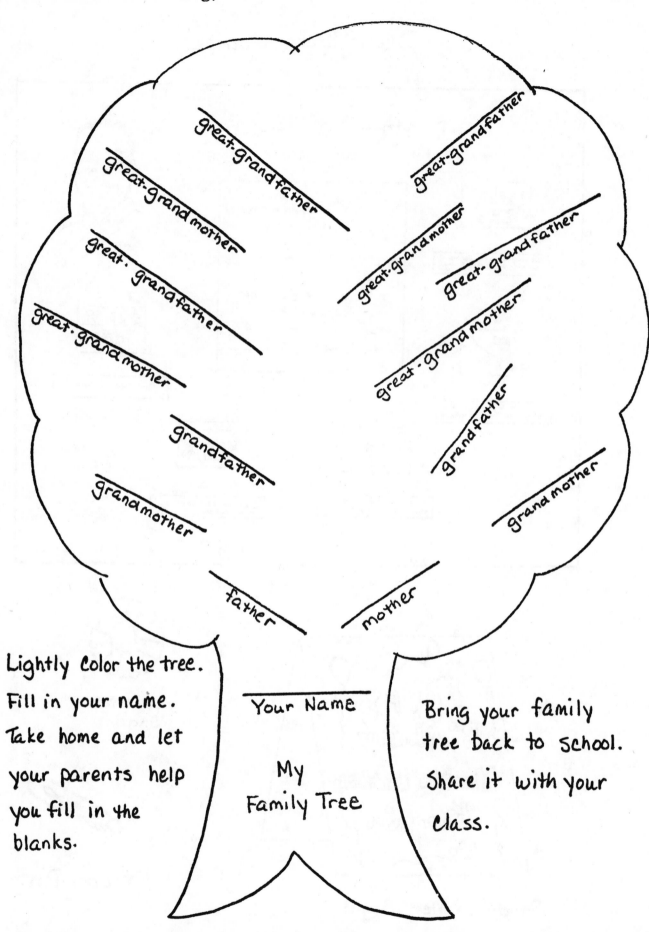

great-grandfather

great-grandmother

great-grandfather

great-grandmother

great-grandfather

great-grandmother

great-grandmother

grandfather

grandfather

grandmother

grandmother

father

mother

Lightly Color the tree.
Fill in your name.
Take home and let
your parents help
you fill in the
blanks.

Your Name

My
Family Tree

Bring your family
tree back to school.
Share it with your
class.

Ebenezer Baptist Church - Dot-to-Dot

Name _____

Martin Luther King, Jr. - Silhouette

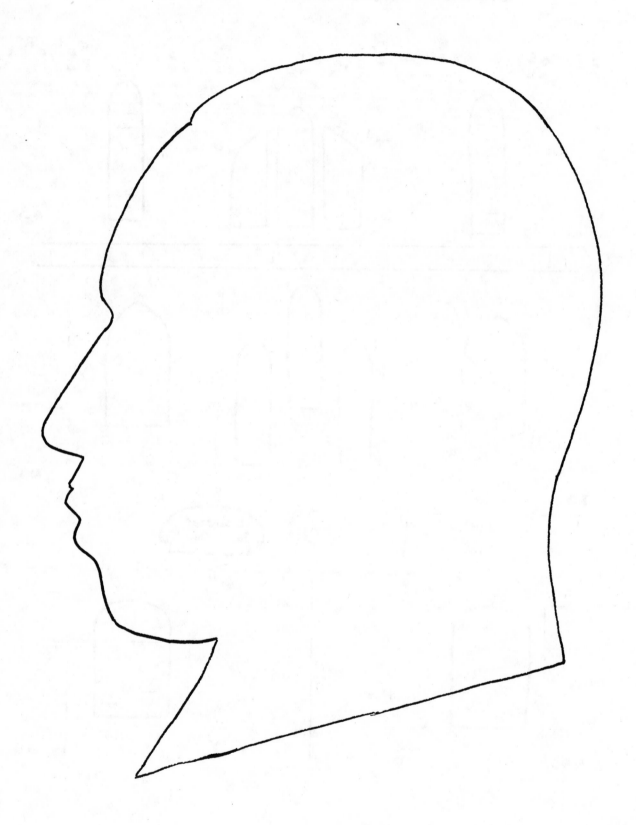

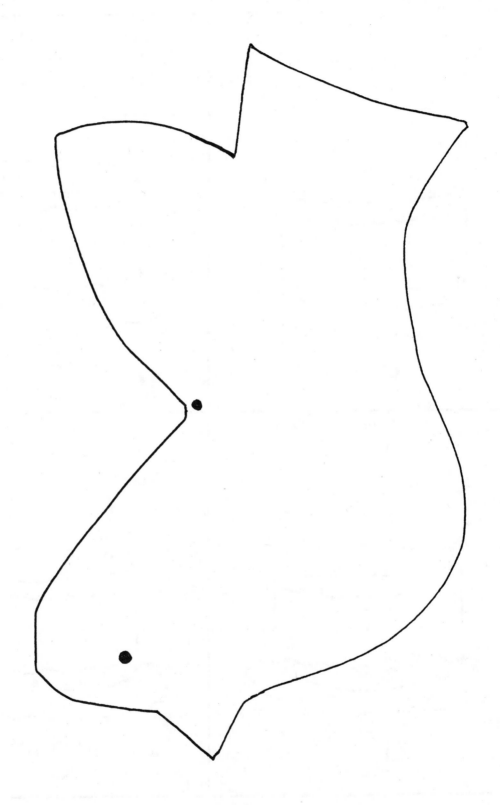

Peace Doves

Birthday Cakes

5

7

4

3

Name ——————————————

THURGOOD MARSHALL

(1908 -   )

ROOM ENVIRONMENT - BULLETIN BOARD

"Steps to the Supreme Court"

Cover and trim the bulletin board as desired and mount the title at the top. In pencil, sketch the Supreme Court building directly on the bulletin board paper. Go over the lines with a black or blue marker. Cut three strips of green and three strips of blue construction paper to fit within the lines of the building steps. On the green strips write "Case A," "Trial Court," and "Appellate Court." On the blue strips write "Case B," "U.S. District Court," and "Court of Appeals." Staple on the building steps in order as shown. (See example on page 154.)

Note: The steps above are simplified for the benefit of young children. For the more detailed steps of how cases reach the Supreme Court, refer to The Supreme Court by Harold Coy.

ROOM ENVIRONMENT - LEARNING CENTERS

Famous Black Americans - (See Room Environment - General - Learning Centers)

Staple a picture of Thurgood Marshall (see page 153) on the learning center. On the remaining space, mount pictures of other Supreme Court justices, the Supreme Court building, and the court building in your town or city. In front of the center, display books such as Thurgood Marshall: Fighter for Justice by Lewis H. Fenderson, The Supreme Court by Harold Coy, The First Book of the Supreme Court by Harold Coy, Let's Go to the Supreme Court by Bernard Rosenfield, Shh! We're Writing the Constitution by Jean Fritz, and The Story of the Constitution by Marilyn Prolman.

Brainwork Center

Using a picture book of Washington, D.C., such as Washington by Janice Anderson, tape-record a description of the buildings and scenes on each page. Include pertinent information. Place the book and the tape recorder in the center. The children look at each page in the book and listen to the taped information.

BIOGRAPHICAL INFORMATION

In 1967 Thurgood Marshall became the first black associate justice of the Supreme Court, the highest court in the United States. From 1934 to 1961, Marshall worked for the National Association for the Advancement of Colored People (NAACP), first as a lawyer, then as chief counsel. In 1961 he was appointed to the U.S. Court of Appeals, and in 1965 he was appointed Solicitor General of the United States.

Thurgood Marshall was born on July 2, 1908, in Baltimore, Maryland. He was named after his grandfather who, when enlisting in the Union Army during the Civil War, had named himself Thorough Good Marshall. Thurgood's parents, William and Norma, sometimes joked that they should have named their son "Thorough Bad" because he was often unruly. At school he spent many hours in the basement memorizing the United States Constitution as punishment for misbehaving.

Marshall's parents knew the value of a good education and taught this to their children. Mrs. Marshall hoped Thurgood's older brother, Aubrey, would be a doctor and Thurgood, a dentist. However, Mr. Marshall felt that Thurgood, who loved to argue, would make a good lawyer. Both boys had after-school jobs and, when the time came, went to college.

Aubrey Marshall and Thurgood Marshall went to Lincoln University in Oxford, Pennsylvania. After three years of college, Thurgood married Vivien Burey whose nickname was "Buster." Both had part-time jobs and Thurgood was able to continue his education.

It was at about this time that Marshall realized he didn't want to be a dentist. He remembered the Constitution he had memorized while being punished and the trials his father had taken him to see when he was a child. He had enjoyed the debating team at college and had always felt that he should do something about the inequality of blacks in America. At that time, blacks were made to sit in the back of buses and were not allowed in white schools or colleges. Marshall thought that as a lawyer, he could work to make these things better.

Marshall went to law school at Howard University, paying his way by working in the law library on campus. Each morning he got up at 5:30, rode the train to Washington, D.C., went to school and worked, then returned home to Baltimore at 9 or 10 at night in time to study awhile before sleeping.

In 1933 Thurgood Marshall graduated from law school at the top of his class and began practicing law in Baltimore. After a year, he figured that he had lost nearly one thousand dollars because he didn't charge those who were too poor to pay.

Then he was hired to be the Baltimore lawyer for the NAACP. The NAACP had been started in 1909 in New York by blacks and whites who believed blacks should be treated fairly. Since that time, the NAACP had grown and had helped many blacks who had been mistreated or whose civil rights had been violated. As a lawyer for the NAACP, Marshall could help.

In 1935 a young man named Don Murray came to Marshall for help. He wanted to attend the University of Maryland law school but couldn't because he was black. Marshall remembered when he, too, had wanted to attend the law school there but couldn't because of his color. Marshall took the case to court where he argued that under the Constitution, a state university had to provide equal treatment for whites and blacks. He won the case, and Donald Murray was the first black allowed to enter law school at the University of Maryland.

In the years that followed, Thurgood Marshall defended many cases. One was a graduate student, a black man named G. W. McLaurin, who was forced to sit outside the college classrooms and eat and study in separate quarters. Another case involved black soldiers in Japan and Korea who were being mistreated. But for Thurgood Marshall, the biggest case was the one to end segregation in schools called "Brown v. Board of Education." After presenting his case to the Supreme Court, Thurgood listened as the decision was read on May 17, 1954. From then on, public schools would be open to all, blacks and whites.

This was Marshall's biggest victory. But then his wife, Buster, became very ill, and the doctors discovered that she had incurable cancer. As fall turned to winter, Marshall spent as much time as possible with Buster. In February 1955, she died.

To help overcome his grief, Marshall kept as busy as possible. The battle for equal rights continued in the South, and despite the threats and dangers, Thurgood Marshall was there. Eventually he began to see people again and go to concerts and lectures. After dating Cecilia "Sissy" Suyat for a while, he asked her to marry him. They married and later had two sons, Thurgood, Jr., and John.

In 1961 President John F. Kennedy appointed Thurgood Marshall to the United States Court of Appeals. Judge Marshall missed the excitement of his job with the NAACP but enjoyed his new job. As usual, his schedule was a busy one.

In 1965 President Lyndon Johnson named him Solicitor General of the United States. Working under the Attorney General, the Solicitor General is the government's chief lawyer and is responsible for presenting cases to the Supreme Court. Also, the Solicitor General helps decide which cases go before the Supreme Court and how to argue such cases. It is one of the government's most important jobs, and Thurgood Marshall was the first black to ever hold such a position.

Almost two years later, President Johnson chose Judge Marshall as associate justice of the Supreme Court. The Supreme Court is made up of the Chief Justice and eight associate justices. All are appointed by the President and approved by the Senate. Thurgood Marshall took his oath of office on October 2, 1967, and became the first black to serve on the high court.

LANGUAGE ARTS - SOCIAL STUDIES - SCIENCE

Discussion

Share the following information with the children: "When people live together, there must be rules or laws to protect the rights of each person. If you like to play your piano late at night, that is your right or privilege. But if you play so loud that your neighbor is disturbed, you are taking away his or her rights. Laws are made to protect or guard our rights. Can you think of any laws? (List them on the chalkboard.)

It is the duty of policemen and courts of law to make sure we obey the law. If you break the law, a policeman will give you a summons—a notice that you must appear in court—or the policeman will arrest you. If you are arrested, it is your right to have a lawyer and to go to court. A lawyer goes to college and law school for many years to learn everything about the laws of our land. The lawyer goes to court with you and "pleads your case"; that is, the lawyer tells your side of the story. The judge and the jury are like umpires. They listen to the lawyers and decide if you broke the law or not. If they believe you did, you are found guilty. If they believe you did nothing wrong, you are found innocent.

Suppose you are innocent but the jury found you guilty. It is your right to go to a higher or more important court and appeal the decision. That means you ask that the case be heard again. Once you go through the higher courts, and you have a good reason to do so, you can go to the highest court in our land, the Supreme Court."

Point out the room displays and summarize the Biographical Information. Show pictures from references (see Famous Black Americans, Room Environment - Learning Centers, page 144). Locate Baltimore and Washington, D.C., on a map.

Supreme Court Activities

Show a film on the Supreme Court or read Let's Go to the Supreme Court by Bernard Rosenfield. Show pictures from references (see Famous Black Americans, Room Environment - Learning Centers). Using the information on the Supreme Court, ask the students questions such as those listed below. Call on volunteers for answers.

1. I am big and white and look like a Greek temple. Inside me important cases are heard. I am _____. (the Supreme Court building)

2. I stand above the columns of the Supreme Court building. Beautiful figures are carved in me. I am _____. (the pediment)

3. There are two of us in the Supreme Court building. We each have four panels with carved figures and weigh 6½ tons. We are bronze. We are _____. (doors)

4. I am black and made of material. I am worn by a justice of the Supreme Court. I am _____. (a robe)

5. There are nine of us. We hear the important cases and decide who is right and who is wrong. We are _____. (the justices of the Supreme Court)

Lawyer's Visit

Invite a lawyer to speak to the class. Tell him or her the ages of the children and what information and items will interest them.

Field Trip

Take the class to city court to see a trial in action. Make sure the trial is for a traffic law violation or a similar minor offense.

Delivery Boy Pantomime and Sheet

Tell the class, "One of Thurgood Marshall's after-school jobs was delivering packages for a department store." Duplicate and distribute the sheet on page 155. After pantomiming the actions of the story below, the children complete the sheet as directed.

It was Saturday morning (make circle of hands and raise). Thurgood was still sleepy (yawn and stretch) but he got out of bed (step out of bed). He took off his pajamas (act out) and put on his clothes (act out), then ran downstairs (run in place). He ate some cereal (say "crunch, crunch"), then brushed his teeth (wiggle fist up and down in front of mouth) and ran (run in place) to work. He went through the revolving door (walk around in a small circle two times) of the department store and said hello (say hello, hello, hello) to the people he saw. His boss (make saluting motion) gave him the deliveries (run in place) for the day. First he delivered (run in place) a hat (make peak with fingers of hands, place on head) to a nice lady (say "thanks, Sonny") and a shirt (act out holding up shirt) to a grouchy man (say "hmmmph"). He delivered (run in place) a bicycle ("steer" with two hands, "pedal" with one foot) to a little boy (say "hot dog!"), and letters (draw rectangle in air) to the post office (act out putting letters in slot). Then he was finished (say "whew") and went home (walk in place).

Complainer's Court

Set up a courtroom using tables and chairs for the judge's bench, the witness stand, the jury box, the lawyers' tables and the audience's seats. Choose students to be the judge and the jury and others to be the two lawyers, the two parties, and the witnesses in each of the cases below. Brief the students on simple court procedures. Let the "lawyers" and their "clients" meet and decide how to present their cases. Let each case come before the court and the jury decide the verdict.

1. Brutus vs. Wilbur: Brutus, a huge man, is accusing Wilbur, a 90-pound weakling, of beating him up on a public beach and kicking sand in his face which caused severe eye damage. Brutus' best friend, Chunky, is his only witness. Wilbur claims Brutus attacked him because he "looked funny" and hurt his own eye when he hit Wilbur's beach umbrella by mistake. Wilbur has two witnesses, a preacher named Rev. William Truth and Corky Washington, the great, great, great, great, (etc.), grandson of George Washington.

2. Mrs. Pincher vs. Rover III: Mrs. Pincher is accusing Rover III, a Chihuahua, of knocking her to the ground, ripping a hole in her purse, and absconding with her wallet. Rover III's owner claims Mrs. Pincher, his next door neighbor, knocked on his door and asked if he had seen her wallet which had fallen out of a hole in her purse. When Mrs. Pincher saw the dog, she screamed "rat!", ran to her house, and tripped over the sign in her yard which reads "Everyone Go Away!" There are no witnesses.

3. Hatfields vs. McCoys: The Hatfield family accuses the McCoy family of trespassing on their property and of group assault with deadly weapons. The McCoy family claims that they heard a party in progress and assumed their invitations were lost in the mail. When they arrived at the party, the Hatfields told them to "go

home" and stuck out their tongues. In self defense, the McCoys pelted the party with eggs they had brought as gifts for the hosts and hostesses. All members of both families claim to be witnesses.

ART

Gavel

Preparation - Collect a cardboard toilet paper roll for each child. Use a pair of scissors to make a hole in the center of the roll. Then make a lengthwise slit by inserting a blade of the scissors in the hole and cutting in each direction (you will be cutting towards the open ends of the roll). The slit should measure 1¼". Give each child a cardboard roll and a third-sheet of brown construction paper (4" x 9"). Provide brown tempera paint, paintbrushes, and transparent tape.

Procedure - Paint the cardboard roll brown and set aside to dry. Starting at one wide edge (9"), roll the construction paper into a tube and secure with tape. This is the handle of the gavel. Mash one end and insert into the slit of the cardboard roll. Gently push the handle until the inserted end touches the inside "wall" of the roll. (See example on page 154.)

Seal of the Supreme Court

Preparation - Purchase a variety of dried peas and beans, macaroni, and (unpopped) popcorn. Duplicate the sheet on page 156. Distribute along with a piece of tagboard of the same size. Set out the peas, beans, macaroni, and popcorn; scissors; crayons or markers; and glue.

Procedure - Glue the seal to the tagboard, dry, then cut out. Color the seal; then fill in the eagle and the symbol above it with the peas, beans, macaroni, and popcorn. Use ample glue to secure. Dry. (See example on page 154.)

MATH

Dot-to-Dot Quill Pen

When the Supreme Court was established, quill pens were used, and as a reminder of this, white goose-feather quills are still placed on the lawyers' tables in the Supreme Court. Duplicate and distribute the sheet on page 157. The children draw lines to connect the numbered dots and, if desired, color the quill pen.

Fingerplay - "Five Lawyers"

Five lawyers standing at the courthouse door   (Hold up 5 fingers)
One went inside and then there were four   (Lower thumb)
Four lawyers entering an innocent plea   (Holding up 4 fingers)
One was dismissed and then there were three   (Lower 1 finger)
Three lawyers arguing as lawyers do   (Holding up 3 fingers)
One went to lunch and then there were two   (Lower another finger)
Two lawyers talking in the noonday sun   (Holding up 2 fingers)
One left for court and then there was one   (Lower another finger)
One lawyer smiling for the case he won   (Holding up 1 finger)
He went home and then there were none.

MUSIC - MOVEMENT - GAMES

Song - "Thurgood Marshall"

Tune: "Davy Crockett"

He was born in Baltimore in 1908,
A lively boy who grew up to debate
Justice for all and equality of man,
Appointed to the highest court in the land.

Chorus:
Thurgood, Thurgood Marshall,
Justice of the Supreme Court,   (Justice - 1 beat, Supreme - 2 beats)
Thurgood, Thurgood Marshall,
Justice of the Supreme Court.

Game - The Judge Says

One player is the judge and stands in front of the other players who are spread out in an open area. The game is played just like "Simon Says" except the player in front says, "The judge says," before giving the commands; and when a player is out, the "judge" points and says "guilty!" The last player standing is the new "judge."

STORY TIME

1. The Snowy Day - Ezra Jack Keats
2. Goggles - Ezra Jack Keats
3. Policeman Small - Lois Lenski

COOKING IN THE CLASSROOM

The Judge's Bow Ties

Wheat bread
Butter
Bacon

Use scissors to cut the crusts from the slices of bread and to cut bacon slices in half. Spread a layer of butter on the bread. Beginning at one end, roll up the bread. Wrap the half piece of bacon around the center of the bread. Bake at 400° on a foil-covered cookie sheet until the bread is toasted.

Dear Parents,

On _____, we will learn about Thurgood Marshall, the first black associate justice of the United States Supreme Court. Please read below to find out ways you can help.

Things To Send: _____
_____
_____

Volunteers Needed To: _____
_____
_____

Follow-Up: At the end of the unit, ask your child the following questions:
_____
_____
_____

Thank you for your cooperation.

Sincerely,

THURGOOD MARSHALL

Bulletin Board, Examples

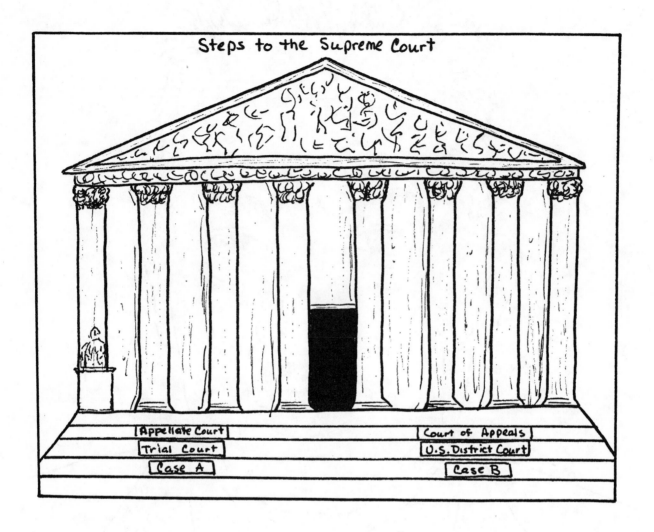

Steps to the Supreme Court

Appellate Court

Court of Appeals

Trial Court

U.S. District Court

Case A

Case B

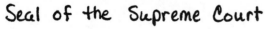

Seal of the Supreme Court

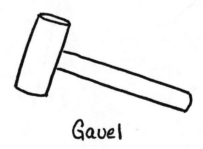

Gavel

Delivery Boy Sheet
Draw lines to match Thurgood's deliveries with the Correct packages.

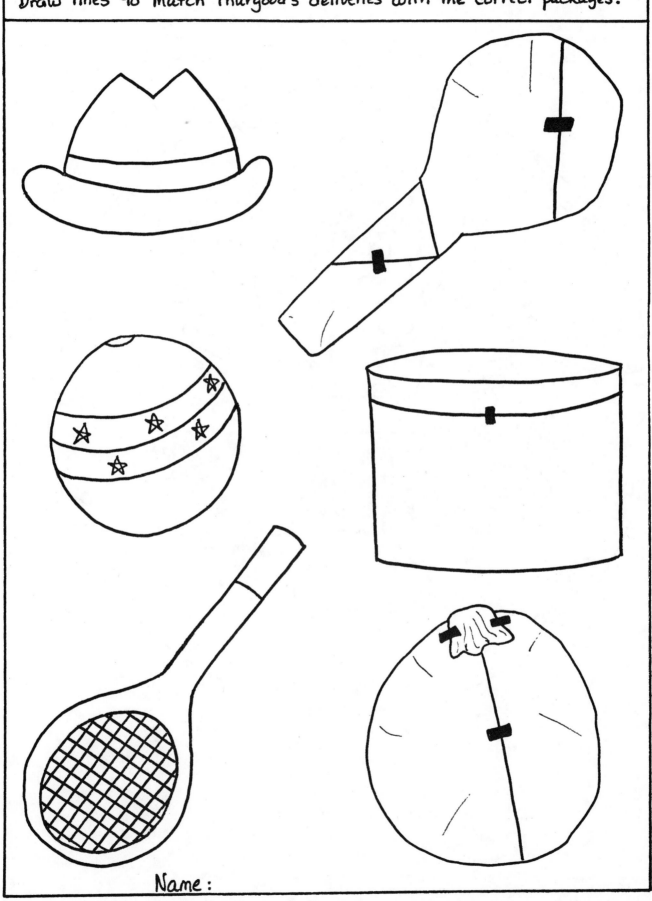

Name:

Pattern

Dot-to-Dot Quill Pen

12 ●

11 ●

10 ●

● 1   ● 13

● 14

9 ●   ● 2

● 15

8 ●

● 3   ● 16

1 ●

● 17

● 4

6 ●   ● 18

● 19

5 ● ● 20

JESSE OWENS

(1913 - 1980)

ROOM ENVIRONMENT - BULLETIN BOARD

"Swifter, Higher, Stronger"

Cover the bulletin board with white paper and trim with a red border.
Cut green construction paper for the title, which is the English version of
the Olympic motto. (If desired, you may use the Latin version. See
Language Arts - Social Studies - Science.) Staple at the top. Draw,
color, and cut out the Olympic rings and the Olympic flame; and copy the
Olympic creed (see Language Arts - Social Studies - Science). Mount on
the bulletin board as shown. Arrange and staple pictures of the various
Olympic events on the remaining areas of the bulletin board. (See example
on page 169.)

ROOM ENVIRONMENT - LEARNING CENTERS

Famous Black Americans - (See Room Environment - General - Learning
Centers)

Staple a picture of Jesse Owens (see page 168) and pictures of various
track events on the learning center. (You may use snapshots of area
track meets.) Display related books such as The Black Athlete, (Volume I
- International Library of Afro-American Life & History), Running,
Jumping, and Throwing – If You Can by Gary Paulsen, Olympic Games in
Ancient Greece by Shirley Glubak and Alfred Tamarin, The Story of the
Olympic Games by John Kieran and Arthur Daley, Hitler and the Germans
by Ronald Gray, The Harlem Globetrotters by Chuck Menville, The First
Book of Cotton by Matilda Rogers, Steel: The Metal With Muscle by Walter
Harter, and India: The Land and Its People by Natasha Talyarkhan.

Brainwork Center

To make picture cards showing sets of sports-related items, cut squares of
tagboard and either draw or glue magazine pictures of the items on the
cards. Make several of these cards with sets of one, several with sets of
two, and so on, ending with sets of five.

Make corresponding number cards by cutting five squares of tagboard and
numbering them 1 though 5.

Put all cards in a ziplock bag and place in the center. The child puts the number cards in order in a row on the table. Then he or she looks at each picture card, counts the items in the set, and places the picture card in a stack below the corresponding number card.

BIOGRAPHICAL INFORMATION

James Cleveland Owens, known as Jesse, was a famous black American track and field star. His performance in the 1936 Olympic Games, where he won four gold medals, made him one of the most famous athletes in the history of sports.

James Cleveland Owens was born in Oakville, Alabama, on September 12, 1913. He was called "J.C." and was one of the seven children of Henry and Emma Owens. His father was a sharecropper, which is a farmer who works another person's land in return for a share of the crops. As a child, J.C., who was frail and sickly, worked in the cotton fields.

In 1921 the family moved to Cleveland, Ohio, where Henry Owens became a laborer in a steel mill. J.C. entered school, and when his teacher asked his name, he answered "J.C." Because of his Alabama drawl, the teacher thought he said "Jesse." J.C. was too shy to correct her, so from then on he was Jesse Owens.

When Jesse Owens was in the fifth grade, the athletic supervisor encouraged him to try out for the track team. By the time he entered junior high, he had become a strong runner. Fairmont Junior High was amazed when Owens ran the 100-yard dash in ten seconds flat, setting a new junior high school record. Coach Charles Riley took over his training and continued as his advisor while Owens attended East Technical High School in Cleveland. There Owens set a world scholastic record of 9.4 seconds for the 100-yard dash.

Many colleges offered Owens athletic scholarships. He decided to attend Ohio State, and he paid his way by pumping gas at a filling station, working as a page in the state House of Representatives, and working as a night elevator operator. At age eighteen, he married Ruth Solomon, and the next year they had a baby daughter.

Guided by Larry Snyder, considered one of the nation's foremost coaches, Owens' performances in track got even better. In 1933, at the Big Ten track and field meet, Owens, who was suffering from a back injury, tied his own world record of 9.4 seconds for the 100-yard dash and set world records in the broad jump, the 220-yard dash, and the 220-yard low hurdles.

After that, Owens' goal was the Berlin Olympics. He traveled there with the American Olympic team in 1936. Adolph Hitler was in power and the Nazi press was quoting Hitler's claims of the superiority of "Aryans," a term used for Germans and certain other people of northern Europe. To him Negroes and Jews were subhuman.   To Hitler's embarrassment and anger, Jesse Owens won four gold medals and the admiration of the German spectators and athletes. Owens won the first two Olympic medals by establishing new records in the 100-meter and 200-meter races. His third gold medal was for a broad jump of 26 feet 5 5/16", a world record which he held for another twenty-five years. The fourth medal was for the 400-meter relay run by the American team of Owens, Ralph Metcalfe, Floyd Draper, and Frank Wycoff. The relay team set a new world record of 39.8 seconds for the race.

Each time Jesse Owens won an event, the American flag was raised above the flags of the competing nations and the "Star-Spangled Banner" was played. America shared his victories, and when he returned home, he was given a hero's welcome.

Unfortunately, Owens had to give up his amateur athletic status. The officials of American amateur sports, in order to raise money and publicity, had scheduled a European tour for the Olympic team to begin after the Olympics. The constant traveling and competing took its toll on Owens. He lost thirteen pounds, and Larry Snyder insisted he needed rest. When the officials scheduled another meet in Sweden, Owens came home. He was then barred from amateur athletics.

Once home, Jesse Owens was met by fans wherever he went. He was voted by Associated Press as America's foremost athlete in 1936. Shortly after that he began making a series of appearances with a touring dance band and toured with black baseball teams. By the end of the year, Owens had made enough money to buy his parents a new house.

In the following years Owens made public appearances, led a swing orchestra, and ran exhibitions—one against a race horse. He appeared in a Hollywood film, owned a dry-cleaning business, worked in public relations for a clothing firm, and was director of personnel for the Ford Motor Company.

Jesse Owens and his wife and three daughters moved to Chicago, Illinois, and in 1950 he joined the board of directors of the South Side Boys Club. In 1951 he revisited Berlin with the Harlem Globetrotters basketball team. Then he started his own public relations firm and became secretary of the Illinois Athletic Commission.

In 1955 Owens traveled to India on a goodwill tour at the request of the State Department.   He returned to his work at the Illinois Athletic Commission where he was dedicated to helping children lead "clean" lives through sports. Jesse Owens died on March 31, 1980, at the age of sixty-seven.

LANGUAGE ARTS - SOCIAL STUDIES - SCIENCE

Discussion

Display a track suit and running shoes and ask the children to guess how Jesse Owens became famous. Define racing and discuss the different kinds—foot races, car races, horse races, etc. Show pictures of a foot race. Point out the room displays and briefly explain the Olympics. Summarize the Biographical Information and show pictures from references (see Famous Black Americans, Room Environment - Learning Centers, page 159). Locate Alabama, Ohio, Germany, Illinois, and India on a map or globe, as they are mentioned in the discussion. Show a film or videotape on the Olympic games. Ask the children, "How do you think Jesse Owens felt after winning four gold medals?"

Olympic Creed, Motto, Flame, and Symbol

Direct the attention of the class to the bulletin board. Read the creed, defining vocabulary words as necessary. Simplify and discuss the meanings of the creed, the Olympic motto, the Olympic flame, and the Olympic symbol.

Creed - "The most important thing in the Olympic Games is not to win but to take part, just as the most important thing in life is not the triumph but the struggle. The essential thing is not to have conquered but to have fought well."

Motto - The Olympic motto, "Citius, Altius, Fortius" or "Swifter, Higher, Stronger" was written by Father Didon, a French educator, in 1895.

Flame - The Olympic flame is a symbol of the first Olympic Games which were held in Greece long ago. Before the Olympic Games can start, the torch is lit by the sun's ray at Olympia, Greece, and then carried to the location of the Games by runners (and ships and planes when necessary). The torch is used to light the huge Olympic flame which burns for the length of the competition.

Symbol - The Olympic symbol is five interlocking rings. The rings represent the five continents—Europe, Asia, Africa, Australia, and America; and the different colors of the rings—blue, yellow, black, green, and red—are taken from the flags of the world. The rings are linked together to symbolize friendship between nations.

Friendship Rings - Friendship and Using Complete Sentences Activity

Direct the children to stand in a circle with their arms by their sides. The first child forms a "ring" with one arm by placing his or her hand on his or her hip and then says, "This is a friendship ring. I will share it with Susan (the child standing next to that arm)." Susan then forms a ring with her other arm and repeats the two sentences, substituting her neighbor's name.   The procedure is repeated until all children have participated and their arms are linked. For the next round, have them add a descriptive sentence about their neighbor's appearance. For example, the first child will say, "This is a friendship ring. I shared it with Susan. Susan has brown hair." Subsequent rounds could include sentences naming an outstanding inner quality, something funny about the child, something the child does well, and so forth.

Note: If this is too difficult for your class, limit the activity to one or two sentences per round rather than increasing the number of sentences with each round.

Poem - My Feet

My feet
walk
here or there,
My feet
jump
up in the air,
My feet
hop
high or low,
My feet
run
fast or slow.
My feet . . .
They're neat.

Book - Read Running, Jumping, and Throwing – If You Can by Gary Paulsen.

ART

Olympic Torch

Preparation - Provide pieces of tagboard or stiff white construction paper, squares of yellow cellophane, crayons, glue, and scissors. On the chalkboard, demonstrate drawing the torch as shown in the example.

Procedure - Draw the torch on your paper and cut it out. Color the handle. Spread glue above the handle and around the edges of the flame. Place the cellophane on this area, directly above the handle and covering the flame. Allow to dry for a short time, then turn the torch over and trim the cellophane close to the edges. (See example on page 169.)

Olympic Necklace

Preparation - Give each child one blue, one yellow, one black, one green, and one red pipe cleaner and a 24" piece of white yarn.

Procedure - Make the blue pipe cleaner into a circle, twisting each end around part of the circle so that it lays flat. Stick the yellow pipe cleaner through the center of the blue pipe cleaner. Then make it into a circle, twisting the ends in the same manner. Repeat with the black, green, then red pipe cleaners. Tie the yarn to the blue pipe cleaner circle. Put the yarn around your neck, adjust to the proper length, and tie to the red pipe cleaner circle. Trim excess yarn. (See example on page 169.)

MATH

Jesse Owens Forming Sets Sheet

Distribute sheets of white unlined paper. Provide crayons. Direct the students to fold the sheet in half, fold it in half once again, and then unfold it. Next they draw lines on the folds to divide the sheet into four blocks. For each block, give the following directions:

1. Jesse Owens was one of seven children. Draw a set of seven children and write the number **7** in the first block.

2. Jesse Owens wore running shoes when he raced. Draw a set of two running shoes and write the number **2** in the second block.

3. Jesse Owens won four gold medals in the 1936 Olympics. Draw a set of four gold medals and write the number **4** in the third block.

4. The Olympic symbol is five rings. Draw a set of five rings and write the number **5** in the fourth block.

Shot Putting

Write large numerals on sheets of white tagboard and place on the floor. The children stand behind a line and attempt to land beanbags on the numbers. When they are successful, they identify the number. If you wish, the children can be divided into teams to compete for points. The numbers on the sheets will equal the points scored if the beanbags land on them. In this case, the higher numbers should be placed farther away from the line.

MUSIC - MOVEMENT - GAMES

Song - "Run, Run, Run the Race"

Tune: "Row, Row, Row Your Boat"

Run, run, run the race,
Running feels so fine,
Round and round the track you race
To cross the finish line.

Song - Sing "The Star-Spangled Banner."

Class Olympics

Have your own Olympic Games in a gym or on the playground. Enlist the help of parent volunteers if you wish the activities to take place simultaneously. Let the children help draw, cut out, and paint the decorations—the Olympic flame, the Olympic flag (white with the five rings in the center) and, if desired, the flags of the "participating countries." (Refer to The International Flag Book in Color by Christian Fogd Petersen.) Form girls' teams and boys' teams for each event and for each "country" if you wish. Make medals by covering cardboard circles with foil of different colors and attaching to yarn. Record "The Star Spangled Banner" on a tape recorder and play when presenting the medals. Materials needed are included in the descriptions of each event.

Broad Jump - Use a jump rope for the line and use sand, hay, leaves, and old blankets or sheets for the pit. The player takes a running start up to the line and then jumps as far as possible. Measure the jumps with a measuring tape.

Discus Throw - Throw frisbees as far as possible. Use different colors for contestants to prevent confusion.

Shot Put - Throw softballs as far as possible. Write names on masking tape and stick on the softballs. The softball thrown the farthest wins.

Javelin - Throw broomsticks or yardsticks as far as possible. If you only have one, mark each thrower's distance with a different colored wooden block.

High Jump - Stand two chairs or stools a few feet apart. Loosely tie a crepe paper streamer to the legs of the chair or stool. Place a gymnastic mat or old blankets underneath. Have a yardstick, tablet, pencil, and more streamers available. Move the streamer up after each jump until the contestant has jumped as high as he or she can. Measure his or her highest jump and record on paper. The highest jump of all wins.

100-, 200-, 400-Meter Races - Convert the meters to inches for each race. Use jump ropes for the starting lines and crepe paper streamers or string held by volunteers or tied to chairs for the finish line. Blow a whistle to begin each race. If desired, use a stopwatch to time the winner.

Hurdles - Using the measurements and setup above, place hurdles at intervals along the track. For each hurdle, place two boxes or chairs a few feet apart and tape a crepe paper streamer or piece of string between them. Have extras available.

Relay Race - Use the 100-inch measurement (see above) and a paper towel cardboard roll for the baton. The three or four members of each team stand at the starting line. The first member of each team runs the distance and back and passes the baton to the next team member. The first team to finish wins. If there is a track on the playground or boundary lines in the gym, the race can be run in a circle with the baton being passed in the usual manner.

Gymnastics - Provide gymnastic mats and a balance board. The contestants perform a free-style floor exercise of forward rolls, log rolls, cartwheels, etc., ending by walking or hopping on the balance board. The best performance wins. The contestants should be barefooted or wearing tennis shoes.

Note: A balance board or walking board stands a few inches above the floor.

Weight Lifting - Fill plastic milk jugs and other similar containers with different amounts of sand. The child who can lift the heaviest jug wins.

Wrestling - Substitute leg wrestling for the "real thing." The contestants lie beside each other with their heads in opposite directions. Inside arms are locked, and at the sound of the whistle, inside legs are interlocked at the knees. Each contestant pushes his or her leg forward. The person who forces the other to roll over backwards is the winner.

Fencing - The contestants fence, using long breadsticks. When a contestant's breadstick is broken until it is too short to use, the match is over and the other contestant wins. If a contestant hits any part of his opponent's body, he or she is disqualified.

Equestrian Events - The 100-, 200-, and 400-inch races (see above) are run with contestants riding piggyback on their teammates' backs. Include the hurdles, making sure they are low enough to be jumped in this fashion.

STORY TIME

1. Jafta's Father - Hugh Lewin
2. The Trip - Ezra Jack Keats

COOKING IN THE CLASSROOM

Egglympic Torches

Eggs, 1 per child
Mayonnaise
Mustard
Salt
Pepper
Sweet pickle relish
Paprika

Cut apart styrofoam egg cartons to make individual cups. Set aside. Hard boil the eggs. Peel and cut each egg in half (holding the pointed end at the top and the rounded end at the bottom, cut at "the equator" halfway between them). Carefully remove the centers with a teaspoon and place in a bowl. Mash well with a fork; then add enough mayonnaise to make the mixture smooth but stiff. Add a small amount of mustard and relish; salt and pepper to taste. Mix well. Use teaspoons to make a "mountain" of the mixture within each egg half. Sprinkle paprika on top. Place in individual egg cups.

Dear Parents,

On _____, we will learn about the famous black American track and field star, Jesse Owens. Please read below to find out ways you can help.

Things To Send: _____
_____
_____

Volunteers Needed To: _____
_____
_____

Follow-Up: At the end of the unit, ask your child the following questions:
_____
_____
_____

Thank you for your cooperation.

Sincerely,

JESSE OWENS

Bulletin Board, Examples

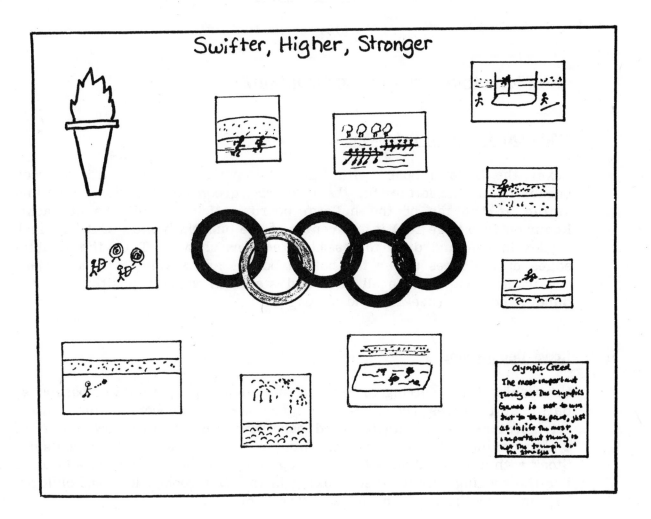

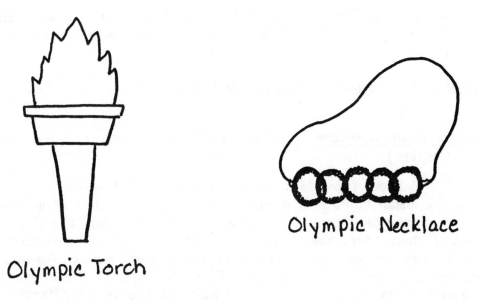

Olympic Torch

Olympic Necklace

JACKIE ROBINSON

(1919 - 1972)

ROOM ENVIRONMENT - BULLETIN BOARD

"Hats Off to Jackie Robinson"

Cover the bulletin board with light blue paper and trim with a green border. Cut the letters for the title from green construction paper and staple at the top of the bulletin board. Mount a picture of Jackie Robinson (see page 180) in the center of the bulletin board. Cut five-inch circles in half and draw to resemble faces as shown. Tuck the straight edges of the faces under the bottom border and staple in place. Make construction paper baseball hats and staple in various positions on the bulletin board. (See example on page 181.)

Room Decorations

Use fishing line or string to hang construction paper cutouts of baseballs, bats, and gloves from the ceiling. Make a popcorn stand from a refrigerator-sized corrugated cardboard box. Cut out a window and staple a sign reading "Popcorn" over the window. Cut out a door from one side. Stock with a small table, a toy cash register, play money, and small sacks. For the cooking activity (see Cooking in the Classroom), let some children bag and sell the popcorn and the others buy it.

Note: By removing the "Popcorn" sign, the popcorn stand can be later used as a puppet theater, a grocery story, a lemonade stand, and so forth.

ROOM ENVIRONMENT - LEARNING CENTERS

Famous Black Americans - (See Room Environment - General - Learning Centers)

Mount a picture of Jackie Robinson (see page 180) on the center. Around it, staple small cutouts of a baseball, glove, and hat; football and football helmet; basketball; tennis racket and tennis ball; and running shoes. In front of the center, place books on Jackie Robinson, the various sports in which he participated in high school and college, and books and magazine articles on major league baseball. Some examples of these are The Jackie Robinson Story by Arthur Mann, Rickey and Robinson by Harvey Frommer, Baseball by Dick Siebert and Otto Vogel, The First Book of Baseball by

Benjamin Brewster, <u>The Game of Baseball</u> by Sam and Beryl Epstein, <u>Baseball</u> edited by Frank F. DiClemente, <u>Volleying and Lobs</u> by Paul J. Deegan, <u>Basketball</u> by David Paige, and <u>The Story of Football</u> by Robert Leckie. Also display sports equipment for the various sports mentioned above.

Brainwork Center - (See Room Environment - General - Learning Centers)

Cut 6" x 9" puzzle cards from tagboard. Cut the cards in half, varying the cutting lines for each card. One card will be cut in half in a zigzag pattern, another in a curving pattern, another in a pattern resembling teeth, and so forth. Fit the cards back together. On one half of a card, draw or glue a picture of a bat; on the other half, write the word "bat." Repeat for each child, drawing or using pictures of a glove, baseball, base, baseball cap, dugout, baseball player, umpire, scoreboard, popcorn, peanuts, cold drink, etc., on one half of the card—and writing the corresponding word on the other half of the card. If you do not wish to use words, draw or glue matching pictures, such as two bats, on the two halves of the cards. (You may also include other sports in the activity.) Mix up the cards and place in a ziplock bag in the center. Purchase inexpensive baseball games and place in the center. One kind resembles a miniature pinball machine and another has small beads which, by holding the game in different positions, land in holes on the gameboard. A collection of baseball cards to view and possibly match would be a "valuable find" to use in the center.

BIOGRAPHICAL INFORMATION

Jackie Robinson was the first black to play major league baseball. He joined the Brooklyn Dodgers in 1947 and played with them for ten years. He retired from professional baseball in 1957.

Jack Roosevelt Robinson was born on January 31, 1919, in Cairo, Georgia. Nicknamed Jackie, he was the fifth and last child of Mallie and Jerry Robinson. Jerry Robinson deserted the family when Jackie was only six months old. Eight months later Mallie and her children moved to Pasadena, California, to live with her half brother, Burton Thomas, and his family. At the time Jackie was fourteen months old, his sister Willa Mae was almost three; and his brothers, Mack, Frank, and Edgar were five, nine, and ten years old respectively.

Mallie Robinson had few possessions and no money, but she had a deep and abiding faith in God which she passed on to her children. She found a job as a maid and worked long hours to support her children. Still, the children were often hungry and aid from the welfare department was necessary to keep the family going.

Mrs. Robinson was determined to have a decent home for her family. Little by little she put money aside and first rented, then bought a house at 121 Pepper Street in Pasadena.

Soon all of the children were attending school at Cleveland Elementary School and working at odd jobs after school. There, and later at John Muir Technical High School, Jackie excelled in soccer, basketball, football, track, and baseball.

After high school Jackie Robinson attended Pasadena Junior College and set new records in track for the broad jump, in baseball for his batting average, and in basketball for individual points. He was well known for his good sportsmanship and his sense of humor.

In 1938 Robinson went to the University of California at Los Angeles and majored in physical education. There, too, he excelled in every sport and became the first student to letter in all four sports. He also won the Negro tennis championship of Southern California.

In 1940 Robinson fell in love with Rachel "Rae" Isum, an honor student and nursing major at UCLA. At about that time, Uncle Burton Thomas became ill and Mallie Robinson was taking care of him. By then, both Edgar and Mack had married and Frank had been killed in a motorcycle accident. Robinson decided to quit college and get a job. He felt it was up to him to help his mother, and he wanted to save money so Rae and he could be married.

Robinson's first job was as an athletic director at a National Youth Administration camp. When the camp closed, Robinson accepted an offer to play in the Chicago-Tribune All-Star Charity football game in Chicago. From that, he received another offer to play professional football for the Los Angeles Bulldogs. When America entered World War II, Robinson was drafted into the army. He served for thirty-one months, became a second lieutenant, and was honorably discharged because of a severe ankle injury.

After coaching for a short time at Sam Houston College in Austin, Texas, Robinson began looking for work with better pay. He accepted an offer to play short stop for the Kansas City Monarchs, a team in the Negro American Baseball League. At that time, major league baseball was all white. Blacks had to play in the Negro league which paid less and was not well organized.

Robinson began playing for the Monarchs for $400 a month, but he was soon discouraged. The constant traveling, the bad hotels, and the heavy schedule of games on poorly lit fields led Robinson to believe he had made a mistake. It was at this time that he was approached by a scout from the Brooklyn Dodgers baseball team.

Years before this, the president of the Dodgers, Branch Rickey, had enlarged the recruiting program. He had hired more scouts to find players who would make the Dodgers the number one major league team. Whether the players were white or black was not important to him. They had to be good ball players. Mr. Rickey also felt that it was past time for blacks to be able to play on major league teams.

After hearing about Jackie Robinson's outstanding abilities, Mr. Rickey sent one of his scouts, Clyde Sukeforth, to set up a meeting. On August 28, 1945, Jackie Robinson met with Branch Rickey. Mr. Rickey talked to Robinson about being the first black in major league baseball. He warned him that he might be called names, threatened, or shunned by other players. To be successful, he would have to ignore these things and play ball.

Jackie Robinson accepted the challenge, and on October 23, 1945, he signed a contract to play for the Dodgers minor league team, the Montreal Royals. After a year with the Royals, where he helped lead the team to victory at the Little World Series, Robinson proved that he was ready for the big league.

On February 10, 1946, Jackie Robinson and Rae Isum were finally married. On April 10, 1947, Robinson signed a contract to play for the Brooklyn Dodgers.

Some of Branch Rickey's warnings proved to be true. Jackie Robinson was called names, threatened, and shunned by some; but he held his head high and played excellent baseball. No one was surprised when he was named the 1947 "Rookie of the Year." Soon other blacks were signed to play major league baseball.

Jackie Robinson played for ten years before retiring from baseball. In those ten years, he played several positions but gained fame as a second baseman. His accomplishments, awards, and honors were many. He was a superior runner, base-stealer, and hitter, finishing his career with a .311 lifetime batting average. Besides his Rookie of the Year honor in 1947, he was named the National League's Most Valuable Player and won the league's batting championship in 1949. In 1956 he was awarded the Spingarn Medal, an annual award given for highest achievement by the National Association for the Advancement of Colored People, and in 1962 he became the first black man admitted to the Baseball Hall of Fame.

Upon his retirement, Jackie accepted a job as a vice-president of Chock Full O' Nuts, a fast food chain that employed many blacks. He spent time with his wife and three children and became active with the Harlem YMCA. He also campaigned for various candidates whom he felt could make the needed changes in America.

On October 14, 1972, Jackie Robinson died of complications caused by advanced diabetes. He was fifty-three years old.

LANGUAGE ARTS - SOCIAL STUDIES - SCIENCE

Discussion

For the discussion, collect a variety of hats such as a policeman's hat, fireman's hat, nurse's hat, etc. Include a baseball hat in the collection. Put the hats in a row in the discussion area. Introduce the subject of the unit and ask, "Which of these hats did Jackie Robinson wear and why?" After obtaining the proper response, ask for volunteers to tell the names of the other hats and the occupations of those who wear them. Summarize the Biographical Information, pointing out Georgia, California, Canada, and New York on a map. Show pictures from various references (see Famous Black Americans, Room Environment - Learning Centers, page 171). Have the children imagine that they are Jackie Robinson, and ask questions about his experience of being the first black player in major league baseball.

Note: To find out how the game of baseball began and how it developed into today's game, read The Game of Baseball by Sam and Beryl Epstein. This children's book also contains pictures of the first uniforms, a diagram of the inside of a baseball, and pictures of many famous players.

Baseball Day

A week or so before presenting the unit, send home the Parents' Survey Letter on page 182. After receiving the responses, you will be able to better plan Baseball Day and can send home another parents' letter concerning the day's events. (Ask parents to label anything being sent for Baseball Day.)

Suggested Activities:

Let the children wear baseball caps and/or uniforms to school. For alphabet recognition, call on a volunteer to name the letter or letters on another child's baseball cap. Continue until all are identified. For color recognition, have all green caps stand up, blue caps stand on one leg, red caps stand and turn in a circle, and so forth. Refer to the letters and colors throughout the day by having all children with red hats line up first, all the children with the letter **A** on their hats pass out papers, etc.

If the children bring baseball items or equipment, let each child "show and tell." Afterwards, seat the children on the floor in a large circle with the items and equipment in the middle and a corrugated cardboard box nearby. Have the children observe the display, then close their eyes. Remove an item and put it in the box. Have the children open their eyes and guess what was removed. Continue in this manner until all items are in the box. Now place 4 or 5 items in a row. Have the children look at them; then cover the items with a cloth or sheet. Call on one child to rename the items in order from left to right. Uncover and check for accuracy. Repeat, but rearrange the order of the items or replace with others from the box.

Pass the Cap

Stand the children in a circle with all but one wearing a baseball cap (or paper hats). As you begin singing the song (below), each child removes the cap from the person on his or her right and puts it on his or her own head. The activity continues in this manner, but vary the tempo so the children pass the caps faster and slower.

Song - "Pass, Pass, Pass the Cap"

Tune: "Row, Row, Row Your Boat"

Pass, Pass, Pass the cap,

Whether fast or slow,

We are passing baseball (paper) caps,

To the right they go.

Note: If you wish it to be a game, stop singing at various times. The child with no cap is eliminated or must perform a stunt.

Film - Show "Casey at the Bat," the animated film version of the poem by Ernest Lawrence Thayer.

Baseball Identification Sheet

Duplicate and distribute the sheet on page 183. The students circle and color the baseball equipment as directed.

Sit On the Base - Following Directions Activity

Give each child a base (a square of white butcher paper). Have the children spread out in an open area, and give directions such as "hold the base in both hands, in your right hand, in your left hand, above your head, in front of you, behind you; put the base on the floor; stand in front of the base, on the base, behind the base; walk around the base; hop around the base." Give the direction "sit on the base" to allow a rest between directions.

ART

Jackie Robinson's Baseball Glove

Preparation - Duplicate the glove pattern (see page 181) on brown construction paper. Distribute along with scissors and two pieces of brown yarn, one 7" and the other 12" in length. Set out hole punchers.

Procedure - Cut out the glove and punch holes on the dots. Tie one end of the yarn to a hole at the top, sew through the remaining holes, and tie the two ends together. Repeat at the bottom, but tie a knot at each end. (See example on page 181.)

Variation: Cut the pattern on white construction paper and let the children sponge-paint the glove with brown tempera paint and sew as directed above.

Note: You will need a large hole puncher to punch the middle holes of the glove. If this is unavailable, punch holes on the top four dots only and decrease the yarn length from twelve to five inches.

Padded Baseballs

Preparation - For each child, cut two 8" circles from white butcher paper. Set out glue, old newspapers, red markers, and staplers.

Procedure - On one side of each circle, draw red stitching lines as seen on a baseball. Turn one circle over and, except for a few inches, apply glue to the edge. Lay the other circle on top of this and dry. Tear and crumple small pieces of newspaper. Stuff through the opening until the baseball is well padded. Staple shut. (See example on page 181.)

MATH

Popcorn Count

Pop popcorn (see Cooking in the Classroom) and set out in bowls. Distribute small paper cups. Give the class directions such as:

1. Put 4 pieces of popcorn in your cup. (Write the number 4 on the board.) Now take out 2 pieces. Count how many are left in the cup. (Write 4 - 2 = 2 on the chalkboard. Explain.)

2. Put 3 more pieces of popcorn in your cup. Count the total. (Write 2 + 3 = 5 on the chalkboard. Explain.)

3. Put a handful of popcorn in your cup. Now count how many you put in. (Continue in this manner. You may also direct one child to put a certain number of pieces in his or her cup and have another child empty the cup and count the pieces aloud to check for accuracy.)

Create a Set

Distribute sheets of unlined paper, and direct the children to create a set by drawing and coloring like items (pertaining to Jackie Robinson) on the sheet. Next they draw a circle around the set, count the items, and write the corresponding number on the paper.

MUSIC - MOVEMENT - GAMES

Song - "Take Me Out to the Ball Game"

Source: Disney's Children's Favorites, Volume I (LP)

Game - Fly Ball

Blow up a white balloon and use a red permanent marker to draw the seams and stitches so that it resembles a baseball. Divide the class into two teams. Assign a different (baseball) position to each player on a team (pitcher, catcher, first baseman, etc.). To avoid confusion, let each player wear a labeled contact paper square or piece of masking tape on his or her shirt.

Seat the two teams in a circle so that like positions are opposite each other. Stand in the center holding the baseball balloon. Call out a position such as "shortstop"; then with your arm raised as high as possible, drop the balloon to the floor. The two shortstop players rush from their seats and each attempts to catch the baseball balloon before it hits the floor. (If this proves too difficult for your class, toss the baseball balloon into the air.) The player who catches it scores a point for his or her team. No points are scored if the balloon hits the floor. Continue in this manner until all players have participated.

Variations: For younger children, make several "baseball balloons" as explained above.   Let pairs of children toss the balloons to each other, or let one child toss the balloon and the other child "bat" the balloon with his or her hand.

Game - Whiffle Ball

Play baseball using a plastic ball and bat. Adjust the dimensions of the field and the number of players in the field according to your children's abilities. You may also wish to use a T-ball stand to hold the ball for the batter.

STORY TIME

1. Willy's Raiders - Jack Gantos and Nicole Rubel

COOKING IN THE CLASSROOM

Popcorn

Microwave popcorn, or pop in a popcorn popper as directed. To pop the old-fashioned way, cover the bottom of a pot with cooking oil and heat. Place one kernel of popcorn in the oil.   When it pops, remove it with a spoon and pour in popcorn so that a single layer covers the bottom. Put the lid on the pot and shake the pot as the popcorn pops.   When the popping is almost completed, remove the pot from the heat and pour the popcorn into a bowl.   Salt to taste.

Mini Hot Dogs

Prepare wieners and cut into thirds.   Cut buns into thirds.   Set out mustard, mayonnaise, pickles, pickle relish, and hot dog chili; and let each child prepare his or her own mini hot dog. Party toothpicks may be used to hold the hot dogs together.

Dear Parents,

On _____, we will learn about Jackie Robinson, the first black major league baseball player. Please read below to find out ways you can help.

Things To Send: _____
_____
_____

Volunteers Needed To: _____
_____
_____

Follow-Up: At the end of the unit, ask your child the following questions:

_____
_____
_____

Thank you for your cooperation.

Sincerely,

JACKIE ROBINSON

Bulletin Board, Examples

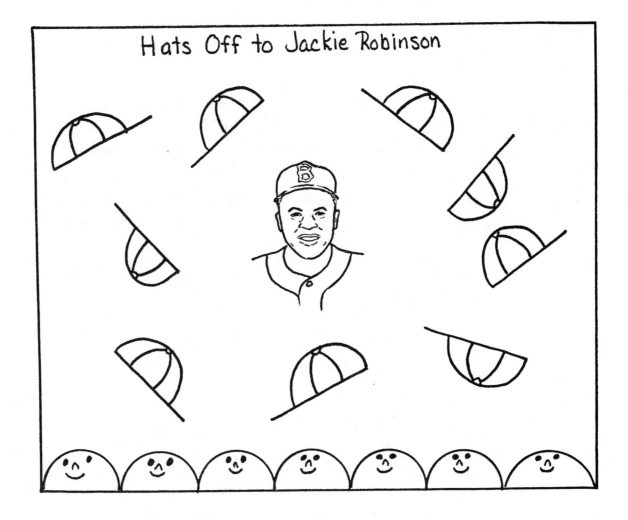

Hats Off to Jackie Robinson

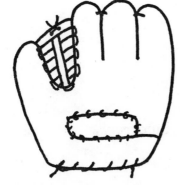

Jackie Robinson's Baseball
Glove

Padded Baseball

Dear Parents,

Next week our class will learn about Jackie Robinson. In conjunction with this unit, I am considering the idea of having "Baseball Day." To facilitate the planning of activities, please answer the following:

____ Yes ____ No   My child has played a game of baseball.

____ Yes ____ No   My child has played organized baseball.

Which of the following can your child wear or bring to school for Baseball Day: (check any)

    ____ baseball cap
    ____ baseball glove
    ____ baseball uniform
    ____ baseball bat
    ____ baseball trophy, medal, or ribbon
    ____ baseball cards
    ____ baseball pictures or posters
    ____ other related items (please list below)

Thank you for your cooperation.

        Sincerely,

Baseball Identification Sheet
Circle the things you see that go with the game
of baseball. Color those items only.

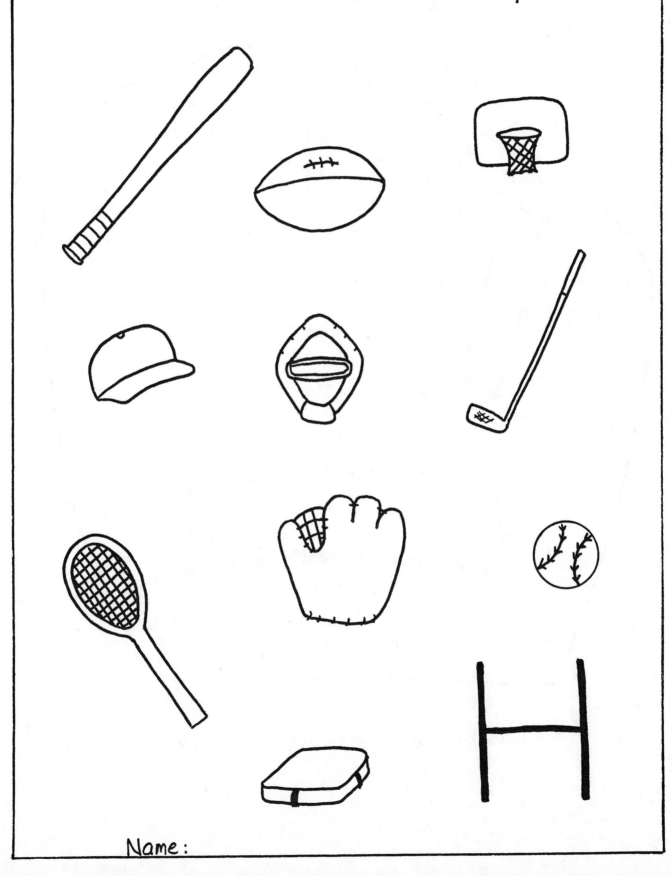

Name:

Pattern

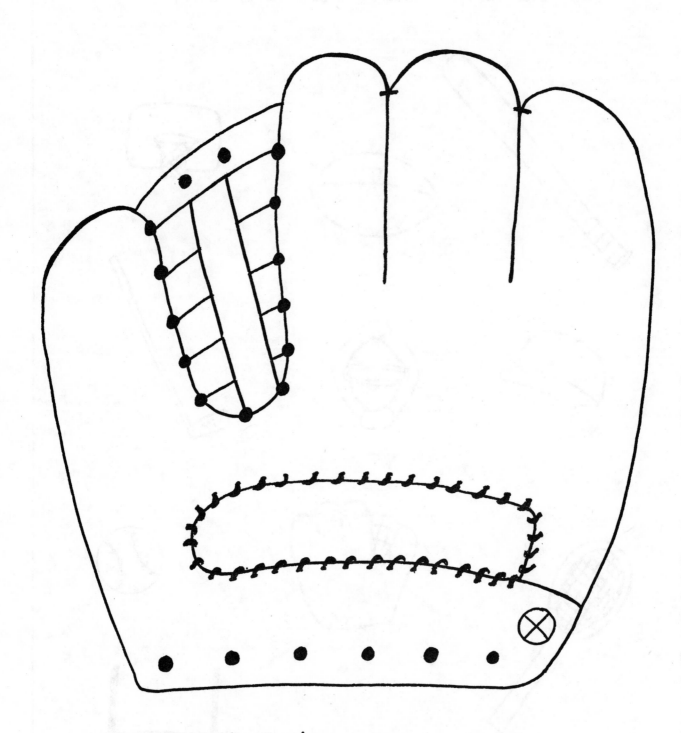

Jackie Robinson's Baseball Glove

WILMA RUDOLPH

(1940 -   )

ROOM ENVIRONMENT - BULLETIN BOARD

"Go for the Gold!"

Cover the bulletin board with white paper and trim with a green border. Make the letters for the title of blue construction paper except for the word "gold" which should be made of gold or yellow construction paper. Mount the title at the top. Write the numerals 1–5 (or more if desired) and the words "Finish Line" on strips of paper and staple across the bulletin board as shown. The rest of the bulletin board will represent a running track. Stretch pieces of black yarn across the bulletin board to make a lane for each child. Tie to stick pins at each side. Tie a piece of red yarn vertically 4 or 5 inches from the right edge of the bulletin board to represent the finish line.

Make a tennis shoe for each child and stick-pin in a lane at the left side of the display. On the chalkboard or on a piece of poster paper, list the five (or more) skills or concepts that must be achieved to cross the finish line. When a child masters one of these, he may move his tennis shoe forward in his lane so that it is under the number **1**. When he masters another, he moves it under the number **2**, and so forth. When he crosses the finish line, his tennis shoe is placed on the far right of the bulletin board and is decorated with a large gold star sticker. (See example on page 198.)

ROOM ENVIRONMENT - LEARNING CENTERS

<u>Famous Black Americans</u> - (See Room Environment - General - Learning Centers)

Staple Wilma Rudolph's name and picture (see page 197) on the bulletin board. Also include a picture of the Olympic symbol (5 rings) and Olympic flame (see unit on Jesse Owens for Olympic background information). Display books such as <u>100 Greatest Women in Sports</u> by Phyllis Hollander, <u>The Black Athlete</u>, (<u>Volume 1 - International Library of Afro-American Life and History</u>), <u>Running, Jumping, and Throwing – If You Can</u> by Gary Paulsen, <u>Olympic Games in Ancient Greece</u>, <u>The Story of the Olympic Games</u> by John Kieran and Arthur Daley, and <u>Basketball</u> by David Paige.

Brainwork Center - (See Room Environment - General - Learning Centers)

From construction paper, make three each of the following: a running shoe, a basketball, a hamburger, a cold drink bottle, a book, the Olympic torch, the Olympic flag, and an Olympic gold medal. Make each of the three objects identical except for the size. Make one small, one medium-sized, and one large. Laminate, mix, and place in a ziplock bag in the center. The children find the like objects, then place them in order of size, from left to right, on the table.

BIOGRAPHICAL INFORMATION

Wilma Rudolph was the first American woman athlete to win three gold medals in Olympic track and field events. At the 1960 Olympics in Rome, Italy, she won the 100-meter dash, the 200-meter dash, and along with three of her teammates, won the 400-meter relay.

Wilma Glodean Rudolph was born the fifth of eight children on June 23, 1940, in St. Bethlehem, Tennessee. St. Bethlehem was a poverty-stricken farming area where tobacco and corn were raised. Wilma's father, Ed Rudolph, was a porter and her mother, Blanche, was a maid. In addition to their eight children, Ed Rudolph had eleven children by a former marriage. After Wilma was born, the family moved to a small house in Clarksville, Tennessee, where Wilma grew up.

Wilma Rudolph weighed only four-and-a-half pounds at birth. Her parents were afraid she would not survive, but gradually she gained weight and became a healthy little girl. Then at age four she developed double pneumonia and scarlet fever which caused her left leg to be completely useless. Her mother took her to specialists at Meharry Medical College in Nashville where she received heat and water therapy to build up the shrunken leg muscles. Then every week for two years, Mrs. Rudolph, on her day off, took Wilma the forty-five miles to Nashville for therapy. Four times each day, the older children in the family and Mrs. Rudolph took turns massaging Wilma's left leg.

For years Wilma Rudolph was confined to a chair or bed. She never complained about the pain and played as well as she could with friends who gathered around her chair or bed.

When she was about seven years old, Wilma Rudolph was able to walk with the help of specially made shoes. She was soon running and playing with her friends, and by the time she was eleven years old, she no longer needed the special shoes.

When she was thirteen years old, Rudolph made the Burt High School basketball team. Her coach, Clinton Gray, nicknamed her "Skeeter" because she resembled a mosquito—little, fast, and always buzzing around. But in two years she grew to her full six foot height, and in her sophomore year she set a new state record in girls' basketball by scoring 803 points in 25 games.

Ed Temple, the women's track coach at Tennessee State University, saw Wilma Rudolph in a tournament and recognized her potential as a runner. He convinced Clinton Gray to start a track team at Burt High School so that she could be trained. After a year of high school competition, Wilma Rudolph became a member of the 1956 U.S. Olympic team. At sixteen years of age, she helped her team win a bronze medal in the 400-meter relay in Melbourne, Australia.

Rudolph returned to high school competition, spending her summers in Nashville at Tennessee State University. There she trained under Clinton Gray and Ed Temple. After she graduated from high school in 1957, Rudolph enrolled at the university and became a member of Coach Temple's track team.

Surrounded by an excellent team, Rudolph ran even faster. Coach Temple was pleased but complained that she didn't eat enough, and when she did, it was only hamburgers and cold drinks. Her teammates laughed because she loved to sleep, and second to that, she loved to read in bed. As a result of this, she would often oversleep, arrive late for practice, and have to run extra laps.

Illness prevented Rudolph from competing in the 1958 season, and in 1959 she had problems with a pulled thigh muscle. But in 1960 she was in good health and ready to compete in the Olympics in Rome.

The 1960 Olympics brought some disappointments for the American spectators. Surprisingly in one day, the great high jumper, John Thomas, who had held all world records, was beaten by two Russians; and the American runners, Ray Norton and David Sime, were beaten by a German in the 100-meter final. Then two Russian women won the 80-meter hurdles and the javelin throw.

The next day the Americans began their comeback, and Wilma Rudolph stunned the crowds with her magnificent performances. In the 100-meter dash, Rudolph finished at least three yards ahead of the field. Next she won the 200-meter dash, set an Olympic record, and became the first American woman to win both sprint gold medals. In the 400-meter relay, Rudolph ran with her teammates who were all from Tennessee State and had named themselves the "Tiger Belles." Martha Judson, Lucinda Williams, Barbara Jones, and Wilma Rudolph won the event and set another world record. She then became the first American woman to win three Olympic gold medals.

Wilma Rudolph, the fastest female runner in the world, became famous, and because of her graceful style, was called La Gazelle Neva (The Black Gazelle) by the people of France and La Perle Noire (The Black Pearl) by the people of Italy.   On tour with her team in Europe following the Olympics, Rudolph drew crowds of admirers wherever she went.   The tour ended in her home town where a parade and dinner were held in her honor.

Following this, Rudolph was honored at dozens of banquets and held many press conferences.   She was awarded the 1960 Helms World Trophy Award, the United Press International's Athlete of the Year's European sports poll, and the 1961 Sullivan Memorial Trophy for her outstanding performance as an amateur athlete.

In 1961 Wilma Rudolph competed in the Millrose Games at Madison Square Garden and won the 60-yard dash, tying her own world record.   Two weeks later she returned and broke this record.   Later she set a new world record in both the 70-yard dash and the 100-meter dash.

Rudolph decided not to compete in future Olympics.   After winning three gold medals, she decided to go on to other things.   She traveled around the country lecturing to young people, engaged in fundraising activities, and worked for Job Corps.   She was also assistant director of athletics for Mayor Daley's Youth Foundation in Chicago.   A few years ago she started the Wilma Rudolph Foundation to help young people who are interested in track.

LANGUAGE ARTS - SOCIAL STUDIES - SCIENCE

Discussion

(For information on the Olympic flame, symbol, flag, creed, and motto, see unit on Jesse Owens.)   Point out the various room displays and briefly explain the Olympics.   Summarize the Biographical Information and show pictures from references (see Famous Black Americans, Room Environment - Learning Centers, page 186).   Locate Tennessee, Australia, Italy, New York, and Illinois on a map or globe as they are mentioned in the discussion.

100-Meter Dash

Write "100-Meter Dash" at the top of the chalkboard.   Draw three parallel lines (4 or 5" apart) horizontally across the chalkboard to represent two running lanes.   Draw two vertical lines at each end to be the starting and finish lines.   Add a tennis shoe before the starting line of each lane.   On the top and bottom lines, make a mark every few inches.   Divide the class into two teams.   Alternating teams, ask questions pertaining to the

Biographical Information or any concepts you desire. For each correct answer, the tennis shoe of that team is moved forward one mark. (Erase the tennis shoe and draw again.) The team that reaches the finish line first wins the game.

Poem - "The Tiny Creatures' Olympics"

Read the poem. If desired use as a choral poem, assigning certain lines to students or groups of students.

Oh, the Tiny Creatures' Olympics
Takes place each year in July,
No human has ever seen it
'Cept me and I'll tell you why.

My house is out in the country
And as I sat by our pond one day,
A small voice said, "Tiny Creatures,
The Olympics is underway!"

A little band began to play
And what a sight to see,
The Grand Parade of Creatures
Led by a buzzing bee.

Around the miniature stadium marched
The grasshoppers, snails, and fleas,
The ants and crickets and beetles,
The mosquitos, flies, and bees.

Then the Tiny Creatures' Olympic Games
Were played and the races run,
And teeny-tiny medals
Were given to those who won.

A fly was first in the four-inch dash
The mosquitos were aghast,
The crickets won the relays,
And the snails, as usual, were last.

A flea was first in the high jump
And a mantis, in the boxing contest,
An ant won the honors in weight lifting,
In fencing the bees were best.

A water bug won best swimmer,
A horsefly, the best horse-rider,
A dragonfly won the rowing contest,
The discus was won by a spider.

When the games were through, they all shook hands
And said, "Goodbye, goodbye!"
But they'll return and I will too,
To the next Olympics in July.

Basic Four Food Group Activities

From old magazines, cut out pictures showing examples of the Basic Four
Food Group. On an experience chart, list the four groups: the Meat
Group, the Fruit and Vegetable Group, the Bread and Cereal Group, and
the Milk and Dairy Products Group. Leave a space under each group.
Explain the groups and call on volunteers to look through the pictures and
find examples of each. Discuss a balanced diet. Under the name of each
group, write the required daily servings (meat - 2, fruits or vegetables
- 4, breads and cereals - 4, milk and dairy products - 3), and let the
children glue that many examples on the chart. Ask if Wilma Rudolph's
(college) diet of hamburgers and cold drinks was a balanced one. Discuss.
Have the children recall the foods they ate at the three meals of the
previous day. Discuss whether or not their diets are balanced.

Wilma's Weird Race - Maze

The children complete the maze (see page 199) as directed.

Rhyme - "Wilma Rudolph" (adapted from Little Boy Blue - Mother Goose)

Wilma Rudolph,
Come run your race,
The coach is on the sidelines,
And he's red in the face.

Where is the girl

Who's in trouble so deep?

She's snug in her bed,

Fast asleep.

Will you wake her?

No, not I,

For if I do

She'll surely cry,

"Oh, no, oh, no, it's ten 'til one,

How many laps must I run?"

ART

Sand-Painted Olympic Flags

Preparation - Purchase blue, yellow, black, green, and red colored sand at a craft store. Cut an 8" x 10" piece of white poster paper for each child. Set out the sand in separate aluminum pie pans. Provide glue and pencils. Draw the Olympic rings on the chalkboard with colored chalk.

Procedure - Draw the Olympic rings in the center of the poster paper. Spread or squeeze glue on the first ring and use your hand or a spoon to trickle colored sand on the glue. Let it dry a few minutes; then tap lightly to remove the excess sand. Return this to the proper aluminum pie pan. Repeat this procedure, using the correct color for each ring. Dry well. (See example on page 198.)

The Big Tennis Shoe

Preparation - Duplicate the pattern (see page 200) on white construction paper. Distribute to each child along with a 36" piece of white yarn. Set out fingerpaints of various colors, hole punchers, spray bottles of water, and scissors. Cover the work area with old newspapers.

Procedure - Cut out the tennis shoe and punch holes on the X's. Lightly spray the tennis shoe with water, and fingerpaint as desired. Dry thoroughly. Lace the yarn through the holes and tie in a bow at the top. (See example on page 198.)

Note: If lacing is too difficult for your students, use a black pen to draw the lacing pattern on the tennis shoe. Duplicate. Direct the children to punch holes in the top two **X**'s only, lace yarn through these holes, and tie in a bow.

MATH

Olympic Rings - Shapes Activity

Before the activity, use chalk to draw a large circle on a concrete area. On the other side of the area, draw five large interlocking circles to represent the Olympic symbol.

To give the children a better understanding of a circle, hold up one made of tagboard and discuss the shape. Have the children find and name circular items in the classroom as you list these, too, on the chalkboard.

Show a picture of the Olympic flag and say, "This is the Olympic flag. Do you see any circles on the flag?" Call on one child to point to one of the circles and another to count aloud the number of circles on the flag. Show that the interlocking circles of the Olympic symbol are actually five complete circles by placing five jar rings (plastic bracelets, milk jug rings, or the outer rims of margarine container tops) in a row on a table. Then overlap them to form the symbol. (If you wish to be completely accurate, you may make a cut in each ring and interlock them.)

Now take the class to the concrete area and have them walk (hop, skip, run, etc.) in single file on the large circle. Repeat the procedure with the interlocking rings.

Note: This activity can be extended to include the rectangular shape of the flag, the oval-shaped track, the triangular base of the flame, and so on.

Hamburger Puzzle

Duplicate and distribute the sheets on pages 201 and 202. The children color the puzzle parts as indicated, cut out, match the number dots on the parts to the numerals on the outline, and glue in place.

Height Activities

Duplicate and distribute the sheets on page 203 and set aside. Obtain a ruler for each child and six extras for the activity. Discuss measuring and how we measure things. Show a ruler and explain that a ruler is also called 1 foot and we use it to measure height or how tall things are.

Tape six rulers end-to-end to a wall with the end of the first ruler touching the floor. Stand next to the rulers and let the children compare your height with that of Wilma Rudolph (six feet). Let the children choose partners with one child standing against the ruler and the other child counting the feet. Record each child's height on the chalkboard. The partner should supply the number of feet, and you should fill in the number of inches. (For this activity, explain inches as parts of a foot.)

Distribute the sheets and write the date on the chalkboard. The children write the correct information in the blanks. Give assistance when necessary. Save the sheets and repeat the activity at the end of the year, using the bottom half at that time.

MUSIC - MOVEMENT - GAMES

Song - "Wilma Rudolph Went to Rome"

Tune: "Twinkle Twinkle Little Star"

Wilma Rudolph went to Rome
Many miles away from home
There beneath the famous flame
Wilma won Olympic fame
Wilma Rudolph went to Rome
And then brought three gold medals home.

Relay Game - Pass the Torch

Divide the class into two even teams and establish two lines. Direct each team to line up behind one line. Darken the room and give the first player in each line a lighted flashlight. At the signal, the players run to the far boundary line and back, holding the flashlights like torches. When they get back to their lines, the "torches" are passed to the next players. The relay continues in this manner. The team whose last player finishes first wins the race.

Note: The room should be dark enough for the children to enjoy the flashlights, but light enough for them to safely run the race.

Games - Mini Olympics

Set up the following games in the classroom so the activities can go on simultaneously. Let the contestants practice each skill a few times before competing.

<u>Races</u> - Cut sheets of tagboard and draw an oval-shaped 2"-wide running track on each.   Draw a vertical line across the track for the finish line and an **X** in front of the finish line to represent the starting block. Laminate.   Place a magnet on the front side of the sheet within the lane and on the **X**, and one directly underneath it on the back side of the sheet.   The two will attract through the sheet and hold each other in place.   Each child holds the tagboard sheet in front of him or her with one hand (as if it is a dinner plate), and with the other hand holds the magnet on the back side of the sheet.   At the signal, the children move the magnets around the track without going out of the running lanes.   The first to cross the finish line wins.

Variation: Make the running tracks for various races different sizes.

<u>Discus Throw</u> - Provide separate drinking straws for contestants and bottle caps from cold drinks.   Have a ruler available.   Set the equipment on a table and use masking tape to make a line near the edge of the table. The contestants place their bottle caps (with the smooth sides down) directly in front of the tape line.   At the signal, they blow as hard as they can through the straws to make the caps move as far as possible. The straws must remain behind the taped line.   The contestants whose cap travels the farthest wins.

<u>Shot Put</u> - Make a masking tape line on a rug or carpet.   Provide marbles. The contestants place their hands behind the tape and shoot the marbles forward in the standard marble-shooting manner.   The contestant's marble that is propelled the farthest wins.

<u>Javelin</u> - Make a masking tape line on the floor or carpet.   The contestants hold a toothpick in one hand and thump it with the other. The contestant whose toothpick travels the greatest distance wins.

<u>Broad Jump</u> - Place the bottom portion of an egg carton on a table so that one narrow edge faces the contestants.   Each contestant sits at the end of the table and attempts to flip a button into one of the cups of the egg carton by pressing on the button's edge with another button (as in tiddly-winks).   The contestant who lands a button in the cup which is the greatest distance away wins.

<u>Swimming Contest</u> - Fill two baby food jars with corn syrup or glycerin. Collect pebbles of various shapes and of approximately the same size and place in a pile next to the jars.   Have a long handled teaspoon available. Each contestant picks a pebble and drops it into one of the jars.   The contestant whose pebble reaches the bottom first wins.   Remove the pebbles with the teaspoon.

<u>Ice Skating</u> - Provide old-fashioned tops and an area with a hard surface. The contestant whose top spins for the longest period of time wins.

STORY TIME

1. <u>Jennifer's New Chair</u> - Charles Bible
2. <u>Holes and Peeks</u> - Ann Jonas
3. <u>Hippo Jogs for Health</u> - Richard Hefter
4. <u>Jafta's Mother</u> - Hugh Lewin

COOKING IN THE CLASSROOM

Tiny Creatures' Olympic-Burgers

Small rolls (bakery-type)
Ground chuck
Mayonnaise
Mustard
Tomatoes, sliced
Lettuce, shredded
Pickles, sliced
Salt
Pepper

Help the children form their own mini-patties. Broil, barbecue, or fry the patties; drain on paper toweling. Let the children assemble their Olympic-Burgers. Serve with chips and milk or cold drinks. (For dessert, see below.)

Gold Medals

Plain sugar (or similar) cookies
Yellow ready-to-spread frosting
Plastic knives or wooden popsicle sticks.

The children spread the frosting on the cookies to make their own gold medals.

Dear Parents,

On _____, we will learn about Wilma Rudolph, the first black American woman athlete to win three gold medals in Olympic track and field events. Please read below to find out ways you can help.

Things To Send: _____
_____
_____

Volunteers Needed To: _____
_____
_____

Follow-Up: At the end of the unit, ask your child the following questions:
_____
_____
_____

Thank you for your cooperation.

Sincerely,

WILMA RUDOLPH

Bulletin Board, Examples

Go For The Gold !

| 1 | 2 | 3 | 4 | 5 | Finish Line |

The Big Tennis Shoe

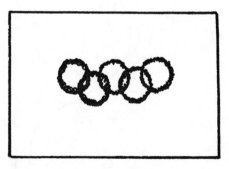

Sand-Painted Olympic Flags

Wilma's Weird Race - Maze

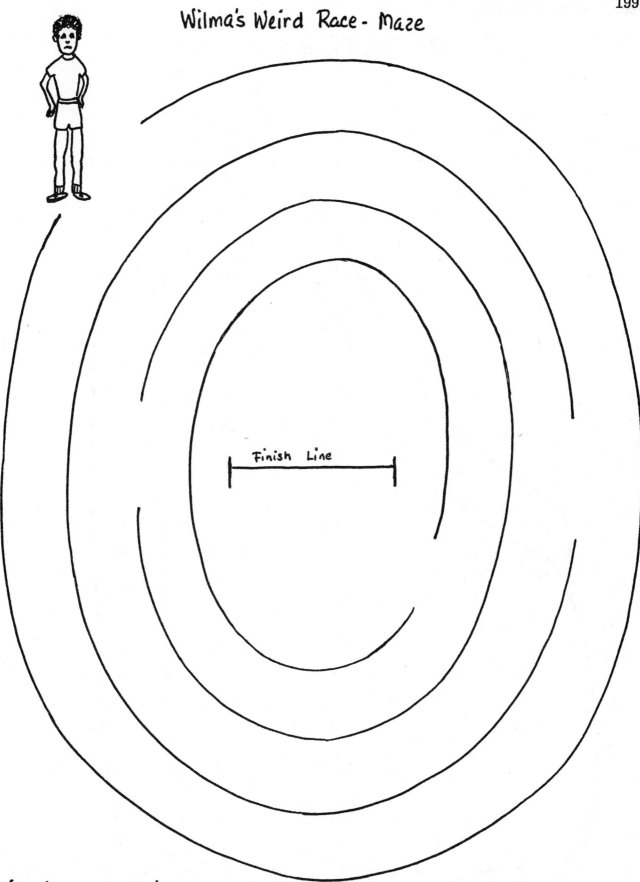

Finish Line

To win this weird race, Wilma has to run around each lane!
Help her find the path to the finish line! Draw a line
with your pencil.

The Big Tennis Shoe

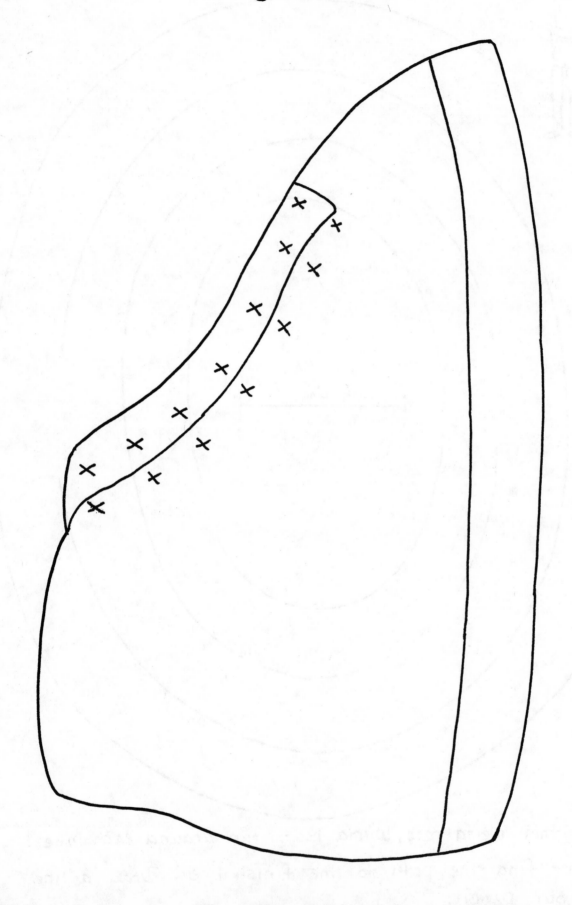

Hamburger Puzzle
Parts

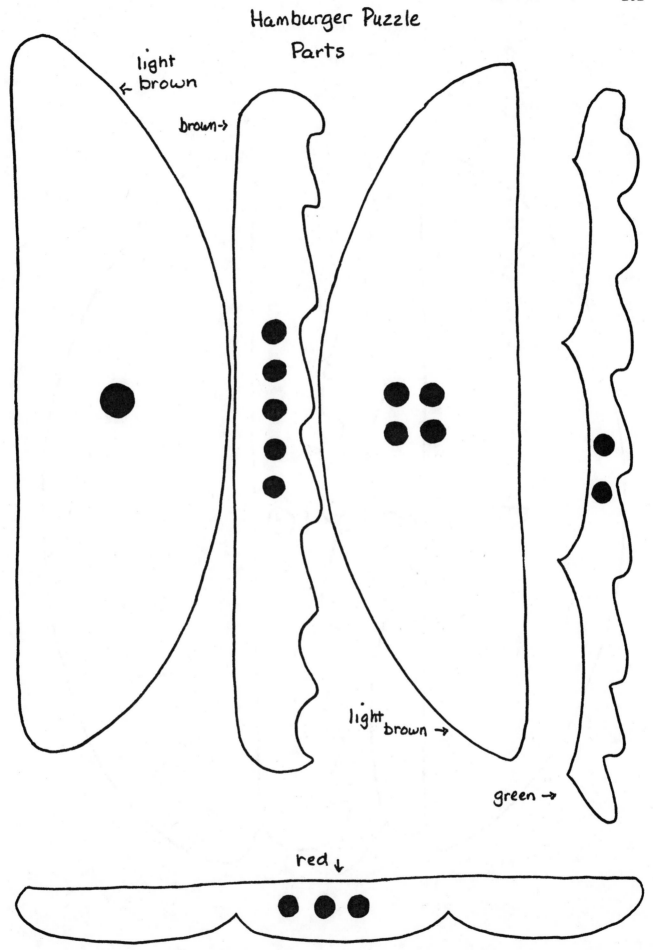

light
← brown

brown→

light brown →

green →

red ↓

Hamburger Puzzle
Outline

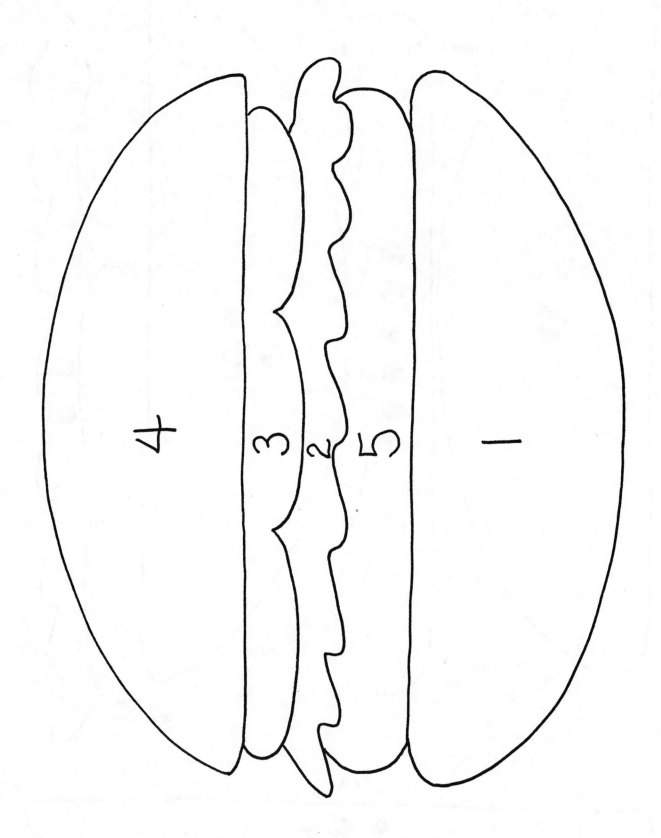

My Height Sheet

Today is _____ .

We learned to measure with a ruler.

I am _____ feet _____ inches

tall!

My Name _____

My Height Sheet

Today is _____ .

We learned to measure with a ruler.

I am _____ feet _____ inches

tall!

My Name _____

SOJOURNER TRUTH

(1797 - 1883)

ROOM ENVIRONMENT - BULLETIN BOARD

"The Learning Journey"

Cover the bulletin board with light blue paper and trim with a red border. Cut the letters for the title from green construction paper and staple at the top. In pencil, sketch a trail as shown on page 215 directly on the bulletin board. Go over the pencil lines with a blue marker. Staple trees and buildings near the trail and a commercially-prepared or teacher-made spinner in the lower right corner. Make a name marker for each child and stick-pin to the bulletin board on the right side.

For the game activities, make simple matching games and use any games or learning materials in your classroom. Put each in a ziplock bag and code with symbols: shapes of different colors, letters, numbers, etc. Store in the Brainwork Center (see Room Environment - Learning Centers). Put these same codes on the squares of the trail. If you lack enough activities to fill all the squares, make the remaining squares solid colors. When a child has free time, he goes to the bulletin board, spins the spinner, then moves his marker that many spaces. He then looks at the symbol and finds the corresponding game or activity and takes it back to his seat. If he lands on a solid square, he spins again. Once he completes the game or activity, the procedure may be repeated. Tack reward stickers to the sun at the end of the trail.

ROOM ENVIRONMENT - LEARNING CENTERS

Famous Black Americans - (See Room Environment - General - Learning Centers)

Staple a picture of Sojourner Truth (see page 214) on the center along with a map showing the areas where she traveled. In front of the center, display books such as Sojourner Truth: Slave, Abolitionist, Fighter for Women's Rights by Aletha Jane Lindstrom, A Pictorial History of Black Americans by Langston Hughes, Milton Meltzer, and C. Eric Lincoln, Abraham Lincoln by Ingri and Edgar Parin d' Aulaire, Lincoln – A Picture Story of His Life by Stefen Lorant, The Abraham Lincoln Joke Book by Beatrice Schenk de Regniers, and The Civil War in Pictures by Fletcher Pratt.

Note: A map showing the areas of Sojourner Truth's travels can be found in the first reference listed above.

<u>Brainwork Center</u> - (See Room Environment - General - Learning Centers)

File games or activities for "The Learning Journey" bulletin board (see above) in a box so that the bags stand and the symbols are at the top. Examples of matching games are numbered chickens with corresponding number-dot eggs; numbered trees with apples to count and place on each tree; one set of white fruit (banana, apple, grapes, etc.) labeled with color words and another set in the correct colors with no words; nests labeled with upper-case alphabet letters and birds labeled with lower-case alphabet letters; and cars and milk carton garages marked with matching shapes. You may also wish to include taped questions on a tape recorder, puzzles, activity sheets, listening station activities, and other center activities. Since ziplock bags cannot be used for all of these, simply code the items themselves with purchased stickers or symbols drawn on masking tape.

BIOGRAPHICAL INFORMATION

Sojourner Truth was a well-known public speaker and former slave who traveled throughout New England and the Midwest speaking out against slavery.

Sojourner Truth's real name was Isabella Baumfree. She was known only as "Belle" until she was freed from slavery. Then she adopted her father's name as her last name. She was born around 1797 in Dutch-settled Western County, New York. Her mother, known as Ma-Ma Bett, and her father, Baumfree, had been the slaves of Colonel Johannes Hardenbergh and his son Charles for many years. Baumfree's first two wives and his many children had been sold and never seen again. Ma-Ma Bett was his third wife. Belle and her brother, Peter, were the only children he had left.

When Master Charles died, Peter was quickly sold and taken away by his new master. No one was interested in buying nine-year-old Belle. So when a flock of the Hardenbergh sheep were sold, she was given as a bonus to the buyer, John Neely.

John Neely and his wife were cruel to Belle. Many times she was beaten until she bled. Soon, however, she was sold to the Schryuers who were kind people. She was happy then and looked forward to the times she could see her parents who lived nearby. They had been given their freedom only because they were too old to work or be sold. So when they were freed, they were also too old to take care of themselves and soon died. Belle grieved deeply for her parents who had been so cruelly mistreated.

A short time later Belle was bought by John Dumont, a wealthy farmer from New Paltz, New York. It was 1810, and Belle was thirteen years old.

Belle worked in the house and around the farm. When she could, she would sit in a secluded spot by the creek and talk to God. She was alone in the world and this was her only comfort.

One evening she met a slave there from the neighboring farm. She and Bob became friends, then fell in love. They hoped to be married, but Bob's master found out and forbid him to return to see Belle. When Bob returned anyway his master beat him, tied him with ropes, and dragged him home. Then he was beaten again and a short time later died.

Belle's master decided it was time for her to have babies so he could have more slaves. He married her to an old slave named Thomas. Belle had four children, Diana, Elizabeth, Peter, and Sophie. When Peter was five, he was sold and taken away before Belle even knew about it. When Belle asked for her freedom so that she could find him, her master promised she could be free in a year. When the year was up, Master Dumont refused to let her go. Belle took her youngest child, Sophie, and went to the home of the Van Wagener's, a Quaker couple who opposed slavery. They arranged for her to work for them, but after a year she was ready to return to slavery just to see her other children. As Master Dumont's wagon approached, Belle was aware of an overpowering light and felt the presence of God. She returned to her room and asked God's forgiveness for trying to return to slavery and for the hatred she had felt towards slave owners. For Belle, this was the start of a new life.

In 1828 Belle was given her freedom under a New York law which freed slaves at a certain age. Belle Baumfree worked for a while at the Van Wagener's, then set out to find Peter. Sophie was left with Diana and Elizabeth at the Dumont Farm.

Peter was finally returned to his mother. So that he could go to school, Belle Baumfree moved to New York and worked as a maid. Soon Peter began roaming the streets and getting into trouble with other teenagers. After he was picked up by the police several times, he decided to get work on a whaling ship. He was lost at sea a year later.

In 1843 Baumfree had another religious experience in which she was told by God to preach and do His work. He had told her to go by the name of Sojourner which means a person who stays in one place for a brief time before moving on to the next. To that, she added the last name Truth because she believed God was Truth and He was her master.

After that, Sojourner Truth traveled from place to place preaching about God and speaking out against slavery. She cared for the sick and never accepted more than 25¢ for any work that she did. She slept at the homes of generous strangers or she slept under the stars. Her daughters, with whom she had kept in touch, were proud of what she was doing.

When Sojourner Truth stood before people in her black Quaker's dress and old shoes, they didn't know what to expect. But then hearing her deep, rich voice ring out in song, they would listen. After singing hymns she had learned or made up, she would speak of sin and slavery and the need to show kindness to one another. She told of the day God appeared and kept her from returning to slavery and how he had commanded her to preach.

Sojourner Truth became well known and was greeted by crowds wherever she went. After traveling many miles, she settled down with other people who were working to abolish slavery.

Friends persuaded her to publish her autobiography which would help turn people against slavery. In 1850 The Narrative of Sojourner Truth: A Northern Slave was published. Booksellers were afraid to stock it, so Sojourner Truth once again traveled from meeting to meeting selling her book.

As she traveled, Sojourner Truth became aware of the crusade for women's rights. She continued to travel and speak, but now she spoke out against slavery and for women's rights.

In 1863 the Emancipation Proclamation went into effect and all the slaves were freed. In 1864 Sojourner Truth was called to Washington, D.C., to meet President Abraham Lincoln. She was then hired by the Freedman's Bureau to help out in Freedman's Village, an area in nearby Arlington, Virginia, where ex-slaves lived. Two years later she went to work as a nurse at Freedman's Hospital in Washington, D.C. She was nearly seventy years old.

After working at the hospital, Sojourner Truth once again traveled around the North, speaking for the rights of blacks and women. She then returned to her home in Battle Creek, Michigan, and spent time with her daughters and grandson. She died on November 26, 1883, at the age of eighty-six. She was buried at Battle Creek's Oak Hill Cemetery where a six-foot monument marks her grave.

LANGUAGE ARTS - SOCIAL STUDIES - SCIENCE

Discussion

Give a paper plate to each child, and direct the children to draw a smiling face on one side and a frowning face on the other side. Summarize the Biographical Information, referring to the room displays and showing picture from references (see Famous Black Americans, Room Environment - Learning Centers). At various points in the story, pause and ask, "How do you think Sojourner (or Belle) felt?" The children hold up the paper plates with either the smiling or frowning face showing. Discuss briefly and proceed with the summarization.

Sequence of Events

Guide the students in recalling the sequence of events in Sojourner Truth's life. As the students dictate, write the information on an experience chart, leaving spaces beside each event. After all information is recorded, let the children add illustrations. Display.

Heart Story

Duplicate and distribute the sheet on page 216. Use one sheet to make a transparency. Place the transparency on an overhead projector. As you tell the story below, use a transparency marker to draw the lines from one dot to the next. Begin at the (top) center dot on the right, draw around the heart, and end at the top center dot on the left. The children do the same on their sheets using pencils or crayons.

Ask the children, "Do you know the most important thing that Sojourner Truth taught others? Let's find out."

1st Dot - Belle was born a slave. She was sold to Mr. Dumont and moved to his farm. (move to next dot)

2nd Dot - Years later she ran away and lived with a Quaker family. One day she felt God tell her to forgive others and not to hate anymore. She left the Quakers. (move to next dot)

3rd Dot - Belle lived in New York and worked as a maid. Then she went to live with a group of people who were working to abolish slavery. (move to next dot)

4th Dot - She lived there awhile and then moved back to New York. She received another message from God, changed her name to Sojourner Truth, and began to travel and preach. (move to next dot)

5th Dot - She stopped at a house and helped nurse a lady back to health. Then she walked on. (move to next dot)

6th Dot - Sojourner Truth saw a crowd of people and stopped to sing and preach. Then she traveled on. (move to next dot)

7th Dot - She preached at a meeting to abolish slavery. People began to recognize her. She was invited to meet the President, so she traveled to Washington, D.C. (move to next dot)

8th Dot - Sojourner Truth met Abraham Lincoln. Then she was asked to help at Freedman's Village. She walked to Arlington, Virginia. (move to next dot)

9th Dot - Two years later she went to Freedman's Hospital in Washington, D.C., to be a nurse. Then she went back to her home in Michigan. (move to next dot)

10th Dot - Sojourner Truth decided to travel again and speak for women's rights. She preached and sold copies of her book. Then she went back home. (move to next dot)

11th Dot - At home she spent time with her family. She died at age eighty-six.

Ask the class, "Now can you guess what Sojourner Truth taught others? Look at the shape you drew. What is it? What does it stand for?" (Love)

The Name Game

Buy or borrow from the library, a book which tells the meanings of names. Discuss the meaning of Sojourner Truth's name and why she chose it. List the children's names on the chalkboard; then ask, "Would you like to know the meaning of your name?" Look up each name and write the meaning next to it on the chalkboard. Call on each child to make sure he or she remembers the meaning of his or her name. Direct the children to form a circle. The group claps softly (throughout the activity) and chants "Name, name, what is the meaning of your name, name?" At the last word of the chant, toss a ball to one child. The child bounces the ball as the others clap and says "Name, name, my name means _____." Then the group repeats the chant, and on the last word, that child tosses the ball to another, who responds in the same way. Repeat until everyone has participated.

Name Sheet

Leave the names and meanings (see activity, above) on the chalkboard. On a ditto master, write the children's names and their meanings. Turn the master after you write each name and meaning so that they are in different positions on the page. Duplicate and distribute. Each child finds and circles his or her own name.

Book - Read Abe Lincoln's Beard by Jan Wahl.

ART

The Life of Sojourner Truth - Mural

Preparation - Set out a long sheet of mural paper, tempera paints in aluminum pie pans, and paintbrushes. Position the children on one side of the paper. If desired, assign different events to various children so that the mural is in chronological order (from left to right).

Procedure - Paint a scene from Sojourner Truth's life on your section of the mural. Paint your name underneath. (See example on page 215.)

Love Coupons

Preparation - Duplicate the sheet of coupons on page 217. Distribute the sheet along with an envelope (3 5/8" x 6 1/2") for each child. Provide crayons or markers and scissors. Read and explain the coupons.

Procedure - Color the coupons and sign your name at the bottom of each. Cut apart. Decorate the envelope, insert the coupons, and seal. Take home the envelope and coupons; unseal and distribute to your family.

MATH

Money

Initiate a discussion on money by asking the students to recall how much Sojourner Truth charged for any jobs that she did (25¢). Hold up a quarter, a dime, a nickel, and a penny. Explain that each coin has two "names." A penny is also one cent, a nickel is also five cents, and so forth. Put assorted change on the table along with a glass piggy bank or a jar with a slit in the top. Using the different "names" of the coins, call on volunteers to put certain coins in the bank. Once the students know the "names" for each coin, integrate counting into the activity by having volunteers put five quarters in the bank, three dimes in the bank, and so forth.

MUSIC - MOVEMENT - GAMES

Song - "Do You Know Sojourner Truth?"

Tune: "The Muffin Man"

Do you know Sojourner Truth, Sojourner Truth, Sojourner Truth?

Do you know Sojourner Truth,

Who traveled far and wide?

Yes, I know Sojourner Truth, Sojourner Truth, Sojourner Truth,

Yes, I know Sojourner Truth,

Who traveled far and wide.

Do you know the things she taught, the things she taught, the things she
taught?

Do you know the things she taught?

To people far and wide?

Yes I know the things she taught, the things she taught, the things she
taught,

Yes I know the things she taught,

To people far and wide.

Song and Game - "Sojourner's Walking Home"

Tune: "Farmer in the Dell"

Cut tagboard cards and on each one, draw a different line—straight, winding, circular, a zigzag, a spiral, a figure eight, an inverted **V**, and so forth.

The players form a large circle and sing the song below. For the second verse, point to a player to be the "walker," and at the same time hold up one of the cards. The "walker" (whose name is sung in the second verse) walks within the circle in the path designated by the line on the card. For example, if the line on the card is a zigzag pattern, the walker "zigzags" across the circle and back to his or her place as the second verse is sung. Continue in this manner until all have participated.

Sojourner's walking home,

Sojourner's walking home,

Home today, she's been away,

Sojourner's walking home.

(child's name)'s walking home,

(child's name)'s walking home,

Home today, she's (or he's) been away,

(child's name)'s walking home.

STORY TIME

1. "Tappin, the Land Turtle" from The People Could Fly told by Virginia Hamilton.
2. Why Mosquitos Buzz in People's Ears - Verna Aardema

COOKING IN THE CLASSROOM

New York Dutch Dumplings

2 packages refrigerated biscuits (20)
3–4 peaches, chopped
5 tablespoons sugar
1 teaspoon cinnamon
2 tablespoons butter, melted
Butter
Flour
Cup of water

Preheat oven to 375°. Mix sugar and cinnamon and place in a salt shaker. Set aside. Remove the biscuits from the cans.

On a floured surface, roll each biscuit into a circle (about 4" in diameter). Place a tablespoon of chopped peach in the center of the dough circles. Sprinkle with the sugar and cinnamon mixture and dot with about $\frac{1}{2}$ teaspoon of butter (divided into 3 small pieces). Wet your fingers in the cup of water and moisten the edges of the circles. Fold the dough in half over the filling to form a half-circle. Press the edges with a fork to seal. Place 2" apart on an ungreased cookie sheet, pierce with a fork, and brush with melted butter. Bake for 12–14 minutes or until golden. Yield: 20 dumplings

Dear Parents,

On _____, we will learn about Sojourner Truth, the former slave, abolitionist, and speaker for women's rights. Please read below to find out ways you can help.

Things To Send: _____
_____
_____

Volunteers Needed To: _____
_____
_____

Follow-Up: At the end of the unit, ask your child the following questions:
_____
_____
_____

Thank you for your cooperation.

Sincerely,

SOJOURNER TRUTH

Bulletin Board, Examples

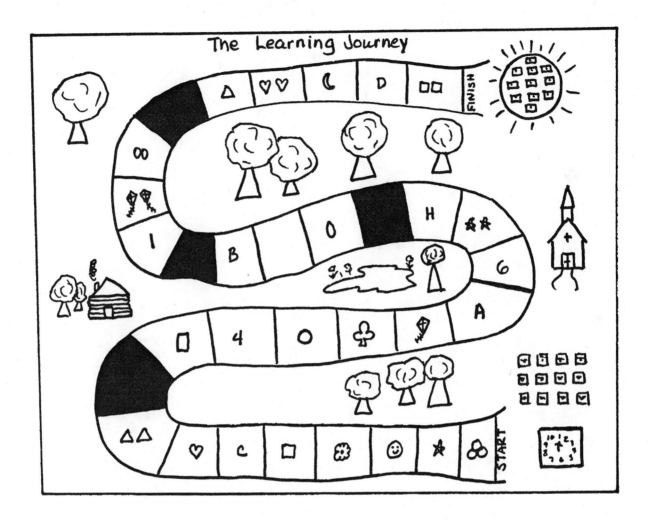

The Learning Journey

The Life of Sojourner Truth - Mural

Heart Story

Heart Story

Washing the Dishes

LOVE COUPON

Love,

Making a Bed

LOVE COUPON

Love,

Taking Out the Trash

LOVE COUPON

Love,

Free Choice

LOVE COUPON

Love,

Yard Work

LOVE COUPON

Love,

Watering Plants

LOVE COUPON

Love,

Dusting

LOVE COUPON

Love,

Free Choice

LOVE COUPON

Love,

HARRIET TUBMAN

(1820 - 1913)

ROOM ENVIRONMENT - BULLETIN BOARD

"Harriet Tubman - Conductor on the Underground Railroad"

Cover and trim the bulletin board as desired and staple the title in the center below a picture of Harriet Tubman (see page 229). After relating the Biographical Information, distribute sheets of white drawing paper and let the children illustrate scenes from Harriet Tubman's life. Mount each sheet on construction paper and staple on the bulletin board. (See example on page 230.)

ROOM ENVIRONMENT - LEARNING CENTERS

Famous Black Americans - (See Room Environment - General - Learning Centers)

Staple Harriet Tubman's name on the center. Trace or draw scenes from her life, including a map of North America, and mount on the display. Place books on Harriet Tubman, the Underground Railroad, the constellations, plants, and animals on the table in front of the center.

Brainwork Center - (See Room Environment - General - Learning Centers)

When she was very young, Harriet Tubman's father taught her the constellations and how to use the North Star as a guide. To teach the constellations, use reference books to make two identical sets of constellation cards. Cut squares of black construction paper and use yellow paint markers to make the stars in each constellation. Use white paint markers to make the connecting lines. Write the name of the constellation at the bottom of each card. Also label the North Star on the two Little Dipper cards. Laminate, mix, and place in the center. The students match identical pairs.

At an early age Harriet Tubman learned to identify all the animals in the area. Make a classification game by cutting two pieces of tagboard to measure 5" x 8". Fold in half so that they will stand. On one, draw water (waves); on the other, draw land. From old workbooks or magazines, cut out animals that live on land and animals that live in water. Glue on tagboard squares. Place in the center for the children to sort.

BIOGRAPHICAL INFORMATION

Harriet Ross Tubman was a black slave who escaped to free territory but returned again and again to help other slaves escape. In all, she guided more than three hundred men, women, and children to freedom.

Harriet Ross was born in 1820 in Bucktown, Maryland. Her mother, Harriet Green, and her father, Benjamin Ross, were both slaves of Edward Brodas. They lived on his plantation in the "slave quarters" which was a group of crudely built one-room log cabins. The cabins had dirt floors, no windows, and no furniture. The families slept on the floor and a fireplace provided heat, light, and a place to cook.

Harriet's father, Ben, was a good worker and was put in charge of the slaves who cut timber on the plantation. Her mother, called "Old Rit," was fortunate enough to work around the "Big House" (the master's house) rather than in the fields like many of the women slaves. Their master, Mr. Brodas, was better than most slave owners; but even so, the slaves lived in constant fear of being sold, chained, and sent down South. Ben and "Old Rit" lost several of their children to Southern slave traders.

Harriet, like the other small children, was cared for during the day by an old woman who was too old to work. The slave children played in the dirt in front of the cabins; listened to the old woman's horror stories of chains, whips, and slave ships; and many times ate corn meal mush and scraps of food from a common trough. Harriet loved the outdoors, and at an early age she was taught how to move silently through the woods and to identify all plants and animals. She learned the constellations and how to use the North Star as a guide.

Starting at age six, Harriet was "hired out" to work for other people as a baby sitter and as a maid. Many times she was beaten and half-starved, but finally she was employed by a man who let her work outdoors. From then on she worked felling trees, hauling logs, and plowing fields. Even though the work was hard and Harriet was barely five feet tall, she was unusually strong and happy to be outside.

In 1843 Harriet spent hours and hours working on her wedding quilt. She had fallen in love and soon married John Tubman, a black who had been freed by his parents' master. Since more and more slaves were being sold, Harriet Tubman lived in constant fear of being separated from her husband. But when she asked John to escape with her and go North where slaves could be free, he threatened to tell the master. After that, she never again trusted him.

In 1849 Harriet Tubman met a white woman who promised to help her if she ever needed it. Soon after this, Harriet Tubman's two sisters were "sold South," and Tubman learned that she, too, would be sold. That night she escaped and went to the woman who gave her the names of the next two places she could safely stop.   Tubman learned that the woman was a member of the "Underground Railroad."   This was not actually a railroad but rather a group of people who believed slavery was wrong and who offered food and hiding places to slaves escaping to the North.   To thank her, Tubman gave the lady her wedding quilt and then went on her way.

For Harriet Tubman, the trip was a rough one.   If caught, she could have been shot, whipped, or sent down South.   She spent a week hiding in a potato hole, slept on the ground, stumbled over grapevines and underbrush, hid in an attic, and traveled only at night.   But she safely reached the state of Pennsylvania where, for the first time in her life, she was free.

Harriet Tubman settled in Philadelphia and found work cooking and washing dishes in a kitchen.   She had decided to work and save money so she could return to Maryland and help her family escape.   However, after living for a while as a free person, Harriet Tubman knew that she would have to help as many slaves as possible escape to freedom.   She eventually made nineteen of these dangerous journeys since she could safely take only a small group of slaves at a time.   But from 1849 to 1859 Harriet Tubman, now called a "Conductor on the Underground Railroad," guided over three hundred slaves, including all of her family, from Maryland to freedom in the North.

To slaves and slave owners alike, Harriet Tubman became known as "Moses" because, like Moses who led the Israelites from bondage in Egypt, Harriet Tubman led her people from bondage in Maryland.   At one time, rewards for her capture totaled $40,000.   But although she lived in constant danger and sometimes longed for the husband and children she'd always wanted, she felt God had chosen her for this special task.

As Harriet Tubman's fame grew, she was invited to lecture at anti-slavery meetings and made many speeches against slavery.

During the Civil War, she worked for the Union Army as a nurse, spy, and scout.   After slavery was forever abolished in 1863, Harriet Tubman lived with her parents in Auburn, N.Y., and helped raise money to build schools for freed slaves.

In 1903 Harriet Tubman gave her house and twenty-five acres in Auburn, N.Y., to the African Methodist Zion Church to be used as a home for the poor and the sick.   She lived there herself until she died on March 10, 1913, at the age of ninety-three.

LANGUAGE ARTS - SOCIAL STUDIES - SCIENCE

Discussion

To introduce the unit, explain the various room displays on Harriet Tubman. Use puppets to tell the story of Harriet Tubman's life. (See Biographical Information, page 219.) One puppet is "Grandmother" who tells the story, and two puppets are the grandchildren who listen and ask questions. (You will need one child to assist you.) Point out the map on display and show where Harriet lived and where she led her escaped slaves.

Book - Read The Story of the Underground Railroad By R. Conrad Stein.

Constellation Discussion and Activities

Tell the children, "How many of you have seen stars in the sky at night? Stars are really clusters of hot gases, and the gases make the stars blaze. Many, many years ago people studied the stars and noticed that different groups seem to form pictures. These groups are called constellations and the people of long ago gave them names."

Using a reference book such as The Stars by H. A. Rey, draw some of the well-known constellations on the board. Discuss each. Read The Big Dipper by Franklyn M. Branley. Teach the following poem to the class:

Star light, star bright

First star I see tonight,

I wish I may, I wish I might,

Have the wish I wish tonight.

Send home the parents' note (see page 231) asking them to point out the Big Dipper, the Little Dipper, and the North Star to their children.

Harriet's Journey to Freedom - Action Story

Once there was a young girl named Harriet Tubman who was sad (look sad). She was a slave and wanted to be free (make X with hands and flap to resemble bird flying). She decided to run away (run in place). She left when the moon was high (make circle with two hands, raise above head). She looked back at the cabin (make peak roof with fingertips together) and blew a kiss (blow kiss) to her sleeping family (hands beside cheek, eyes closed). She ran through the woods (run in place) and swam across the stream (swimming motion). When the sun came up (make circle with two hands, raise above head) she slept in a cave (cup left hand, place curled right pointer finger on palm). When night came, she ate some berries (eating motion) and drank some water (drinking motion) and then walked (walk in place). She heard some horses (say "clippity-clop" and quickly hid behind a big rock (make fist). Then she walked (walk in place) for miles and miles until she reached another state. She was tired (rub eyes) but she was happy (big smile) because at last she was free (make **X** with hands, flap to resemble bird flying).

Weather Activities

Predicting the Weather Discussion - Tell the children, "Harriet Tubman's father was known for his ability to predict the weather. Since he had none of the modern instruments and equipment we now have, how do you think he did this? (Call on children to answer.) Probably Mr. Ross learned by watching the weather and the world around him for many years. Possibly he studied the color of the sky and its cloud formations, the behavior of animals and birds, and the 'feel' of the air. (Discuss each of these.) Sometimes parents taught their children certain weather signs to look for such as 'a halo around the moon means rain the next day,' 'high clouds mean good weather,' and 'flies always swarm before a big storm.'"

Weather Vanes - Another sign of the weather is the wind. One prediction says "winds from the west bring good weather; winds from the east bring rain." To test this prediction, make a class weather vane. Push a straight pin through the center of a plastic drinking straw and into the eraser of a pencil. Cut a triangular piece of cardboard and cover with aluminum foil. Slit one end of the straw and insert the triangular piece. If necessary, secure with dots of glue. Fill a pint-sized plastic tub with sand and make a hole in the lid slightly larger than the pencil. (The pencil should be able to turn freely.) Put the lid on the plastic tub and using a permanent marker, mark north, south, east, and west on the tub. Make sure the positions are correct. Push the pencil through the hole and into the sand until it touches the bottom of the tub. Place the weather vane in an open area, preferably visible from the classroom, with the markings in the correct positions. (Use a compass if necessary.) Observe the weather vane each day.

Weather Chart - Obtain a large calendar. Observe the weather each morning. Let one child draw a weather symbol (sun, raindrop, gray clouds) on the calendar for that day. On Fridays, review the weather of the previous week.

Cornhusking Bee

One of the few forms of entertainment for the slaves on the Brodas plantation was the cornhusking bees held at harvest time. Slaves from neighboring plantations were invited and the groups competed. Cover the area with old newspapers; then give each child an ear of corn to husk. Demonstrate; then divide the class into two teams. At the signal, the children say the chant below and husk the corn. Applaud the group that finishes first. The corn can then be boiled until tender (or microwaved) and eaten.

Chant:

All:　　　　Give us children some corn to husk
　　　　　　Shuck, shuck, shuck without a fuss.

One Team:　We can husk it quicker than you!

Other Team: Look at us, we're almost through!

(Repeat both verses until cornhusking is finished.)

ART

Harriet's Escape - Crayon Resist

Preparation - Thin black tempera paint and set out in aluminum pie pans. Provide paintbrushes, crayons, and light colored construction paper. Remind the children that this will be a night scene.

Procedure - Draw and color Harriet's escape on the construction paper. When you are finished, paint over the entire picture with the black tempera paint. Dry. (See example on page 230.)

North Stars

Preparation - Duplicate the sheet on page 232 and cut apart the patterns. Give each child one pattern, a sheet of waxed paper, a bottle of white glue (the kind that dries hard), an 18" piece of string or strong thread with a paper clip attached to one end, and a piece of cardboard or section of newspaper to work on. Set out shaker bottles of gold glitter.

Procedure - Place the cardboard or newspaper on the table in front of you. Put the pattern in the center and cover with the waxed paper. Completely open the twist-top on the glue bottle and use to "draw" the star on the waxed paper. Follow the lines of the pattern and squeeze the bottle so that the lines are thick. Sprinkle on glitter until the glue lines

are completely covered. Dry for at least 48 hours. Remove waxed paper.
Carefully attach the string for hanging. (See example on page 230.)

MATH

Rescue Counting Activity

Choose one child to be "Harriet." Harriet stands on the opposite side of
the room from the other students. Hold up a number card to signify how
many slaves "Harriet" should rescue. "Harriet" reads the number, then
"sneaks" across the room, chooses that many slaves, then they all "sneak"
back. Have the class count aloud the "rescued slaves" and look again at
the number card. Is the number correct? Now the students count the
"rescued slaves" and Harriet. What is the new total? Hold up the
corresponding number card, and if desired, write the addition equation on
the board ("numerical version of Harriet plus escaped slaves equals total").
The "rescued slaves" stay where they are and a new "Harriet" is chosen.
Hold up a different numeral card and follow the same procedure until each
child has been "Harriet."

Stars Counting Sheet

Give each child a black sheet of construction paper. Set out star-shaped
cereal, white or yellow crayons, and glue. Have the children fold the
sheet in half, and then in half once again. Next they unfold the sheet
and draw lines on the folds to divide the sheet into fourths. Call out
four numbers. (You may also write them on the chalkboard.) The
children write one number at the bottom of each section, then glue that
many stars above the number.

Variation: Use star stickers instead of cereal, or have the children draw
the stars with white or yellow crayons.

MUSIC - MOVEMENT - GAMES

Song - "Harriet Was Brave As Could Be"

Tune: "My Bonnie Lies Over the Ocean"

Oh, Moses guided his people,   (3 beats on Moses)
Oh, Moses parted the sea,
Her friends called Harriet, Moses
Because she helped them to be free.

Chorus:

Harriet, Harriet,

Oh, she was as brave as could be, could be,

Harriet, Harriet,

Helped so many be free.

Go Down Moses

This was one of Harriet Tubman's favorite songs and one she sometimes sang to signal her arrival. Words and music can be found in The Family Music Book, collected by Grosset and Dunlap, published by G. Schirmer, Inc., or in Sinful Tunes and Spirituals by Dena J. Epstein.

Dance - Juba

African slaves did a dance called "Juba." The meaning of the word is unknown, but it might have originated from the slaves' term "jibba" which meant giblets or leftovers. More information on "Juba" and other dances, games, and songs of the Afro-American heritage can be found in the book Step It Down by Bessie Jones and Bess Lomax Hawes.

Seat the children in a large circle. Stand in the center to lead the activity. Teach the Juba chant and actions; then begin the activity.

Verse 1:	Actions
Juba, Juba, what's my name, Juba, Juba, it's all the same, Call me this and call me that, Call me skinny, call me fat.	(Throughout the verse, slap hands together, then slap thighs - 2 beats - in time to the chant.)
Chorus:	
Juba up and Juba down, Juba, Juba, all around	(The children stand up, squat down, and stand up again. Then they walk in the circle swinging both arms up and down and bending the knees more than usual with each step.)

Verse 2:

Juba pick and Juba husk,   (Repeat actions, Verse 1)
Juba eat the corn bread crust,
Juba kill a hog today,
Take the foot and run away.

Chorus:

Juba up and Juba down,   (Repeat chorus actions)
Juba, Juba, all around

Verse 3:

Juba plow a crooked line   (Repeat actions, Verse 1)
Juba, Juba, feeling fine,
Juba got an old straw hat.
Call me this and call me that.

Chorus:

Juba up and Juba down,   (Repeat chorus actions)
Juba, Juba, all around

STORY TIME

1. Harriet and the Promised Land - Jacob Lawrence
2. The Quilt Story - Tony Johnston and Tomie de Paola
3. "A Wolf and Little Daughter" from The People Could Fly - Virginia Hamilton. (This type of story was told by the slaves who tended the slave owners' children.)
4. "Carrying the Running-Aways", a slave story of freedom, from The People Could Fly - Virginia Hamilton

COOKING IN THE CLASSROOM

Trail Food

Trail Food is food that can be carried in a kerchief. It is healthy and good for long trips, hikes, or even "escapes." You may purchase kerchief or bandanna material and cut it into squares to hold each child's portion. (Secure with a twist tie.) Or you may prefer to show the children a kerchief and let them decorate small paper bags in similar designs. To make the Trail Food, mix any of the following:

Honey Graham cereal
Wheat Chex
Rice Chex
Cheerios
Peanuts
Raisins
Wheat germ
Miniature marshmallows
Dates
Sesame Seeds

Pecans
Sunflower seeds (shelled)
Pieces of hard cheese
Pretzels
Walnuts
Oyster crackers
Brown sugar
Dried fruit
Granola
M & M's

Dear Parents,

    On _____, we will learn about Harriet Tubman, an escaped slave who became part of the famous Underground Railroad and helped many other slaves to freedom. Please read below to find out ways you can help.

Things To Send: _____

_____

_____

Volunteers Needed To: _____

_____

_____

Follow-Up: At the end of the unit, ask your child the following questions:

_____

_____

_____

    Thank you for your cooperation.

                    Sincerely,

HARRIET TUBMAN

Bulletin Board, Examples

Harriet's Escape

North Stars

Dear Parents,

As part of the unit on Harriet Tubman, our class learned that a star is really a cluster of gases. We also learned that many, many years ago people noticed that different groups of stars seem to form pictures. They gave these constellations names such as the Big Dipper, the Little Dipper, the Lion, and the Twins.

On a clear night, please take your child outside and show him or her these constellations, particularly the Big and Little Dippers (see below). Since Harriet Tubman traveled by the North Star, you may also wish to point it out to your child. (See diagram below.)

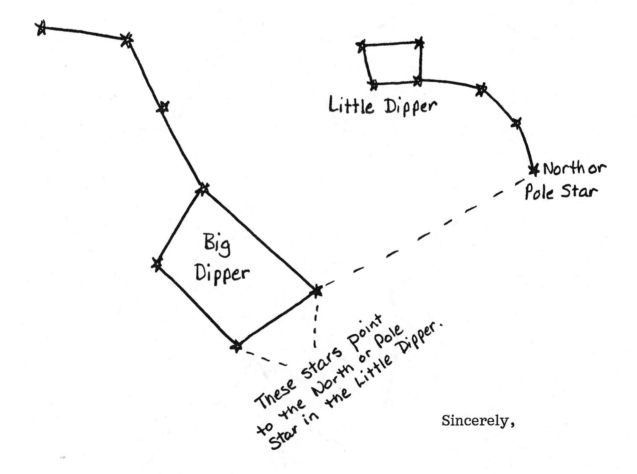

Little Dipper

North or Pole Star

Big Dipper

These stars point to the North or Pole Star in the Little Dipper.

Sincerely,

North Stars

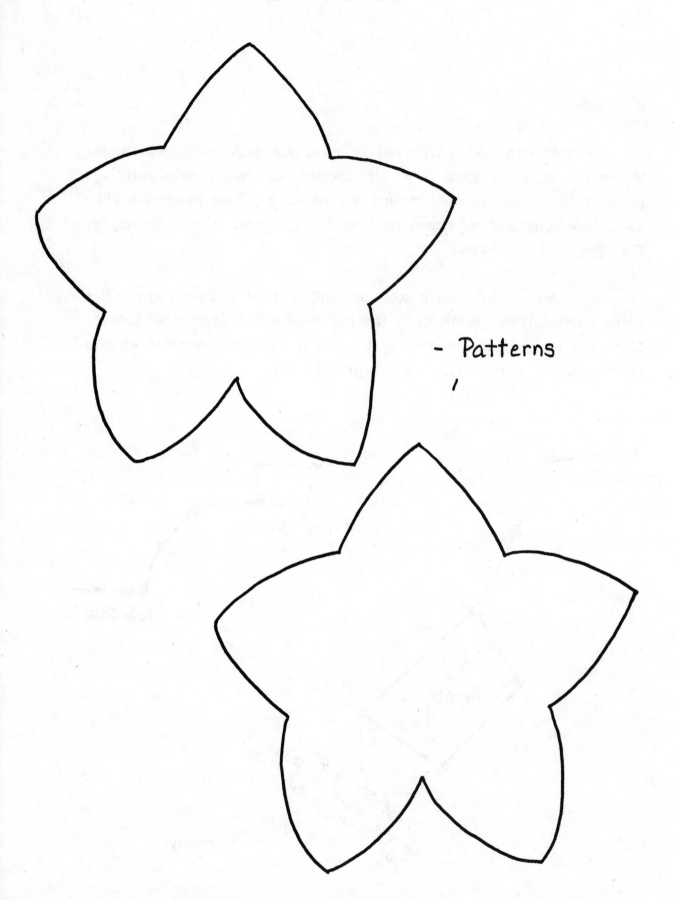

- Patterns

BOOKER T. WASHINGTON

(1856 - 1915)

ROOM ENVIRONMENT - BULLETIN BOARD

"Booker T. Washington - Educator"

Cover and trim the bulletin board as desired. Staple a picture of Booker T. Washington (see page 243) in the center of the bulletin board with the title below it. On labels of different colors of construction paper, write "Slave," "First Home," "Worker in the Salt Furnaces," "First Day at School," "Working for Mrs. Ruffner," "Traveling to Hampton," "At Hampton Institute," "Teaching School," "Starting Tuskegee Normal and Industrial Institute," "Building Tuskegee," and "Speaking for Education." Let the children draw pictures to go with the labels. (Before they begin, you may wish to show pictures of Booker T. Washington and various scenes of his life from the references listed below.) Mount the pictures and labels on the bulletin board. (See example on page 244.)

ROOM ENVIRONMENT - LEARNING CENTERS

Famous Black Americans - (See Room Environment - General - Learning Centers)

Staple Booker T. Washington's name and sketches of a log cabin and Tuskegee University on the learning center. In front of the center, place references such as Booker T. Washington: Ambitious Boy by Augusta Stevenson, Up From Slavery by Booker T. Washington, A Pictorial History of Black Americans (mark sections on Booker T. Washington and Tuskegee Institute) by Langston Hughes, Milton Meltzer, and C. Eric Lincoln, Salt by Augusta Goldin, Coal by Bill Gunston, and Let's Find Out About School by Martha and Charles Shapp.

Note: For slides, maps, and pamphlets of Tuskegee Institute, postcards of Booker T. Washington's home, and other related materials, send for a mail order list from:

Eastern National Park and Monument Association
P. O. Drawer #10
Tuskegee Institute, Alabama 36088-0010

Brainwork Center - (See Room Environment - General - Learning Centers)

One of the trades taught at Tuskegee Normal and Industrial Institute was carpentry. To familiarize the children with the tools of this trade, place the book, <u>Toolbox</u> by Anne Rockwell, in the center. Cut a piece of poster paper into fourths. On each section, outline the tools from a toolbox—hammer, nail, screwdriver, screw, pliers, etc. Set the tools and outline cards in the center. The children place the tools within the correct outlines.

Note: You may wish to use toy tools or a mixture of both. With the toy variety, larger tools, such as a saw, can be included in the activity.

BIOGRAPHICAL INFORMATION

Booker Taliaferro Washington was a former slave who became the foremost educator of his time. He was founder and head of the Tuskegee Institute in Tuskegee, Alabama.

Booker Washington was born in 1856. He and his family were slaves on the Burroughs Plantation in Hales Ford, Virginia. He never knew his father, but his mother Jane was the plantation cook. The log cabin in which they lived was also the kitchen for the plantation. It had one room with a dirt floor, openings for windows, a potato hole for storing potatoes, and an open fireplace for cooking. Also, like all the mansions and cabins in Virginia, it had a "cat-hole," a square opening in the wall to let cats pass in and out of the house. There was little furniture; the family slept on bundles of rags laid on the dirt floor and ate standing up. In the winter, with the wind coming through the cracks and openings in the walls, the cabin was extremely cold. In the summer, the open fire for cooking made it very hot.

Booker, his older brother John, and his sister Amanda, spent most of their time working on the plantation. Amanda helped her mother while Booker and John cleaned the yards, carried water to the men in the fields, and took huge bags of corn on horseback to the mill three miles away. When John was only eleven years old, he began doing the work of an adult in the cotton fields. Booker's favorite job on the plantation was pulling the fan rope which hung over the dining table in the big house and was used to scare the flies away.

At an early age, Booker felt a deep desire to learn to read, but slaves were not allowed to go to school. None of the slaves on the plantation could read or write.

When Booker was nine years old, the United States government freed all the slaves. Booker and his family loaded their few possessions in a cart and walked several hundred miles to their new home in Malden, W. Virginia. There they joined their stepfather, Jim, who had gotten a job at a salt furnace.

Booker's mother wanted all of her children to go to school, but they had no money and little food. Soon Booker and John, who were only nine and twelve years old, were working twelve hours a day at the salt furnace. Their stepfather was pleased because the family needed the money, but Jane was disappointed. When a school for blacks opened in Malden, she persuaded Jim to let Booker go.

Booker's first day of school was the most exciting day of his life. He still had to work seven hours a day but was allowed to take off to go to school—but for him it was worth it. His teacher was pleased that Booker learned so quickly and liked each of his subjects so well.

Up until this time, Booker, like all slaves, had no last name. When his new teacher asked him his name, Booker decided he liked "Washington," and from then on, his name was Booker Washington. Later he found out his mother had given him the name Booker Taliaferro after he was born. So he became Booker Taliaferro Washington.

Before long, Booker Washington had to return to work full-time, so he learned any way that he could. He went to night school or found teachers to teach him at night. When he was twelve years old, he heard about the Hampton Institute, an industrial school in Hampton, Virginia, where blacks could go to school and also work to pay their expenses.

To save money to go to Hampton, Washington worked in the coal mines, then worked for Mrs. Lewis Ruffner doing yard work. She taught him the value of cleanliness and of doing any job well. He learned that his clothes could be old but they must be clean and neat. He learned to keep the yard tidy, the fence painted and repaired, and the gardens weeded and beautiful. When Mrs. Ruffner's housekeeper was ill, he learned how to clean a room thoroughly. In later life, Booker Washington said that the things he was taught by Mrs. Ruffner were as important as any education he ever got.

After a year Washington had little money saved. What he had earned had been used to help his family. But he was thirteen years old and decided it was time for him to go to Hampton to get his education. With only a few dollars in his pocket, he traveled the five hundred miles to Hampton by train, by stagecoach, and then on foot. When he presented himself to the head teacher, Miss Mary F. Mackie, he was tired, dirty, and hungry. He could tell she was doubtful about letting him enter the school. When she asked him to sweep out a nearby room, Washington had a chance to prove himself. As Mrs. Ruffner had taught him, he swept the room three times and dusted it four times.   After Miss Mackie inspected the room, Booker Washington became a student at the Hampton Institute.

Booker T. Washington worked as a janitor at the school to pay his way. More than anything he wanted to grow up to be like General Samuel C. Armstrong, founder and head of the school.   General Armstrong had seen the need of newly freed slaves to learn a skill as well as to learn from books.   The students were taught to bathe each day, to use a toothbrush regularly, and to eat meals at certain hours, things which were not possible during their years of slavery.   Besides cleanliness and nutrition, they were taught good manners and good citizenship.   They learned from books, and they each learned a skill that they could use to support themselves.

In 1875 Washington graduated and returned to Malden to teach school.   He was then able to help his brother John and his adopted brother James go to Hampton.

From 1879 to 1881 Washington, himself, taught at the Hampton Institute. In 1881 two men in Alabama wrote General Armstrong.   They wanted someone to take charge of a school for blacks in their town of Tuskegee. General Armstrong recommended Booker for the job.

Booker T. Washington moved to Tuskegee and started the Tuskegee Normal and Industrial Institute in two buildings, an old abandoned church and a shanty.   Like Hampton, the students at Tuskegee Normal and Industrial Institute were taught certain trades such as farming, mechanics, carpentry, and laundering.   There, too, the values of cleanliness and good citizenship were impressed upon the students.   The school's name was later changed to Tuskegee Institute (now Tuskegee University), and as the school grew, the students themselves built the buildings.   They also raised livestock, vegetables, and made bricks—for their own use and to sell to support the school.

Booker T. Washington spent most of his time running the school, raising money for it, and bringing up his three children.   As a result of his many speeches, the school became well known and he was in demand to speak at different events.   His opinions on the future of blacks in America was much respected, and he advised governors, congressmen, and presidents. For the rest of his life, he remained principal of Tuskegee and also sought ways to improve the lives of all people.   He died on November 14, 1915, at the age of fifty-nine and was buried on the campus of the school he created.

LANGUAGE ARTS - SOCIAL STUDIES - SCIENCE

Discussion

Before the discussion, using a tape recorder and disguising your voice, tell the story of Booker T. Washington's life. Speak directly to the children as if you are Booker T. Washington. Have reference pictures (see Famous Black Americans, Room Environment - Learning Centers, page 233) available to show as the tape recording is played. For the discussion, play the recording and show the pictures. Point out Virginia, West Virginia, and Alabama on a map. Discuss Booker T. Washington's determination to learn and why he became famous.

The Story of the Flax Shirt

Tell the children the story below. Afterwards, have the children imagine how the flax shirt would feel; then ask, "Why do you think John did this for his brother?" Discuss the feelings of both boys and the value of good deeds. Encourage the children to think of a good deed they have done or a good deed someone has done for them. Distribute drawing paper and crayons, and let them illustrate the good deed.

Slave children did not wear pants and shirts or dresses. They all wore long shirts made of rough material. During the Civil War, when conditions became severe on the plantation where Booker T. Washington lived, there was no cotton to make the material for the shirts. Flax was used instead, and the points of the flax made the material scratch and prick the skin. Only after weeks of wear would the material become soft. When Booker was small and his shirt had worn out, he received a new one. He threw it on the floor and refused to wear it, saying it would feel like hundreds of pins sticking him. The next morning before Booker awoke, his brother John put on the new flax shirt and went to work in the fields. He knew how much it would hurt Booker and decided to "break it in" himself. When Booker found out, he couldn't keep from crying. Many years later, when Booker was famous and wrote a book about his life, he included this story and said it was one of the kindest things anyone had ever done for him.

Booker T. Washington's Log Cabin - Following Directions Activity

Cut out shapes from tagboard. Distribute crayons and drawing paper. Direct the students to draw a horizontal line across the paper to represent the ground. Holding up the proper shape as an example, give the following directions:

1. Draw a large square on top of the ground.
2. Draw a tall rectangle at the center bottom of the square.

3. Draw a small square on either side of the rectangle.

4. Draw a large triangle on top of the large square with the point at the top.

5. Draw a circle in the top right corner of the paper.

6. Color the house, ground, and sun.

7. Draw lines on the house to represent logs, and lines around the sun for rays.

8. Now you have a picture of Booker T. Washington's log cabin.

Poem - "Booker T."

Booker T. worked in a coal mine,
Booker T. worked on the land,
Booker T. started his life as a slave
But became a famous man.

I only work at school and my chores,
But I hope to grow up to be
A person good and kind and smart
A person like Booker T.

Momma Jane's Alphabet Soup

Seat the children in a circle. Place a large pot and a big wooden spoon in the center of the area along with plastic or cardboard alphabet letters, upper and lower-case. Tell the children, "Today we are going to make alphabet soup." Call on a child to find a certain letter such as the upper-case **A**. Call on another child to find the lower-case **A**. Each child shows the letter to the class, then puts it in the pot and stirs the "soup" with the spoon. After all the letters are in the pot, "serve" the soup by placing each letter on the wooden spoon and giving it to a different child. Each child names the letter he or she is served.

Tuskegee Learning Skills

Use the following activities to exemplify the skills taught at Tuskegee Institute:

Setting the Table - Use plastic dinnerware to teach the children how to set a table. If desired, make place mats from butcher paper and trace around a plate, a glass, and utensils to show the proper positions.

Manners - Discuss and list examples of good manners; then have the students act out different scenes to demonstrate them. Prompt when necessary.

Brushing Teeth and Bathing - Play the songs and let the children act out "Take a Bath" and "Brush Away" from Learning Basic Skills Through Music: Health and Safety (LP) by Hap Palmer.

Cleaning House - Explain, then assign cleaning jobs to each child. Have them wash windows, dust, clean tables, sweep, and mop. Provide cleaning materials and supervision.

Painting - Collect large paintbrushes and fill buckets with water. Let the children paint the outside of the building or playground equipment with water.

Making Bricks - Mix clay, soil, and water and mold into bricks. Children may experiment with adding different ingredients—sand, hay, pine straw, leaves, etc. Dry in the sun.

Building - If possible, invite a carpenter to build a simple project for the class. Obtain scrap lumber, hammers, and nails with large heads. Let the children hammer the nails into the wood.

ART

Booker T. Washington - Wet Chalk Picture

Preparation - Set out construction paper, colored chalk, paintbrushes, and water in aluminum pie pans.

Procedure - Brush water over the construction paper to cover. Use the colored chalk to draw Booker T. Washington or a scene from his life. Touch the paper with the chalk only to prevent smearing. (See example on page 244.)

Variations: Use dry paper and let the children dip the chalk in water, buttermilk, or liquid starch diluted with water.

Note: After the pictures have dried, you may wish to use hairspray or fixative spray to prevent smearing.

Paper Plate Snake

Preparation - On a paper plate for each child, draw a spiral as shown on page 244. Give each child a plate and a 15" piece of string. Set out crayons, scissors, and hole punchers. Tell the children that when Booker T. Washington and his family were moving to W. Virginia, they got tired of sleeping on the ground. When they saw an abandoned cabin one night, they decided to sleep there. As Booker and John built a fire in the fireplace, a long black snake crawled out of the chimney and onto the floor. Everyone ran from the cabin and slept under a tree far away.

Procedure - Color both sides of the paper plate to resemble a snake. Cut on the spiral line. Cut off the point on the outer rim. On the outer end, draw an eye on either side and punch a hole a half inch from the end. Tie one end of the string to the hole. (See example on page 244.)

MATH

Animal Sounds Math

On the plantation where Booker Washington lived as a child were many types of animals. Review the sounds various animals make. Write a number on the chalkboard and say the name of an animal, such as cow. Call on a child. The child reads the numbers and "moos" that many times. Repeat with different numbers, animals, and children. All the children may respond together, if desired.

Number Story

Give each child (or two) a number card from 1–10. Read the story. When the child hears his or her number, he or she holds up the card.

Booker was **1** busy boy. He stopped for a minute and looked at the **5** pigs playing in the mud. He never got tired of looking at them but today he didn't have time. It was **2** days before Christmas and Miss Clara was expecting **6** guests. Booker carried **2** hams to his mother who was the plantation cook. "Thank you, Booker," she said. "Now will you get me **8** sweet potatoes from the potato hole? I also need **4** onions and **7** eggs." Booker got the sweet potatoes and onions, then hurried to the chicken house. On the way there he saw **4** men carrying the huge yule log to the big house. Miss Clara burned the yule log for good luck. As long as the Christmas log burned, the slaves could celebrate Christmas. No work! Booker collected eggs and then counted them. **10** eggs! His mother would be pleased. On the way back, Booker dropped **1** egg. He was very upset, but then he thought "**9** eggs will do and the master's **3** dogs will enjoy that egg." Booker gave his mother the **9** eggs. He sat down a minute to rest and watched the other activities on the plantation.

MUSIC - MOVEMENT - GAMES

Song - "Blue-Tail Fly"

Source: Disney's Children's Favorites, Volume I (LP) and Best Loved Songs of the American People (book) compiled by Denes Agay

Song - "Old MacDonald Had a Farm"

Source: Disney's Children's Favorites, Volume I (LP)

Game - Train Ride

Seat all the players except one in chairs arranged in a circle. The player with no chair sits in the center of the circle. Give each player the name of some part of the train—the wheels, the axles, the horn, the brakes, the engineer, the passengers, and the different cars. Begin telling a story about a train ride, including these different parts. When a player hears his or her part named, he jumps up and runs around his chair. At some point in the story yell "train wreck!" At that, everyone scrambles for a new seat, including the player seated in the middle of the circle. Continue in this manner as long as the players are interested in the game.

Variation: Let the child in the middle of the circle tell the story.

STORY TIME

1. Who's in the Rabbit House? - Verna Aardema
2. Jafta - Hugh Lewin

COOKING IN THE CLASSROOM

Yule Logs

Slices of wheat bread
Peanut butter
Apple jelly

Cut the crusts from the bread and flatten with a rolling pin. Spread peanut butter on the bread, and beginning at one edge, roll it up so that it resembles a log. Secure with a toothpick if necessary. Spread apple jelly on top.

Dear Parents,

On _____, we will learn about Booker T. Washington, the famous black educator and founder of Tuskegee Institute in Alabama. Please read below to find out ways you can help.

Things To Send: _____
_____
_____

Volunteers Needed To: _____
_____
_____

Follow-Up: At the end of the unit, ask your child the following questions:
_____
_____
_____

Thank you for your cooperation.

Sincerely,

BOOKER T. WASHINGTON

Bulletin Board, Examples

Booker T. Washington -
Wet Chalk Picture

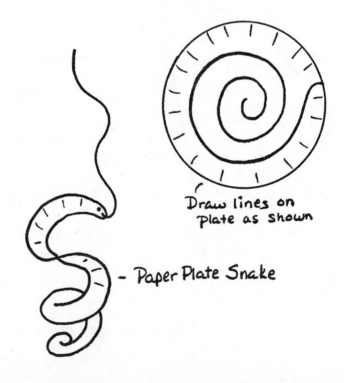

Draw lines on
plate as shown

- Paper Plate Snake

PHILLIS WHEATLEY

(c. 1753 - 1784)

ROOM ENVIRONMENT - BULLETIN BOARD

"Our Poems"

Cover and trim the bulletin board as desired. Write the title on a circle of paper and staple in the center. Mount the illustrated poems from "Learning About Poetry" (see Language Arts - Social Studies - Science) on sheets of construction paper and staple on the bulletin board. Use yarn to connect the poems to the title. (See example on page 257.)

ROOM ENVIRONMENT - LEARNING CENTERS

Famous Black Americans - (See Room Environment - General - Learning Centers)

Staple Phillis Wheatley's picture (see page 256) on the learning center. In front of the center, display items from colonial times such as a quill pen, a three-cornered hat, and a tin lantern. Also display books such as Phillis Wheatley: America's First Black Poetess by Miriam Morris Fuller, The Poems of Phillis Wheatley edited by Julian D. Mason, Jr., The Golden Book of the American Revolution - American Heritage, George Washington by Ingri and Edgar Parin d 'Aulaire, The Story of the Liberty Bell by Natalie Miller, The Story of the Boston Tea Party by R. Conrad Stein, and The Story of the Declaration of Independence by Norman Richards. Include various books of poetry for children and books on African culture.

Brainwork Center - (See Room Environment - General - Learning Centers)

Set up a listening station using "listen and look" records and books of Mother Goose and other poems. The record "reads" each page and beeps for the child to turn the page of the book. Or instead, tape-record the poems of your choice, announcing a number before each poem. Illustrate each poem on a sheet of construction paper and number accordingly. Place in order in the center.

BIOGRAPHICAL INFORMATION

Phillis Wheatley was the first recognized black American poet. Brought from Africa as a slave at age eight, she had her first volume of poems published when she was twenty years old.

The date of Phillis Wheatley's birth is uncertain. When she was bought at a Boston slave auction by John Wheatley, she had lost all of her baby teeth. So Mr. Wheatley assumed she was about eight years old.

When the little girl was placed on the auction block, no one seemed interested in buying her. She stood with heavy chains around her thin ankles and was obviously terrified. Then John Wheatley, a well-to-do tailor, saw her. He noticed her delicate features and sensed that she possessed an inborn dignity. He also felt sorry for her and quickly purchased her and took her home.

The Wheatleys lived in Boston in a large two-story house surrounded by trees and flowers. When the little slave arrived, she was met with kindness. John's wife Susannah was a gentle mistress and the children, fifteen-year-old Mary and her twin brother Nathaniel, treated her as a friend. Aunt Sukey, the elderly slave who did the housekeeping, became like a mother to Phillis.

Phillis was kidnapped from Senegal, West Africa. She could speak no English and her name was unknown. Mrs. Wheatley decided to name her Phillis, and Mary began teaching her the English language. At that time it was against the law in some parts of the country and was not the custom in any area to teach slaves to read and write. The Wheatleys chose to ignore this and soon Phillis, who proved exceptionally bright, was reading and writing. Nathaniel taught her Latin and science, and Mrs. Wheatley introduced her to literature. Aunt Sukey taught her how to perform the household chores.

By the time she was thirteen, Phillis was healthy and happy. She lived in a nice home with her own room and people who loved her. It was 1776 and the Thirteen Colonies were having problems with King George III. The Stamp Act, a law requiring colonists to buy special stamps from England to be put on newspapers, books, etc., caused new resentment. When the King repealed the Stamp Act, the people rejoiced and Phillis wrote her very first poem in honor of King George. The Wheatleys were pleased and encouraged her to continue her writing.

After that, Phillis wrote poems whenever she could, giving many of them as gifts. She also enjoyed reading the Bible and books by Milton, Dryden, and her favorite writer, Alexander Pope. Soon her poems were widely discussed and she was received in the homes of the Wheatley's friends. Others, including publishers, claimed a slave could not possibly be the author of such beautiful poems. So the Wheatleys arranged a meeting with Governor Hutchinson and a group of prominent men including the statesman, John Hancock. Phillis answered their questions, recited from the Bible, and spoke in Latin. Satisfied, the men signed an affidavit which stated that Phillis was indeed the author of the poems.

The Wheatley's house seemed empty. Aunt Sukey had died, Mary lived with her husband across town, and Nathaniel was away at school. Phillis was twenty years old, and the year before, the Wheatleys had given the young poet her freedom. They even hired a maid so that she had time to write. It was at this time that she took Wheatley as her last name.

Earlier Phillis Wheatley had written a poem for the Countess Huntingdon in England. The Countess had the poem published and then invited Phillis Wheatley to come to England as her guest. So she sailed to England where she met many intellectuals and attended many parties given in her honor. Countess Huntingdon had previously found a publisher interested in Phillis Wheatley's poems and surprised her with a copy of her first book <u>Poems on Various Subjects, Religious and Moral</u>.

Meanwhile, in Boston, Mrs. Wheatley was very ill. Phillis Wheatley returned as quickly as possible, but soon afterwards Mrs. Wheatley died. It was 1774 and there was much unrest in Boston. After the incident called the Boston Tea Party, the British government had closed the Boston harbor. British solders began arriving and patrolling the streets, and the colonists united and prepared for war.

The American Revolution began, and Phillis Wheatley became a nurse caring for the wounded soldiers. George Washington had been chosen as the Commander of the Continental Army, and Phillis Wheatley was inspired to write a poem about him. Mary insisted that the poem be sent to the General who replied and asked the poet to visit him. His letter was delivered by a black soldier named John Peters whom Phillis Wheatley later married.

On July 4, 1776, the Declaration of Independence was signed, breaking the colonists' ties with England. Food and fuel were scarce, but the colonists continued to fight for their independence for five more years.

Meanwhile, Mr. Wheatley's health declined and he died in 1777. Later that year, Phillis Wheatley and John Peters were married and went to live behind John's grocery store. Mary became ill, and although Phillis Wheatley did her best to nurse her back to health, she died.

Times were hard. The war continued and John lost the grocery store. The couple traveled from town to town until John found work. Their first son, Johnny, was born in an old barn where John and Phillis lived for several months.

On October 19, 1781, Phillis Wheatley heard the news that the war had ended. For the first time in many months she wrote a poem, considered one of her best, called "Liberty and Peace."

John Peters spent most of his time looking for work. The family was poor and near starving. Phillis Wheatley went to a former publisher who promised to print a new volume of poems. She worked hard on the new poems, but the publishing company went out of business.

Johnny became seriously ill and died a few weeks late. The new baby, named Susie, also died. A year later another baby was born, and John Peters was put in debtor's prison for the money he owed on the grocery store.

Phillis Wheatley worked in a boardinghouse scrubbing floors, barely earning enough money for food. Both she and the baby became ill and they died within minutes of each other. It was 1784, and the first American editions of Phillis Wheatley's poems were just appearing in Boston.

Friends were shocked to learn of Phillis Wheatley's death. Possibly she was too ashamed to ask for the help they would have readily given. She died in poverty but has never been forgotten. Many schools and clubs are named after her. Several editions of her poems have been published since then, and some of her poems appear in textbooks and other collections. Through her poems, generations have come to know the love, patience, and courage of Phillis Wheatley.

LANGUAGE ARTS - SOCIAL STUDIES - SCIENCE

Discussion

Explain that a poem is an arrangement of words that have rhythm much like a song and most have words that rhyme. Read several children's poems; then read the last verse of Phillis Wheatley's poem to George Washington. (The language and figures of speech make the first verses of the poem—and most parts of Ms. Wheatley's other poems—too difficult for young children to understand. Ask for her book of poems at the public library.) Summarize the Biographical Information, referring to the room displays and showing pictures from references (see Famous Black Americans, Room Environment - Learning Centers). Locate Boston, England, and West Africa on a map or globe. Look at pictures of early America. Compare the clothing, transportation, architecture, etc., with that of today's. Discuss Phillis Wheatley's life and amazing accomplishments. Have the students imagine being kidnapped from their homes, put on a crowded slave ship, sent to a strange country, and sold to people who spoke a different language.

Rhyming Exercise and Sheet

Explain what rhyme means and give examples of words that rhyme. Display items such as a toy boat, a shoe, a comb, a book, a jar, and a hat. Direct the students to look at the items; then ask, "Do you see something that rhymes with coat?" After receiving the correct response (boat), ask if anyone can think of other words that rhyme with coat and boat (float, goat). Repeat this procedure for each item.

Items and Sample Rhyming Words:

       boat - coat, float, goat, moat, oat, throat
       shoe - blue, clue, do, flew, new, stew
       comb - dome, foam, gnome, home, roam
       book - brook, cook, hook, look, shook, took
       jar - are, bar, car, far, star, tar
       hat - bat, car, fat, mat, rat, sat

Duplicate and distribute the sheet on page 258. The students draw lines to match the two items that rhyme, then color the items.

Learning About Poetry

Read a Mother Goose rhyme. Now read the rhyme again and lead the children in clapping in time to the rhythm. Read the poem once again and have the children emphasize the words that rhyme.

Now seat the children on the floor, and with a pencil and tablet in hand, show them how a poem is composed. Brainstorm for a subject, then a first line. Guide the children in thinking of a word that rhymes with the last word in the first line and a second line to fit the word. Read and highly praise the children's first poem.

Divide the class into small groups with an aid, mother helper, or older student to guide the group. Each group composes and illustrates a poem, then shares it with the class.

Book - Read The Story of the Liberty Bell by Natalie Miller and An American ABC by Maud and Miska Petersham.

Flags - Information and Activity

From an encyclopedia or Flags of the U.S.A. by David Eggenberger, show pictures of the Cambridge or Grand Union flag, the Betsy Ross flag, and the current American flag.   Share the following information about each flag.

- The Cambridge or Grand Union flag was the first flag of our country and was first raised in 1776 at George Washington's headquarters of the Continental army in Cambridge, Massachusetts.

- The Betsy Ross flag was the first flag of the new United States in 1777. It was adopted by the Continental Congress and, many believe, was designed by George Washington and sewn together by Elizabeth (Betsy) Ross, an expert seamstress who lived in Philadelphia.

- The current flag evolved from the flag of 1794. At that time, the stars were put in rows to make room for additional states. Today our flag has the same thirteen stripes which symbolize the original thirteen colonies, but has fifty stars. The last two stars were added in 1958 and 1960 when Alaska and Hawaii became states.

Cut three pieces of butcher paper and divide the class into three groups, one for each flag. Let the groups sketch and color the flags. Have a picture in view for each group. Display the flags.

Mother Goose Rhyme - "Oh, Soldier"

Oh, soldier, soldier, will you marry me,
With your musket, fife, and drum?
Oh no, pretty maid, I cannot marry you,
For I have no coat to put on.

Then away she went to the tailor's shop
As fast as legs could run,
And bought him one of the very, very best,
And the soldier put it on.

Oh, soldier, soldier, will you marry me,
With your musket, fife, and drum?
Oh no, pretty maid, I cannot marry you,
For I have no shoes to put on.

Then away she went to the cobbler's shop
As fast as legs could run,
And bought him a pair of the very, very best,
And the soldier put them on.

Oh, soldier, soldier, will you marry me,
With your musket, fife, and drum?
Oh no, pretty maid, I cannot marry you,
For I have no hat to put on.

Then away she went to the hatter's shop
As fast as legs could run,
And bought him one of the very, very best,
And the soldier put it on.

Oh, soldier, soldier, will you marry me,
With your musket, fife, and drum?
Oh no, pretty maid, I cannot marry you,
For I have a wife at home.

ART

Pierced Tin Lanterns

Preparation - For each child you will need a piece of slightly stiff gray paper (lightweight watercolor paper is best, but white typing or ditto paper will do), a piece of tracing paper, and a piece of corrugated cardboard of the same size or larger than the paper. Set out extra white paper, pencils, sewing needles of various sizes, scissors, masking tape, and staplers. Show the children a tin lantern or a picture of one.

Procedure - On the tracing paper, draw the design that you want on your lantern. Place the tracing paper on top of the white sheet of paper and tape both to the piece of cardboard. Using the sewing needles, poke holes through both sheets, following the lines of your design. Remove the tape and discard the tracing paper. Roll the pierced sheet into a cylinder and staple to secure. Cut a strip of the extra paper for the handle and staple to the top of the lantern. (See example on page 257.)

Spatter Paint Liberty Bell

Preparation - Make cardboard patterns of the Liberty Bell on page 259, one for every two or three children. Mix black tempera paint to a thin consistency and pour into spray bottles. Set out gray, white, or light blue construction paper. Cover the area with old newspapers and collect rocks or other objects to anchor the patterns on the paper.

Procedure - Place the construction paper on the newspaper and lay the Liberty Bell pattern in the center of the sheet. Anchor with the rock. Spray the sheet with the tempera paint; then carefully remove the pattern. Dry thoroughly.

Variation: Use spatter-paint frames and toothbrushes. The children dip the toothbrush in the paint and rub it over the screen until the paper below is adequately spattered.

MATH

Our Own Boston Tea Party

Explain the Boston Tea Party. (See reference in Famous Black Americans Learning Center.) To have your own tea party, let different children put a cup, a paper plate, and a napkin at each child's place and pour tea or lemonade into each cup (one to one correspondence). Set out cookies, raisins, and slices of bananas on paper plates accessible to each child. Give directions such as those listed below:

1. Put one cookie on your plate. (one to one correspondence, counting)
2. Place one more cookie on your plate. How many cookies are on your plate? (counting, addition)
3. Eat one cookie. How many are left? (counting, subtraction)
4. Put six raisins on your plate. (counting)
5. Look at the food on your plate. Which is larger? Which is smaller? (comparing, concept of size)
6. Are there more cookies or more raisins? (concept of more)
7. Place three banana slices on your plate. Are there less raisins or less banana slices? (concept of less)
8. Which food was the first you put on your plate? Which was second? Which was third? (ordinal numbers)
9. Which food is the largest? Which is the smallest? (concept of size)
10. How many people are ready to enjoy the refreshments? (Let the children have the tea party.)

Counting Book - Read <u>Moja Means One</u> by Muriel Feelings.

MUSIC - MOVEMENT - GAMES

<u>Song</u> - "Yankee Doodle"

<u>Verse 1</u>:

Father and I went down to camp,
Along with Cap'n Gooding
And there we saw the men and boys,
As thick as hasty pudding.

<u>Chorus</u>:

Yankee Doodle keep it up
Yankee Doodle Dandy
Mind the music and the step
And with the girls be handy.

<u>Verse 2</u>: Substitute "Da" for the words and clap out the rhythm.

<u>Verse 3</u>: Repeat Verse 1.

<u>Song</u> - "When Johnny Comes Marching Home Again" - Patrick Gilmore - 1863

When Johnny Comes marching home again, Hurrah, hurrah,
We'll give him a hearty welcome then, Hurrah, hurrah;
The men will cheer, and the boys will shout,
The ladies they will all turn out,
And we'll all be there when Johnny comes marching home!

<u>Song</u> - "Old Colony Times"

Source: <u>Best Loved Songs of the American People</u> (book) - Denes Agay

Outside Game - War

Divide the class into two armies, the "Colonists" and the "Redcoats." The armies stand back-to-back in the middle of the playing area. Each army will be facing its goal which can be marked with a rope or with two chairs at each end. The teacher calls the name of one of the armies such as the "Redcoats." The Redcoats run for their goal with the "Colonists" chasing them. If a "Redcoat" is tagged, he or she must join the "Colonists'" army. The game begins again with the armies standing back-to-back and continues in the same manner. It should be played for a designated length of time or number of "rounds." The army with the most soldiers wins the war.

STORY TIME

1. <u>Ashanti to Zulu: African Traditions</u> - Margaret Musgrove
2. <u>I Am Eyes = Ni Macho</u> - Leila Ward

COOKING IN THE CLASSROOM

Little Boston Cream Pies

Donuts, cream filled
Chocolate Syrup

Drizzle chocolate syrup over the donuts. Refrigerate until chilled.

Variation: Purchase plain cake-type donuts. Cut in half and spoon instant vanilla pudding on the bottom half. Replace the top of the donut and top with chocolate syrup. Chill.

Dear Parents,

    On _____, we will learn about the first recognized black poet, Phillis Wheatley. Please read below to find out ways you can help.

Things To Send: _____
_____
_____

Volunteers Needed To: _____
_____
_____

Follow-Up: At the end of the unit, ask your child the following questions:
_____
_____
_____

Thank you for your cooperation.

            Sincerely,

PHILLIS WHEATLEY

Bulletin Board

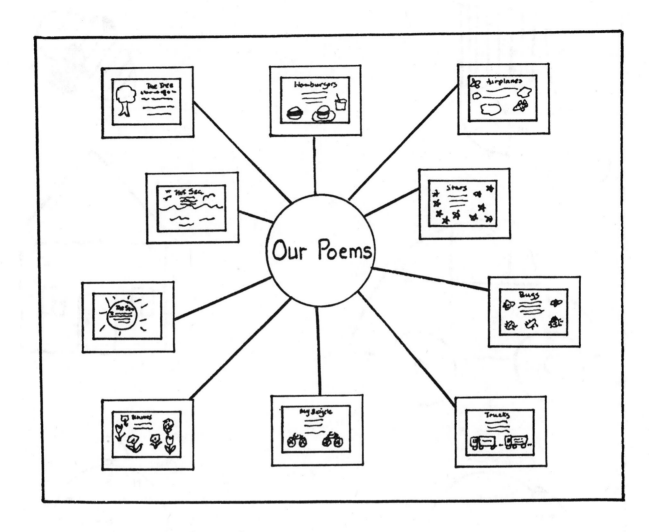

Spatter Paint Liberty Bell

Pierced Tin Lanterns

Pattern

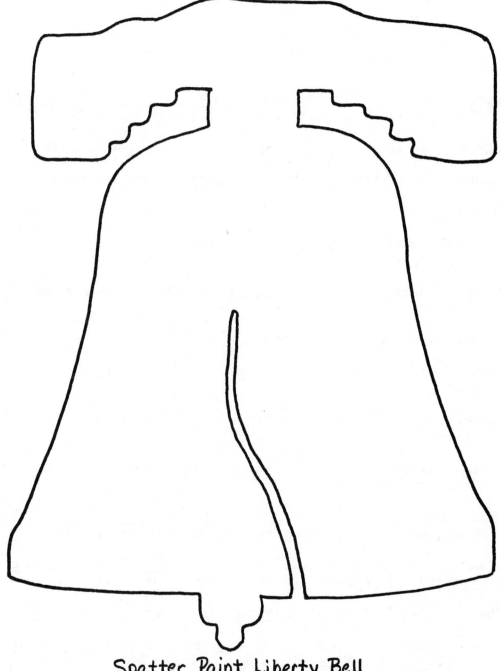

Spatter Paint Liberty Bell

BIBLIOGRAPHY

Adams, Russell. "Phillis Wheatley." Great Negroes Past and Present. Chicago, Illinois: Afro-AM Publishing Company, Inc., 1969.

"Anderson, Marian." Current Biography. 1950 Volume, pages 8–10.

"Bethune, Mary McLeod." Current Biography. 1942 Volume, pages 79–81.

"Bluford, Guion S., Jr." Current Biography. 1984 Volume, pages 29–32.

Brownmiller, Susan. Shirley Chisholm. Garden City, New York: Doubleday and Company, Inc., 1970.

"Chisholm, Shirley." Current Biography. 1969 Volume, pages 92–95.

Eaton, Jeanette. Trumpeter's Tale: The Story of Young Louis Armstrong. New York: William Morrow and Company, 1955.

Embree, Edwin R. 13 Against the Odds. New York: The Viking Press, 1945

Fenderson, Lewis H. Thurgood Marshall: Fighter for Justice. New York: McGraw-Hill Book Company, 1969.

Frommer, Harvey. Rickey and Robinson. New York: Macmillan Publishing Company, Inc., 1982.

Fuller, Miriam Morris. Phillis Wheatley: America's First Poetess. Champaign, Illinois: Garrard Publishing Company, 1971.

Graham, Shirley, and George D. Lipscomb. Dr. George Washington Carver: Scientist. New York: Jullian Messner, Inc., 1944

"Gibson, Althea." Current Biography. 1957 Volume, pages 203–204.

Gibson, Althea. (as told to Ed Fitzgerald). I Always Wanted to Be Somebody. New York, New York: Nobel and Nobel Publishers, Inc., 1958.

Gibson, Althea. (with Richard Curtis). So Much to Live For. New York: G. P. Putnam's Sons, 1968.

Hamilton, Charles V. "Shirley Chisholm." World Book Encyclopedia. Volume 3. 1988 Edition, page 515.

Hanley, Reid M. Who's Who in Track and Field. New York: Arlington House, 1973.

Harris, Jacqueline. Martin Luther King, Jr. New York: Franklin Watts, 1983.

Haskins, Jim, and Kathleen Benson. Space Challenger: The Story of Guion Bluford. Minneapolis: Carolrhoda Books, 1984.

Henderson, Edwin B., and the Editors of Sport Magazine. The International Library of Afro-American Life and History: The Black Athlete. Cornwells Heights, Pennsylvania: The Publishers Agency, Inc., 1978.

Hollander, Phyllis. 100 Greatest Women in Sports. New York: Grosset and Dunlap, 1976.

Holt, Rackham. George Washington Carver. Garden City, New York: Doubleday, Doran and Company, Inc., 1943.

Holt, Rackham. Mary McLeod Bethune. Garden City, New York: Doubleday and Company, Inc., 1964

Hughes, Langston. Famous American Negroes. New York: Dodd, Mead and Company, 1954.

Hughes, Langston, Milton Melter, and C. Eric Lincoln. A Pictorial History of Black Americans. 1956, 5th Revised Ed., New York: Crown Publishers, Inc., 1983.

Iverson, Genie. (Ill. by Kevin Brooks). Louis Armstrong. New York: Thomas Y. Crowell Co., 1976.

Jones, Bessie, and Bess Lomax Hawes. Step It Down. New York: Harper and Row Publishers, 1972.

Jones, Max, and John Chilton. Louis: The Louis Armstrong Story. Boston: Little, Brown, and Company, 1971.

Kitchens, John W. "George Washington Carver." World Book Encyclopedia. Volume 3. 1988 Edition, pages 268–269.

Kranz, Eugene F. "Guion S. Bluford, Jr." World Book Encyclopedia. Volume 2, 1988 Edition, page 437.

Kugelmass, J. Alvin. Ralph J. Bunch: Fighter for Peace. New York: Julian Messner, 1965.

Lerner, Gerda, Ed. Black Women in White America. New York: Pantheon Books, a division of Random House, 1972.

Lindstrom, Aletha Jane. Sojourner Truth: Slave, Abolitionist, Fighter for Women's Rights. New York: Julian Messner, 1980.

Mann, Arthur. The Jackie Robinson Story. New York: Grossett and Dunlap, 1950. (additional material copyright 1951, 1956, 1963).

Mariani, John F. "Louis Armstrong." World Book Encyclopedia, Volume 1. 1988 Edition, page 723.

McKissack, Patrick. Martin L. King, Jr.: A Man to Remember. Chicago: Children's Press, 1984.

Nightingale, Dave. "Jackie Robinson." World Book Encyclopedia. Volume 16. 1988 Edition, pages 374–375

"Olympic Information." The World Almanac and Book of Facts: 1986. New York: Newspaper Enterprise Association, Inc., page 803.

"Owens, Jesse." Current Biography. 1956 Volume, pages 475–477.

Petry, Ann. Harriet Tubman, Conductor on the Underground Railroad. Binghamton, New York: Vail-Ballou Press, Inc., 1955.

Richardson, Ben. Great American Negroes. New York: Thomas Y. Crowell Company, 1945.

Richardson, Ben A., and William A. Fahey. Great Black Americans. New York: Thomas Y. Crowell Company, 1976.

Rowan, Carl T. "Thurgood Marshall." World Book Encyclopedia. Volume 13. 1988 Edition, page 230.

"Rudolph, Wilma." Current Biography. 1961 Volume, pages 399–401.

Saylor, Galen. "Mary McLeod Bethune." World Book Encyclopedia. Volume 2. 1988 Edition, page 275.

Smock, Raymond W. "Booker T. Washington." World Book Encyclopedia. Volume 21. 1988 Edition, pages 88–89.

Stevenson, Augusta. Booker T. Washington: Ambitious Boy. Indianapolis, New York: The Bobbs-Merrill Company, Inc., 1950.

Stevenson, Augusta. George Carver: Boy Scientist. Indianapolis, New York: The Bobbs Merrill Company, 1944.

Toppin, Edgar A. A Biographical History of Blacks in America Since 1528. New York: David McKay Company, Inc., 1969.

Washington, Booker T. Up From Slavery: An Autobiography. Garden City, New York: Doubleday and Company, Inc., 1900.

Watson, Richard L., Jr. "Ralph Johnson Bunche." World Book Encyclopedia. Volume 2. 1988 Edition.